Lecture Notes in Computer Science 6739

Commenced Publication in 1973
Founding and Former Series Editors:
Gerhard Goos, Juris Hartmanis, and Jan van Leeuwen

T0074252

Thorsten Holz   Herbert Bos (Eds.)

Detection of Intrusions and Malware, and Vulnerability Assessment

8th International Conference, DIMVA 2011
Amsterdam, The Netherlands, July 7-8, 2011
Proceedings

 Springer

Volume Editors

Thorsten Holz
Ruhr-Universität Bochum
Fakultät für Elektrotechnik und Informationtechnik
AG "Embedded Malware"
Universitätsstrasse 150, 44801 Bochum, Germany
Email: thorsten.holz@rub.de

Herbert Bos
Vrije Universiteit Amsterdam
Computer Systems Section
1081 HV Amsterdam, The Netherlands
E-mail: herbertb@cs.vu.nl

ISSN 0302-9743   e-ISSN 1611-3349
ISBN 978-3-642-22423-2   e-ISBN 978-3-642-22424-9
DOI 10.1007/978-3-642-22424-9
Springer Heidelberg Dordrecht London New York

Library of Congress Control Number: 2011930927

CR Subject Classification (1998): C.2, K.6.5, D.4.6, E.3, H.4, K.4.4

LNCS Sublibrary: SL 4 – Security and Cryptology

Typesetting: Camera-ready by author, data conversion by Scientific Publishing Services, Chennai, India

Printed on acid-free paper

Springer is part of Springer Science+Business Media (www.springer.com)

Preface

On behalf of the Program Committee, it is our pleasure to present to you the proceedings of the 8th Conference on Detection of Intrusions and Malware & Vulnerability Assessment (DIMVA 2011). Each year DIMVA brings together international experts from academia, industry and government to present and discuss novel security research. DIMVA is organized by the Special Interest Group *Security – Intrusion Detection and Response* (SIDAR) – of the German Informatics Society (GI)

The DIMVA 2011 Program Committee received 41 submissions. All submissions were carefully reviewed by at least three Program Committee members or external experts. The submissions were evaluated according to the criteria of scientific novelty, importance to the field and technical quality. The final selection took place at a Program Commitee meeting held on March 25, 2011, at Ruhr-University Bochum, Germany. Eleven full papers and two short papers were selected for presentation at the conference and publication in the conference proceedings. The conference took place during July 7-8, 2011, at Vrije Universiteit Amsterdam, The Netherlands. The program featured both practical and theoretical research results grouped into five sessions. The keynote speech was given by Manuel Costa, Microsoft Research. Another invited talk was presented by Ahmad-Reza Sadeghi, TU Darmstadt. The conference program further included a poster session.

We sincerely thank all those who submitted papers and posters as well as the Program Committee members and our external reviewers for their valuable contributions to a great conference program. In addition we thank Marc Kührer for helping during the preparation of these proceedings. For further details about DIMVA 2011, please refere to the conference website at http://www.dimva.org/dimva2011.

July 2011

Thorsten Holz
Herbert Bos

Organization

DIMVA was organized by the Special Interest Group *Security – Intrusion Detection and Response* (SIDAR) – of the German Informatics Society (GI).

Organizing Committee

General Chair	Herbert Bos, Vrije Universiteit Amsterdam, The Netherlands
Program Chair	Thorsten Holz, Ruhr-University Bochum, Germany
Sponsoring Chair	Damiano Bolzoni, University of Twente, The Netherlands
Publicity Chairs	Damiano Bolzoni, University of Twente, The Netherlands
	Konrad Rieck, TU Berlin, Germany
Local Chair	Asia Slowinska, Vrije Universiteit Amsterdam, The Netherlands
Workshops Chair	Lorenzo Cavallaro, Vrije Universiteit Amsterdam, The Netherlands

Program Committee

Michael Bailey	University of Michigan, USA
Herbert Bos	Vrije Universiteit Amsterdam, The Netherlands
Juan Caballero	IMDEA Software, Spain
Lorenzo Cavallaro	Vrije Universiteit Amsterdam, The Netherlands
Marco Cova	University of Birmingham, UK
Sven Dietrich	Stevens Institute of Technology, USA
Ulrich Flegel	Offenburg University of Applied Sciences, Germany
Felix Freiling	University of Erlangen-Nuremberg, Germany
Thorsten Holz	Ruhr-University Bochum, Germany
Martin Johns	SAP Research, Germany
Engin Kirda	Eurecom, France
Christian Kreibich	International Computer Science Institute, USA
Christopher Kruegel	University of California, Santa Barbara, USA
Pavel Laskov	University of Tübingen, Germany
Wenke Lee	Georgia Institute of Technology, USA
Corrado Leita	Symantec Research Labs, France
Lorenzo Martignoni	University of California, Berkeley, USA

Michael Meier	Technical University of Dortmund, Germany
Paolo Milani Comparetti	Vienna University of Technology, Austria
Konrad Rieck	TU Berlin, Germany
Robin Sommer	ICSI/LBNL, USA
Dongyan Xu	Purdue University, USA

Additional Reviewers

Zinaida Benenson	Achim D. Brucker	Andreas Dewald
Christian Dietrich	Hans-Georg Eßer	Jan Göbel
Mathias Kohler	Tammo Krüger	Zhiqiang Lin
Christian Moch	Tilo Müller	Lexi Pimenidis
Sebastian Schinzel	Thomas Schreck	Guido Schwenk
Moritz Steiner	Benjamin Stock	Carsten Willems

Steering Committee

Chairs	Ulrich Flegel, Offenburg University of Applied Sciences, Germany
	Michael Meier, Technical University of Dortmund, Germany
Members	Roland Büschkes, RWE AG, Germany
	Danilo M. Bruschi, Università degli Studi di Milano, Italy
	Herve Debar, France Telecom R&D, France
	Bernhard Haemmerli, Acris GmbH & HSLU Lucerne, Switzerland
	Marc Heuse, Baseline Security Consulting, Germany
	Marko Jahnke, Fraunhofer FKIE, Germany
	Klaus Julisch, IBM Zurich Research Lab, Switzerland
	Christian Kreibich, International Computer Science Institute, USA
	Christopher Kruegel, UC Santa Barbara, USA
	Pavel Laskov, University of Tübingen, Germany
	Robin Sommer, ICSI/LBNL, USA
	Diego Zamboni, IBM Zurich Research Lab, Switzerland

Table of Contents

Host Security

Protecting against DNS Reflection Attacks with Bloom Filters

Sebastiano Di Paola and Dario Lombardo

Telecom Italia S.p.A., Via Reiss Romoli 274, 10148 Torino, Italy
{sebastiano.dipaola,dario.lombardo}@telecomitalia.it

Abstract. Nowadays the DNS protocol is under the attention of the security community for its lack of security and for the flaws found in the last few years. In the Internet scenario, the reflection/amplification is the most common and nasty attack that requires very powerful and expensive hardware to be protected from. In this paper we propose a robust countermeasure against this type of threats based on Bloom filters. The proposed method is fast and not too eager of resources, and has a very low error rate, blocking 99.9% of attack packets. The mechanism has been implemented within a project by Telecom Italia S.p.A., named *jdshape*, based on Juniper Networks® SDK.

1 Introduction

The DNS protocol is one of the most important protocol of the TCP/IP suite. It is used to convert names into numeric addresses and is the base of any high-level service. Due to its early birth it lacks the basic security features that a modern protocol has. Many attacks have been documented against this protocol: in this paper one will be analyzed in deep, the DNS reflection attack. It is a DoS attack where the victim is flooded with DNS responses. The paper will describe a defense approach based on Bloom filters: they are used to store the observed DNS queries, and checked against a response. This method allows to couple a query and a response that belong to the same DNS transaction. All the responses that don't have a coupled query are part of the attack. The Bloom filter approach is fast and effective despite of an error rate due to its statistic origin. The filter is a trade-off between the desired precision (error rate and packet rate) and the memory consumption. We used two filters of about 8,22 MB that can store 3 seconds of traffic at a 800000 pkts/s each. The two filters are needed to have a lock-free implementation that runs on an expansion card of a Juniper router (MS-PIC) and are swapped every predefined time-slot. The proposal has been developed and tested in a simulated environment to verify its behavior. It has been also tested running on the router in lab with both test and real traffic. It has been demonstrated to be effective with respect to the preset error rate (0.1%).

The remainder of the paper is organized as follows. Section 2 describes major DNS protocol security concerns. In section 3 reflection attack are outlined.

T. Holz and H. Bos. (Eds.): DMIVA 2011, LNCS 6739, pp. 1–16, 2011.

Section 4 provides an high level overview of Bloom Filter data structure. In section 5 an exaustive approach to solve the problem is analyzed and in section 6 our solution is proposed. In section 7 real world implementation design parameters are evaluated and chosen. In section 8 performances and experimental result are reported and finally in section 9 conclusions and possible improvements end the paper.

2   Security Concerns in the Domain Name System

DNS (Domain Name System) is the protocol used to convert symbolic names (such as www.google.com) into IP addresses (such as 72.14.255.104). It is an ancient protocol, ancient as the Internet itself, and it was developed when protocols were designed without security concerns.

It is the prototype of the insecure protocol:

- it's based on IP than is connection-less and not authenticated
- the most common transport for DNS is UDP, that is connection-less (while TCP is connection-oriented), so easier to attack
- it is unauthenticated itself, allowing easy information forging[1].

Despite its insecurity, this protocol, as IP and the others belonging to the TCP/IP suite, is commonly used in modern networks. In the plethora of the network protocols, IP has the role of the "center of the hourglass". This means that there are many layer-2 protocols, and many layer 4-7 protocols, but IP is the only layer-3 used, so it is a sort of bottleneck (as in the hourglass). The DNS has a similar role in the services context. If a public service is stopped, others can continue to work (e.g. if the Web is stopped for some reason, the email service still works). If the DNS is stopped all the other services are stopped too, because they depend on it: web addresses cannot be resolved, e-mails cannot be delivered, generally speaking servers can't be reached. This is due to the wide use of the symbolic names instead of IP addresses. It is not forbidden to use IP addresses instead of names, but it's not done because of the possibility of dynamic changes in that association. Moreover non-technical users have no idea of what an IP address is, so they use just symbolic names.

   In summary our proposal is an application of the Bloom filters [6] to mitigate DNS DoS attacks, and has been implemented on a Juniper router using Juniper SDK [16]. The solution was designed taking into account both development platform functionalities and real networks measures (as packet rate, packet sizes, latency, and so on).

3   DNS Reflection Attacks

Due to its lack of security, attacks based on IP spoofing are widely used against DNS infrastructures. The most common one is called the *reflection attack* (see [1],

---

[1] DNSSEC digital signature should solve the problem.

[2], [3]). In the scenario of figure 1 the attacker sends a spoofed datagram using the victim IP as source address. This datagram is sent to a DNS server, that sends the response to the victim, causing an unsolicited traffic aimed to the spoofed address. The attack is very easy to achieve because IP addresses are not authenticated, and UDP datagrams are connection-less. So it is very trivial to send such datagrams but very difficult for the victims to protect themselves from them. To bypass the ACLs that the victim could put in place, the attacker could change continuously the reflection servers, so the victim can't guess which reflection server will be next.

The attacker running this attack aims at saturating the victim's network link, but this requires an high amount of data. In this situation the victim could limit the rate (e.g. acting on network elements of its service provider), but this has the side-effect that a portion of the legitimate traffic is cut out too.

Another aim of this attack is the consumption of the resources of the DNS server software. The response, even out of a correct DNS transaction, can't be dropped by the operating system, but must be passed to the application (e.g. BIND), that discards it. With a large amount of data the server can suffer and drop legitimate packets too.

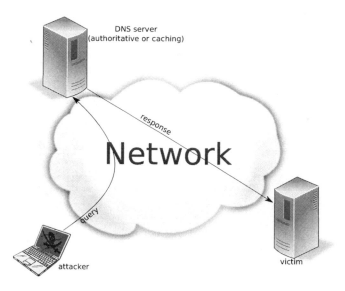

Fig. 1. DNS reflection attack

3.1 Making it Stronger

The described attack is not so threatening because of the large bandwidth the attacker must generate. In fact, to saturate a network link, the traffic must be $S_R \cdot X pps$, where X is the packets per second rate and S_R the size of the DNS response used for the attack. To have this traffic the attacker must generate the same pps rate using queries of S_Q size.

For example: making a query to the domain www.google.com (74 bytes = 592 bits), the response packet is 182 bytes (= 1465 bits). Consequently if the attacker wants to saturate 50% of the bandwidth of a 1 Gigabit link they must have

$$10^9 \cdot 50\% = S_R \cdot X \,\text{pps} \tag{1}$$

that means that the needed packet rate is $X \cong 343406\text{pps}$. In order to generate this rate the attacker must use $S_Q \cdot X \,\text{pps} = 203296352\text{bit/s} \cong 200\text{Mbit/s}$ of bandwidth, that is a very high rate.

To increase the power of this attack, two techniques are used together: amplification and caching (see [4]) as depicted in fig. 2. In standard transactions, responses are greater than queries. The ratio $R = \frac{S_R}{S_Q}$ is about 2:1, that means that the amplification occurs in the base attack too (in this case the bytes are doubled). To improve further this ratio, the attacker must use a DNS domain under their control. Inside this domain they create a TXT record, a type of record that can host more data than responses of type A. This record can be up to 512 bytes[2], with an overall size of the whole packet of 512 (DNS) + 8 (UDP) + 20 (IP) + 14 (Ethernet) = 554 bytes, and resides in the attacker's DNS server.

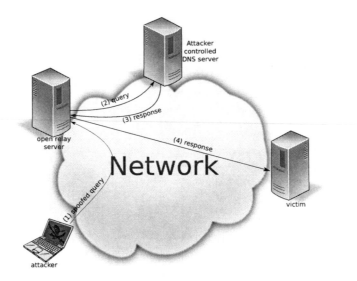

Fig. 2. DNS amplification attack

The next step is to find an open relay server (caching). The attacker sends the datagram to the relayer, that forwards the query to the controlled domain, loads the TXT record and sends the datagram back to the victim (because of the spoofing). With this technique the attacker sends a datagram that is about

---

[2] This limit is described in [5], and has been expanded in DNSSEC that has larger records.

60 bytes long and that is amplified by $\frac{554}{60} \cong 9.23$ times. This amplification rate is much more higher than amplification rate using A records.

The first time the attack is run steps 1 through 4 (referring to fig. 2) are done entirely, and the record is loaded and cached in the caching name server. Subsequently the attacker sends a packet and steps 2 and 3 are jumped, so the attack is quicker than before (possibly using many DNS servers in parallel).

The amplification ratio and the speed of the attack make this attack very disturbing, easy and stealthy. Even if an attacker can't totally block a network because of modern link speeds and servers protection, this attack can create many problems to ISPs and customers because when DNS service is down, other services are down too.

4   Bloom Filters

Bloom Filters [6] are data structures that allow a space-efficient representation of a set of elements in order to support membership queries. This compact representation is achieved using a probabilistic method, so this kind of structure allows a false positive rate. Given a set $E = \{e_1, e_2, ..., e_n\}$ of n elements called keys, the idea is to allocate an array A of m bits initially set to 0 and then choose k independent hash function $h_1, h_2, ..., h_k$ whose output is in the interval $[1, m]$. For each element $e \in E$ the k hash functions are calculated and the corresponding output bits are set in the A array. So given an element b to check for membership, all k hash function $h_1(b)$, $h_2(b)$,...,$h_k(b)$ are calculated and the results are used to access A array at position $A[h_1(b)]$,...,$A[h_k(b)]$. If any of the elements of A is equal to zero, we can surely state that b element does not belong to the E set. In case all elements are $1's$ we can state that the element belongs to the set, although there is the probability equal to the false positive rate that we are wrong.

Assuming that the chosen hash functions select bits positions with equal probability then the expectation of all of k bits being set to 1 giving a false positive is

$$\left(1 - \left(1 - \frac{1}{m}\right)^{kn}\right)^k \approx \left(1 - e^{-kn/m}\right)^k \tag{2}$$

This expression is minimized when

$$k = \ln 2 \cdot \left(\frac{n}{m}\right) \tag{3}$$

giving a false positive probability (as described in [7] and [8]) of

$$P = (1/2)^k \approx (0.6185)^{m/n} \tag{4}$$

Hence, once n is fixed, m and k have to be chosen carefully to have the correct balance between acceptable "false positive" rate (i.e. the smaller is k, the less we have to spend time calculating hash functions, but the higher is the "false positive" rate) and memory usage.

4.1   Partitioned Bloom Filters

A variant of Bloom filters consists in partitioning the array A of m elements among the k hash functions, creating k slices of $m' = m/k$ elements (see [9] and [10]). Every hash function h_i, $1 \leq i \leq k$ will produce an output in the interval $[1, m']$ bits so every element inserted will be surely characterized by k bits as different hash functions insist on different portion of the filter. Hence a more robust filter derives as no element is particularly sensitive to false positive. For every slice the probability of a bit to become 1 after inserting an element is $1/m'$ and the probability of remaining 0 is $1 - 1/m'$. After inserting n element we will have $(1 - 1/m')^n$ and so the probability of having an element set to 1 is

$$p = 1 - \left(1 - \frac{1}{m'} \right)^n .\tag{5}$$

So for the whole filter this probability $P = p^k$. This probability increases with n and decreases with m' and k. In order to maximize the number of elements n and keep the error rate P below a certain value the following formula (see [10]) can be used

$$n \approx m \cdot \frac{\ln p \cdot \ln(1 - p)}{-\ln P}\tag{6}$$

For any given P and size m this n is maximized when $p = 1/2$ (i.e. the fill factor of every slice is equal to $1/2$). Using that value the number of elements that can be stored in the filter is given by this formula:

$$n \approx m \cdot \frac{(\ln 2)^2}{|\ln P|}\tag{7}$$

and for the same p the number of hash functions k can be calculated as described in [10].

$$k = \log_2 \frac{1}{P}\tag{8}$$

5   Protecting from the Attack: The Exact Approach

Previous works have been done for protecting against the attacks described in section 3. Some of them (as [11], [12]), used anti spoofing techniques to block the attack queries: this approach was used to protect the owned servers by being abused as reflection servers. These methods are good and should be put in place by anyone to avoid spoofing. But if other networks in the Internet don't use these countermeasures, our network is still prone to reflection attacks, so a defense countermeasure is necessary.

The most obvious way to protect a network by the reflection attacks is to allow only responses for which we observed the relative query before. To achieve this goal it is necessary to classify all the observed queries, then, when responses arrive, to search for the relative query in the database. If the key is found the response is legitimate, otherwise no.

The parameters in a DNS transaction that uniquely identify it are source IP, destination IP, source port, destination port, protocol, transaction id (tid). We can ignore some of these parameters because they are not necessary in our solution. Thedestination port is always 53, because we are taking into account just public DNS service, that runs always on port 53. We omitted the source port because we used just the tid to identify a DNS transaction: this allowed us to shorten the search key, that speeds up the hash functions execution process. The source port was recently cheated in the well-known poisoning attacks, but these attacks are not related with the reflection attacks: the poisoning aims at spoofing a real answer, while in the reflection attack the answers are not part of a true transaction, so adding the source port to the key would not have added benefits. We decided to manage just UDP packets, because DNS transactions based on TCP protocol are very difficult to spoof: besides the typical difficulties related to three-way handshake, there is also the transaction id to guess.

What we have at the end is source IP (4 bytes), destination IP (4 bytes) and transaction ID (2 bytes). These parameters form our search key (10 bytes long).

In this approach we have to save a key (related to a query) into a database in order to get it back when the response arrives. This database must take into account the following aspects:

- fast insertion: insertion occurs for every query
- fast search: queries must be searched for duplicates, responses for matching
- fast deletion: deletion occurs for every matching response
- starvation: old entries must be purged

Common data structures have one or more of these features, but not all. Usually fast insertion could mean slow deletion or slow search.

The proposal made in [13] is similar to the exact approach, but this method is not quick enough to face the packet rates we are interested into (for a complete description of our scenario see [16]).

We would like to manage 800000 pkts/s. This is a very high DNS packets rate, higher than the packet rate observed in our production network, but our analysis wants to be a bit oversize. This number is related to the network equipment we used (as described later in section 7), so this was our target rate. However the method applies to any given rate: the filter parameters must be recalculated according to the desired scenario. In figure 3 and 4 we have plotted real DNS data that come from the Telecom Italia public network [3]. The histogram shows in a logarithmic scale how short transactions occur much more than the long ones, and we have calculated that the average transaction time value is around 50 ms. As shown by figure 4 too, values are concentrated in the first 0.1s time slice, that means that queries are typically answered in less than one tenth of second.

---

[3] Data processed anonymously, according to Italian privacy law.

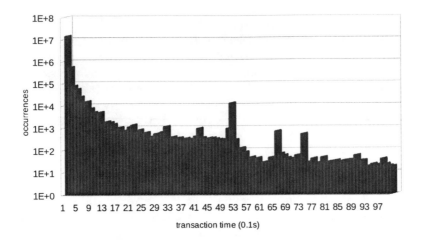

Fig. 3. DNS transaction time distribution (logarithmic scale)

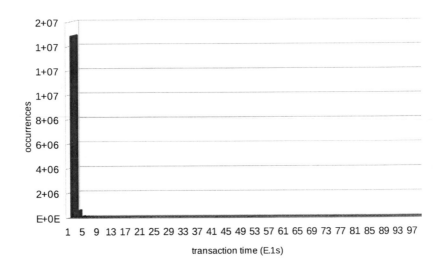

Fig. 4. DNS transaction time distribution (linear scale)

We decided to allow transactions up to 3 seconds, to allow a large amount of long transactions too. The transactions durations hold in the 2 filters used are up to 6 seconds. This value is considered wide enough to catch the most part of the transactions according to what observed in the production network: the transactions that fall out of the filters scope are 0.01% of the total.

The amount of data needed to store all the search keys is

$$800000\text{pkts/s} \cdot 3\text{s} \cdot 10\text{B/pkts} \cong 22,8\text{MB} \ . \tag{9}$$

The conclusion is that the problem has a very easy solution in theory, but it's very difficult when needs to be implemented. Especially if it should run on a parallel machine (such as a network processor platform), there are many issues related to resource sharing, locks and so on. To avoid the slow packet-by-packet locking we need something different from the exact approach.

The solution proposed in this paper is a trade-off between the precision (kept above a desired rate) and the resource consumption: the more resources we use (memory) the more precise we can be, assuming to process a predefined packet rate. This approach is described in the following sections.

6   Protecting with Bloom Filters

The exact approach could be extremely slow: it requires a huge amount of memory and requires a lot of locks in a multithreaded environment.

To go beyond those limits we can use bloom filters, with a modified approach. In our proposal, we create a key from the network packets that we use as bloom filter population. This key is the one described in section 5 and is used as follows:

- query: the key is stored in the filter. This creates the population of elements of the Bloom filter;
- response: the key is checked against the filter to find a match.

The Bloom filter is a one-way structure, that means that elements can just be added and not deleted unless counting bloom filter are used [15]. In order to avoid the filter to fill and become inefficient (saturated filter), we have to clean it periodically. The effect is to have an empty filter every predefined time slice. This periodical cleaning introduces an issue that is not present in the Bloom filters traditional use.

If a query arrives at T_q and the relative response arrives at T_r, we call $T_t = T_r - T_q$ the DNS transaction time. Let's say that the filter gets cleared at time T_n so that it is filled between T_{n-1} and T_n (it lasts for T_f). The issue arises if $T_n - T_q < T_t$: this means that the response arrives after the filter has been cleared, so it can't be found even if is a legitimate response.

To solve this limitation we used two filters, the so-called "new" and "old". The new is updated every query, the old is never updated. The responses are checked against both of them, in order to widen the time window in which the

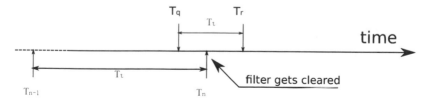

Fig. 5. Filter problem

transaction is valid. When the filter timeout expires, the old filter is cleared, and the filters are swapped. Then the new filter is updated as described before. This assures that the key related to a query is kept at least for T_f in the filter before getting cleared. There are still a couple of issues related to this approach:

1. cold start: when the system starts, old and new collapse, so the system requires to wait for a complete cleaning cycle before it can work correctly;
2. long transactions: if $T_t > T_f$, it is not guaranteed that the good query is still present in the filter (it is assured only if $T_l \leq T_f$). The described approach mitigates the problem described above, but it is still present for long transactions.

These limitations are marginal: they don't affect the overall effectiveness of the approach.

A similar approach to solve this problem has been described in [14], but there are some differences from our work. The main difference is that they use a two-steps method that consists in a detection and a filtering phase. We decided to use a single-step approach that consists in examining/checking all the traffic: this prevents the errors of the detection and filtering phases to add up. We chose not to use the UDP source port in order to shorten the search key. This allowed us to reduce the computational overhead, but the cost of this choice was a slight increase in the number of packets that reach the destination. Anyhow both solutions are not effective during a DNS poisoning attack, because the attack packet would pass throught the filter no matter if you consider the source port or not. Moreover they used 4 hash functions (with a false positive rate of about 6%) while we used 10 functions (with an fpr of 0.1%): the more functions you use, the more precise you are. We think that this compromise best fits our needs according to our experience. Finally these design criteria have been tested on a fully implemented system, as described in section 7.

How wide the filter must be, how often we should clean it, are design parameters, that will be described in the following section.

7   Practical Implementation

The proposed solution is part of the project called *jdshape* for DNS protection in Telecom Italia [16]. The developed software runs on a Juniper router[4] and contains a component called *stateful-check*, that is based on the current paper proposal. The resulting software has been tested for correct behavior and for performance using the Lab Be-Secure^{TM} testing environment (Spirent® TestCenter^{TM}).

To describe the details of our proposal we calculate the values of the variables described in section 6. These values are k (number of hash functions), P (error probability), n (number of storable elements), m (size of the Bloom filter), t (Bloom filter cleaning interval), r (packets rate). Some of them are our desired or observed values, others are derived from them.

---

[4] Supported Juniper routers are T, M and MX series, equipped with MS-PIC or MS-DPC expansion cards.

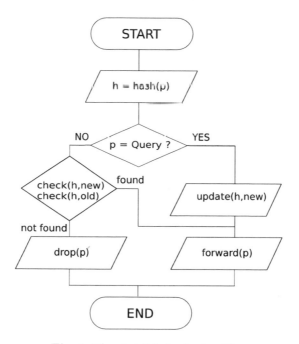

Fig. 6. The stateful-check algorithm

The filter must be designed in order to achieve the following values:

- $P = 0.1\%$: this is the maximum error rate allowed;
- $t = 3s$: as described in 5;
- $r = 800000\text{pkts/s}$: as described in 5.

The other values are derived as follows

- given P, $k = 10$: this is the number of hash functions (from eq. (8));
- given r and t, $n = 2400000$: this is the number of packets that cross the router in 3 seconds
- given n and P, $m = 34500000$ bit (about 4,11 MB), this is the size of our filters (from eq. (7)).

The overall amount of memory required for the 2 filters is about $8,22\text{MB}$. This filters are able to manage 800000pkts/s with a cleaning time of 3 seconds.

The overview of the used algorithm is shown in figure 6. The picture describes the packet-driven management of the two bloom filters. There is also a time-driven phase in which filters are swapped and the old one is cleared (with lock-safe guards).

We have chosen the following, well-known, hash functions, publicly available in the "General Purpose Hash Function Algorithms" library [17]:

1. RSHash by Robert Sedgwicks
2. JSHash by Justin Sobel

3. PJWHash by Peter J. Weinberger
4. BKDRHash by Brian Kernighan and Dennis Ritchie
5. SDBMHash by SDBM Project
6. DJBHash by Daniel J. Bernstein
7. DEKHash by Donald E. Knuth
8. BRPHash by Bruno R. Preiss
9. FNVHash by Fowler/Noll/Vo
10. APHash by Arash Partow

8 Test Environment and Results

The above implementation has been tested using a simulator and a traffic generator. The simulator is a software written by us that creates keys as they were extracted from real packets and runs the *stateful-check*, checking its output. In the second test scenario, the software was loaded into the Juniper router (an M7i equipped with a MS-PIC-100) and the traffic generator was connected in a "loop" configuration in order to measure the performance of the system.

The simulator can generate three kinds of keys and behaves as follows:

- query: a key (src IP, dst IP, txid) is randomly generated. The key is used to update the filter, and is stored in a list (to be used afterwards);
- fake answer: a key is randomly generated, and the filter is checked. The expected result for this case is not to find it, so if it doesn't happen a false positive counter is incremented.
- right answer: to have a right answer, a key is taken from the query list, and its IPs are swapped (to simulate the returning packet), then the filter is checked. The expected result is to find it, so if it doesn't happen a false negative counter is incremented.

The simulations have been run for an amount of 10^{12} packets, and the false positive and negative counters have been checked. The expected result was to have the false negative counter equal to 0, and the false positive counter equal or below the desired error rate (0,1% as explained above). The random numbers have been generated by the `random()` function of FreeBSD, and the seed has been initialized using 4 bytes taken from the `/dev/urandom` device.

All the test runs have reported the following results:

- All the good responses have been correctly found. This means that the legitimate traffic was not affected by the filter. A result that differs from 0 would have implied an error in the filter design or implementation;
- The attack responses were blocked with an error below 0.1%, according to the filter design. That means that less than 0.1% of wrong responses were allowed to flow. This error is embedded in the Bloom filters technique, and is the variable that the protection designers set as desired result.

After the simulated tests, the system has been put under tests in a laboratory environment, in order to measure its performances. The used traffic generators were TestCenter with Structured traffic (TCS) and TestCenter with Unstructured traffic (TSU). Tests have been conducted using queries (about 80 bytes long). The legitimate responses were about 130 bytes long, while attack packets were 542 bytes long. Data in table 1 are reported as transactions per second (tr/s, in this case to have the packets per second rate this number must be doubled) or packets per second (pkts/s). The rate of the legitimate transactions during the attack is very low: in this case the input interface is overloaded by the attack, so legitimate queries can't reach the servers. If the attack doesn't fill the interface more queries can flow, so the number of good transactions is higher. The reported data refer to the worst situation the system could face.

Table 1. Performance tests on jdshape stateful-check implementation

Type of traffic	Generator	Rate
All legitimate without stateful-check	TCS	400000 tr/s
All legitimate	TCS	250000 tr/s
Attack	TCU	216000 pkts/s (965 Mbit/s)
Legitimate traffic	TCS	30000 tr/s

In figures 7, 8, 9, 10, we have plotted how the traffic flows are affected by the *stateful-check*. The traffic sent to the router is a mix of a massive DoS (flood of fake responses) and legitimate queries, as reported in 1. Data have been collected via SNMP using the IF-MIB[5].

In figure 7 and 8 it is reported the traffic originated by the servers (legitimate responses). It can be observed that with and without the *stateful-check* the traffic is almost the same. This is due to multiple factors. The first factor is that in

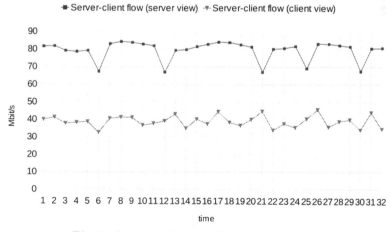

Fig. 7. Server to client traffic without stateful

---

[5] Spikes in the graphs are due to the sampling method used: however average value is correct

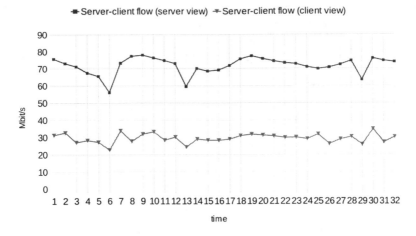

Fig. 8. Server to client traffic with stateful

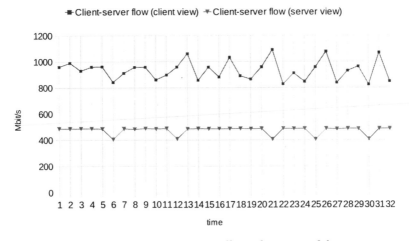

Fig. 9. Client to server traffic without stateful

the proposed scenario, the client link is saturated and the routers is overloaded by the attack, so a low percentage of the legitimate queries can reach the router and then the servers. So, from the clients point of view, the processed responses come from how many queries can reach the servers (that are less than how many queries are generated in total).

In figure 9 and 10 you can see the traffic originated by the clients (both legitimate and not). When *stateful-check* is not active, the mix of traffic hits the DNS server at a rate of about 600Mbit/s. When *stateful-check* is activated the legitimate part of that mix reaches the servers, while at least 99,9% of the attack packets are discarded. That protects the servers from the attack: the load that they must face is significantly lower when *stateful-check* is active. The computational cost

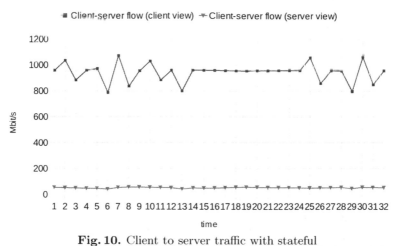

Fig. 10. Client to server traffic with stateful

of the proposed solution can be observed from table 1 comparing the packet rate
values of legitimate traffic with and without stateful check.

9   Conclusions

The described solution has been demonstrated to be effective, both in a simulated environment and in a real application running on a Juniper router. It gives
great advantages because it protects the DNS infrastructure and endpoints, but
doesn't waste resources (as router memory). Its trade-off is between the precision of the results and the resources required (processor speed and memory
occupation). We have been able to find a good compromise that allowed a low
false positive rate with a not-so-high memory consumption.

There is anyway room for improvements. Using the approach proposed in [7],
the time spent during the computation of hash functions could be reduced. This
would lead the system to reach an higher throughput. This is a work in progress
(in order to improve the results reported in section 8). Another aspect that could
be taken into account is that speeding up the hash computation process could
make possible to use more hash functions, reducing the error rate with the same
throughput. To have a error rate of 0,01% (10 times more precise than actual)
we would need 14 hash functions.

References

1. Paxson, V.: An analysis of using reflectors for distributed denial-of-service attacks.
   In: ACM SIGCOMM Computer Communication Review Homepage, vol. 31(3)
   (July 2001)
2. Handley, M., Rescorla, E.: Internet Denial of-Service Considerations. RFC4732
   November (2006)

3. Silva, K., Scalzo, F., Barber, P.: Anatomy of Recent DNS Reflector Attacks from the Victim and Reflector Point of View. Verisign White paper, April 4 (2006)
4. Vaughn, R., Evron, G.: DNS Amplification Attack (March 17, 2006)
5. Mockapetris, P.: Domain names - implementation and specification, RFC1035 (November 1987)
6. Bloom, B.: Space/time trade-offs in hash coding with allowable errors. Communications of ACM 13(7), 422–426 (1970)
7. Kirsch, A., Mitzenmacher, M.: Less hashing, same performance: Building a better bloom filter. In: Azar, Y., Erlebach, T. (eds.) ESA 2006. LNCS, vol. 4168, pp. 456–467. Springer, Heidelberg (2006)
8. Bose, P., Guo, H., Kranakis, E., Maheshwari, A., Morin, P., Morrison, J., Smid, M., Tang, Y.: On the false-positive rate of Bloom filters. Information Processing Letters 108(4), 210–213 (2008)
9. Chang, F., Chang Feng, W., Li, K.: Approximate caches for packet classification. In: Twenty-third AnnualJoint Conference of the IEEE Computer and Communications Societies, INFOCOM 2004, March 7-11, vol. 4, pp. 2196–2207 (2004)
10. Almeida, P.S., Baquero, C., Preguiça, N., Hutchinson, D.: Scalable bloom filters. Information Processing Letters 101(6), 255–261 (2007) ISSN 0020-0190
11. Handley, M., Greenhalgh, A.: Steps towards a DoS-resistant internet architecture. In: Proceedings of the ACM SIGCOMM workshop on Future directions in network architecture (FDNA 2004)
12. Akinori, M., Yoshinobu, M.M.: Implement anti-spoofing to prevent DNS Amplification Attack. In: SANOG, Karachi, Pakistan, July 27 - August 4 , vol. 8 (2006)
13. Kambourakis, G., Moschos, T., Geneiatakis, D., Gritzalis, S.: A Fair Solution to DNS Amplification Attacks. In: Workshop on Digital Forensics and Incident Analysis, Second International Workshop on Digital Forensics and Incident Analysis (WDFIA 2007), pp. 38–47 (2007)
14. Sun, C., Liu, B., Shi, L.: Efficient and Low-Cost Hardware Defense Against DNS Amplification Attacks. In: Proc. IEEE GLOBECOM, New Orleans, LA, November 30-December 4 (2008)
15. Fan, L., Cao, P., Almeida, J., Broder, A.Z.: Summary cache: a scalable wide-area Web cache sharing protocol. IEEE/ACM Transactions on Networking 8(3), 281–293 (2000)
16. Brusotti, S., Gazza, M., Lombardo, D.: Network Embedded security: new scenarios (article in Italian, english translation will be available as soon as possible). Notiziario Tecnico Telecom Italia   (3) (2010)
17. http://www.partow.net/programming/hashfunctions/

Effective Network Vulnerability Assessment through Model Abstraction

Su Zhang[1], Xinming Ou[1], and John Homer[2]

[1] Kansas State University
{zhangs84,xou}@ksu.edu
[2] Abilene Christian University
jdh08a@acu.edu

Abstract. A significant challenge in evaluating network security stems from the scale of modern enterprise networks and the vast number of vulnerabilities regularly found in software applications. A common technique to deal with this complexity is attack graphs, where a tool automatically computes all possible ways a system can be broken into by analyzing the configuration of each host, the network, and the discovered vulnerabilities. Past work has proposed methodologies that post-process "raw" attack graphs so that the result can be abstracted and becomes easier for a human user to grasp. We notice that, while visualization is a major problem caused by the multitude of attack paths in an attack graph, a more severe problem is the distorted risk picture it renders to both human users and quantitative vulnerability assessment models. We propose that abstraction be done *before* attack graphs are computed, instead of after. This way we can prevent the distortion in quantitative vulnerability assessment metrics, at the same time improving visualization as well. We developed an abstract network model generator that, given reachability and configuration information of a network, provides an abstracted model with much more succinct information about the system than the raw model. The model is generated by grouping hosts based on their network reachability and vulnerability information, as well as grouping vulnerabilities with similar exploitability. We show that the attack graphs generated from this type of abstracted inputs are not only much smaller, but also provide more realistic quantitative vulnerability metrics for the whole system. We conducted experiments on both synthesized and production systems to demonstrate the effectiveness of our approach.

Keywords: enterprise network security, attack graph, quantitative vulnerability assessment, abstraction.

1 Introduction

Network security control is an issue that increases in difficulty with growths in network size and the number of vulnerabilities. Automated approaches are needed to quickly and reliably evaluate the current security state of the network. Attack graphs are a common approach to security evaluation [1–3, 8, 10–13, 17–21, 23, 24, 26]. They show how an attacker can combine multiple vulnerabilities

T. Holz and H. Bos. (Eds.): DMIVA 2011, LNCS 6739, pp. 17–34, 2011.
© Springer-Verlag Berlin Heidelberg 2011

in a system to launch multi-stage attacks to gain privileges in the system. Attack graphs are often used in conjunction with risk assessment tools to provide recommendations to system administrators on how to mitigate the discovered problems [4, 6, 9]. There are two main utilities of attack graphs: visualization and risk assessment. A major obstacle in these utilities is the size and complexity of attack graphs from even moderate-size networks. The large number of attack paths towards the same target not only makes the graph too dense to read, but also distorts risk assessment results by ignoring the fact that many of the attack steps are similar and not independent.

Figure 1 shows a simple network. An attacker could launch attacks from the Internet against the web server, which then provides him a stepping stone to exploit the database server in the internal network. The lower part of the figure shows a MulVAL attack graph [18, 19] generated from this network model. The labels of the graph nodes are shown at the right-hand side. Diamond-shaped nodes represent privileges an attacker could gain in the system; circle nodes represent attack steps that achieve the privileges; rectangular nodes represent network configuration settings.

Figure 2 shows the topology and attack graph of a similar scenario, but with five identical servers in the DMZ zone. We can see that the attack graph gets very complicated. Human users, like a system administrator, may have difficulty tracing through the many identified attack paths. An abstracted view of the attack graph can highlight the real underlying issues in the network. We must also consider whether the multitude of attack paths shown in this attack graph reflects a realistic risk picture. The dotted lines in the network topology illustrate a subset of the attack paths identified in the graph. There are five ways to attack the database server, utilizing five different sources in the DMZ. However, the five servers in DMZ are identically configured. Thus if an attacker can exploit any one of them, he can exploit the others as well. In this case, having four more servers will not significantly increase the attacker's chance of success.

Prior research has proposed various techniques to address the visualization challenge [7, 15, 30]. However, we have not found substantial discussion in the literature addressing the distortion problem in risk assessment caused by the redundancy in attack graphs, especially in the context of quantitative security assessment. Traditional approaches [6, 27, 28] would assess all the attack paths to the attacker's target without taking the similarities of these paths into consideration. Consequently, the explosion in the attack-graph's size could yield high risk metrics, often misleading the system administrator's judgment. While one could post-process the graph and remove such redundancy, like in previous works [15, 30], we believe a better approach is to pre-process *the input* to attack-graph generation so that such redundancy is removed by abstracting the network model, instead of the attack graph. There are a number of benefits of abstracting the network model:

– From a human user's perspective, removing redundancy in the network description provides a better high-level view of both the system and the security vulnerabilities identified therein. The semantics of the abstract network model

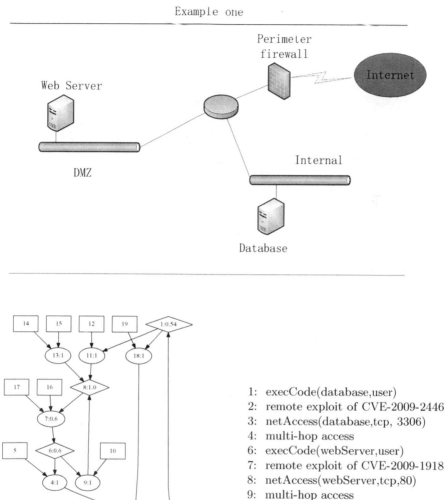

1: execCode(database,user)
2: remote exploit of CVE-2009-2446
3: netAccess(database,tcp, 3306)
4: multi-hop access
6: execCode(webServer,user)
7: remote exploit of CVE-2009-1918
8: netAccess(webServer,tcp,80)
9: multi-hop access
11: multi-hop access
13: direct network access
15: attackerLocated(Internet)
18: multi-hop access

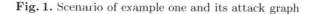

Fig. 1. Scenario of example one and its attack graph

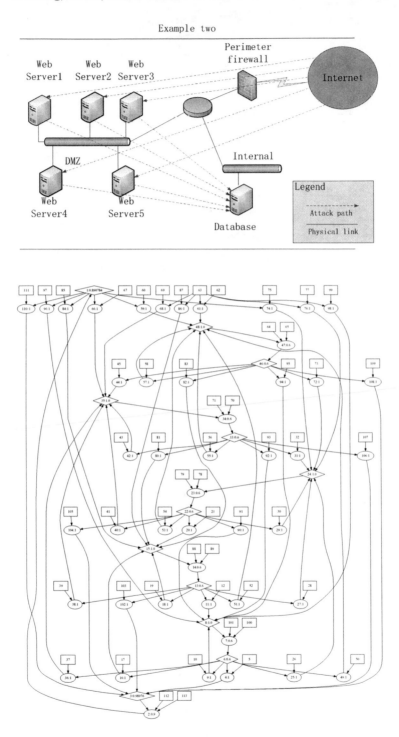

Fig. 2. Scenario of example two and its attack graph

matches better with how a human would manage a large network system, and as a result the output of the attack-graph analysis is natural to communicate to human users.

- After abstracting the network model, the distortion in quantitative security assessment results due to repetitive similar attack paths will be rectified.

We design algorithms to create abstract network models for large-scale enterprise networks, based on network reachability and host configuration information. The algorithms make reasonable assumptions about available input describing the network structure and host configuration information. The abstracted models dramatically reduce the complexity of attack graphs, improving the visualization and also correcting skewed quantitative vulnerability assessment results. Moreover, by using the abstracted models, the quantitative vulnerability assessment process is hastened. We evaluate our methods on both synthesized and production systems, demonstrating the effectiveness of the approach.

The rest of the paper is organized as follows. Section 2 discusses the abstraction criteria and algorithms. Section 3 describes experimental evaluation of the abstraction method. Section 4 discusses related work and section 5 concludes.

2   Network Model Abstraction

2.1   Abstraction Criteria

Similarity among hosts. For large enterprise networks, it is not unusual to have thousands of machines in a subnet with same or similar reachability and configuration. If an attacker could compromise one of the machines, he is likely able to do the same for the others. This would result in a large number of similar attack paths in the attack graph. These attack paths should not be considered independent when assessing the system's security risk: if the attacker failed in compromising one of the hosts, he would probably fail on the others with the same properties (reachability and configuration) as well. Network reachability and host configuration determine to a large extent the exploitability of a host machine. For this reason, the machines with the same reachability and similar configurations can be grouped and treated as a single host.

Similarity among vulnerabilities. A single host may contain dozens or even hundreds of vulnerabilities, each of which may appear in a distinct attack path to further compromise the system. However, not all these paths provide unique valuable information since many vulnerabilities are similar in nature. They may belong to the same application, require the same pre-requisites to be exploited, and provide the same privilege to the attacker. From a human user's perspective, it is more important to know, at a higher level, that *some* vulnerability in the application could result in a security breach, rather than enumerating all the distinct but similar attack paths. Since vulnerabilities in the same application are often exploited by the same or similar mechanisms, if the attacker fails in exploiting one of them, it is reasonable to assume a low chance of successful attack by similar exploits. For this reason, these vulnerabilities can be grouped together as a single vulnerability and an aggregate metric can be assigned as the indicator on the success likelihood of exploiting any one of them, instead of combining them as if each exploit can be carried out with an independent probability. For example, when a host has 10 vulnerabilities in Firefox, we can say with X likelihood an attacker can successfully exploit any one of them, where X is computed based on each vulnerability's CVSS score [14], taking into consideration the similarity among the 10 vulnerabilities. One simple approach would be to use the highest risk probability value as representative of the whole set.

2.2   Abstraction Steps

Our network model abstraction process is carried out in three steps.

1. *Reachability-based grouping.* Hosts with the same network reachability (both to and from) are grouped together.
2. *Vulnerability grouping.* Vulnerabilities on each host are grouped based on their similarities.
3. *Configuration-based breakdown.* Hosts within each reachability group are further divided based on their configuration information, specifically the types of vulnerabilities they possess.

Reachability-based grouping. We group all the hosts based on their reachability information. We first give two definitions.

Definition 1. *reachTo(H) is a set of triples (host, protocol, port) where H can reach host through protocol at port. Similarly, reachFrom(H) is a set of triples (host, protocol, port) where host can reach H through protocol and port.*

Definition 2. *Let H_1 and H_2 be two hosts. We say $H_1 \equiv_r H_2$ if reachTo(H_1) = reachTo(H_2) $\wedge$ reachFrom(H_1) = reachFrom(H_2)*

We put hosts into the same reachability group if they belong to the same equivalence class $\equiv_r$. Then all the hosts in the same reachability group can be abstracted as a single node. Figures 3(a) and 3(b) illustrate this idea, and Algorithm 1 explains the grouping process. The grouping is applied to all the machines in a subnet. We interpret a subnet as a collection of machines communication among which is unfiltered. We incrementally add reachability information into a set. If host H's reachability has been recorded, we find the existing group through a hash map and put H into the corresponding group. Otherwise we store the reachability information, create a new group label and map it to a singleton set with H in it. We do this for all the hosts in each subnet. The time complexity for this algorithm is $O(n^2)$ where n is the number of hosts in the network. We need to go over all the hosts within the subnet and for each host we need linear time to identify its reachability information.

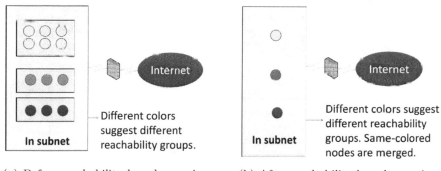

(a) Before reachability-based grouping   (b) After reachability-based grouping

Fig. 3. Before and after reachability-based grouping

Algorithm 1. Pseudocode for reachability-based grouping

Input: A set of (reachTo(h), reachFrom(h)) for each host h in a subnet.
Output: A hash map L, which maps a group label α to a list of hosts having the same
reachability (reachTo and reachFrom).
Lr $\leftarrow$ {} {Lr is a set of triples (α, reachToSet, reachFromSet).}
Queue Q $\leftarrow$ all the hosts of the given subnet
L $\leftarrow$ *empty map* {initialize the return value}
while Q is not empty **do**
  $n \leftarrow$ dequeue(Q)
  if Lr contains (α, reachTo(n), reachFrom(n)) **then**
    L[α] $\leftarrow$ L[α]$\cup$\{n\} {if the reachability of n is the same as some other host that
    has been processed, add n to its equivalent class.}
  else
    create a fresh α
    Lr $\leftarrow$ Lr $\cup$(α, reachTo(n), reachFrom(n)) {Otherwise put its reachability infor-
    mation into Lr}
    L[α]$\leftarrow$ \{n\}
  end if
end while
return L

Vulnerability grouping. We group vulnerabilities on each machine based on
the application they belong to. Typically vulnerabilities in one application will
be of the same type (local, remote client or remote service). For example, vulnerabilities of Adobe Reader are remote client since they are always triggered when
a user opens the application on a malicious input, possibly sent by a remote
attacker. Security holes in IIS, on the other hand, most likely belong to remote
service vulnerabilities. After grouping based on applications, we can provide the
system administrator a clearer view of the system's vulnerabilities — instead of
showing a long list of CVE ID's, we show the vulnerable applications that affect

the system's security. One issue that needs to be addressed is how to assign an aggregate vulnerability metric to the virtual vulnerability after grouping. Such vulnerability metrics, like CVSS scores, are important in quantitative assessment of a system's security. Intuitively, the more vulnerabilities in an application, the more exploitable the application is. But the degree of exploitability does not simply grow linearly since many of the vulnerabilities will be similar. Our current grouping algorithm (Algorithm 2) simply takes the highest value, but it will be straightforward to plug in a different aggregation method.

Algorithm 2. Pseudocode for vulnerability grouping

Input: A set of ungrouped vulnerabilities on a machine (S_u)
Output: A hash map L that maps an application to its vulnerability score
   Lr ←{} {Lr is a set of applications that have appeared so far}
   L ← *empty hash map*
  while $S_u \neq \{\}$ **do**
    take v from S_u
    if Lr contains (v.application) **then**
      if L[v.application] < v.score **then**
        L[v.application] = v.score
      end if
    else
      L[v.application] = v.score
      Lr.add(v.application)
    end if
  end while
  return L

Configuration-based breakdown. For hosts in the same reachability group, their configurations could be different from one another. Thus, if an attacker is able to exploit one host within the group, it does not mean he could compromise the others as well. This means grouping based on reachability alone is too coarse. In order to reflect differences in attackability, we need to "break down" the merged node based on configuration settings. In our current implementation, we have only included software vulnerability as the configuration information. When deployed on production systems, one can rely upon package management systems to decide whether two hosts have the same or similar software set up. Algorithm 3 shows the process of configuration-based grouping. The algorithm iterates over all the hosts in a reachability group and records its configuration information. If a host's configuration matches one previously recorded, meaning some other hosts have the same types of vulnerabilities, this host will not be recorded in the set. At the end of the algorithm, the returned set only contains one representative host for each group of hosts with the same reachability and configuration. The complexity of the algorithm is linear in the number of hosts.

Algorithm 3. Pseudocode for configuration-based break down

Input: A list L, each element of which is a set of machines belonging to the same
reachability group, and with the vulnerabilities grouped.

Output: Further-refined group S_c based on vulnerability information. Each element
in S_c is a representative for a group of hosts with the same reachability and configuration.

  while L≠{} **do**

    remove h from L

    Lr ← *empty map*; {Lr is a set of pairs (hostname, configuration). It is used to
    store the distinct configurations that have appeared so far.}

    if Lr contains (_, h.configuration) **then**

      continue {if its configuration has appeared before, skip}

    else

      Lr.add((h, h.configuration)) {if its configuration has not appeared before, record
      it}

    end if

  end while

  $S_c = \bigcup\limits_{(h,\_)\in Lr} h$ {collect all representative hosts in Lr and put them into S_c}

  return S $_c$

---

3   Experimentation Result

To evaluate the effect of model abstraction on quantitative security assessment of
computer networks, we apply probabilistic metric models [6, 27] on the generated
attack graphs. In such metric models, each attack step is associated with a
(conditional) probability indicating the success likelihood of the exploit when its
pre-conditions (predecessor nodes) are all satisfied. The model then computes
the absolute probability that a privilege can be obtained by an attacker based
on the graph structure. We use MulVAL [18, 19] attack-graph generator in the
evaluation. Our security metric implementation follows Homer's algorithm [6].

We created one scenario to illustrate the visualization effect and rectification
on the distortion in metric calculation generated by the large number of similar attack paths. The topology information of the example is shown in Fig. 5.
There are three subnets: Internal Servers, DMZ, and Normal Users. Each subnet has ten machines, evenly divided into two different types of configuration
(one is Linux and the other Windows). Machines with different shapes represent
different configurations. Machines in the same group have the same configuration and reachability. There are two types of vulnerabilities on each host, and
the types of vulnerabilities could be either local, remote server or remote client.
The reachability relations among those host groups can be found in Table 1.
The table does not include reachability within a subnet, which is unfiltered. If
a group does not have any inter-subnet reachability, it will not show up in the
table.

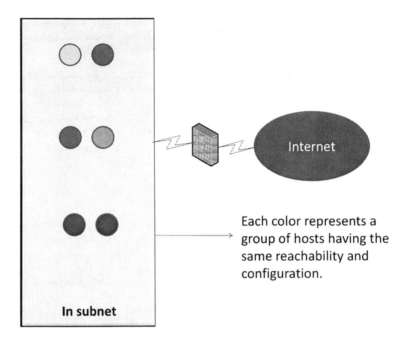

Fig. 4. After configuration-based breakdown

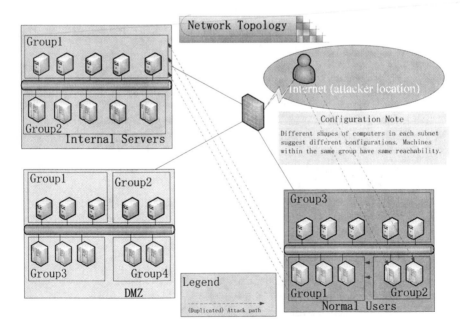

Fig. 5. Network topology

Table 1. Reachability Table

source		destination		protocol	port
subnet	group	subnet	group		
Internet		DMZ	1	tcp	80
DMZ	1	Internet		tcp	25
Internet		DMZ	4	tcp	80
DMZ	4	Internal	2	tcp	1433
User	2	Internet		tcp	80
User	3	Internet		*	*
Internet		User	2	tcp	80
User	1	Internet		*	*
User	1	Internal	1	nfs	
User	1	Internal	1	Tcp	3306

3.1 Attack Graph Generation

We created the input for MulVAL based on the configuration of the network, and we ran our abstraction model generator to generate an abstracted input. We ran MulVAL with both original and abstracted input and obtained two different attack graphs, shown in Figures 6(a) and 6(b). The size of the attack graph was reduced significantly after abstraction (281 arcs and 217 vertices, to 55 arcs and 47 vertices). We verified that all the "representative" attack paths leading to the attacker goal are retained in the abstracted model.

3.2 Quantitative Security Metrics

We compared the quantitative metrics results obtained from the original input and the abstracted input. There is a significant difference between the risk metrics on the original network (0.802) and the abstracted one (0.486) for a three-hop attack which is the deepest chain in this experiment (illustrated in the red dotted lines in Fig. 5). This attack chain includes three sets of attack steps: 1) from Internet to Group2 in the "Normal Users" subnet, via client-side vulnerabilities; 2) from Group2 to Group 1 in the "Normal Users" subnet, via service vulnerabilities; 3) from Group1 in the "Normal Users" subnet to Group1 in the "Internal Servers" subnet, via service vulnerabilities. Each group here refers to a set of hosts with the same reachability and configuration (vulnerabilities). Usually there are multiple attack paths between two groups since there are multiple hosts within each group and they have similar configurations; thus the multiple attack paths have similar natures. From a pure probabilistic semantics, the more paths between two groups, the higher success likelihood the attacker will gain in moving on these paths. However, these paths are not independent and failure on one of them would likely indicate failures on the other; therefore the higher risk metrics are not justified. Moreover, the hosts in the two groups are equivalent in terms of the network access they provide the attackers. Due to the above reasons, the attack paths should be merged into one, before

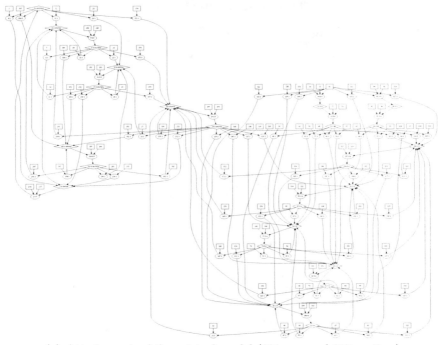

(a) Attack graph of the original model (281 arcs and 217 vertices)

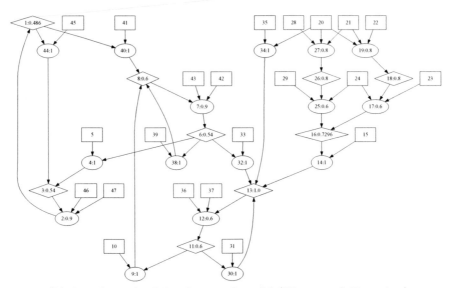

(b) Attack graph of the abstracted model (55 arcs and 47 vertices)

Fig. 6. Comparison of attack graphs from original and abstracted models

quantitative risk assessment. By removing redundancy in the attack graphs through model abstraction, we avoid distortion in the risk assessment result.

To demonstrate the effect of vulnerability grouping on the quantitative security assessment result, we used the network topology shown in Fig. 1, assuming there are five client-side vulnerabilities (from the same application) on the web server and the remote service vulnerability has been patched. We then computed the likelihood that the web server could be compromised through any of the client-side vulnerabilities, assuming the client program may occasionally be used on the server. The nature of client-side vulnerabilities from the same application are similar from both attacker and the victim's perspective, because the victim would open the same application to trigger the exploits, and due to the similar functionalities (and therefore program components) of the same application, the security holes are also similar. If an attacker knows the structure of the application very well, he should be able to utilize the vulnerability easily; if he does not understand the mechanism of the software, he probably will not be able to utilize any of the security holes with ease. Therefore viewing the same type (client-side or service) of security holes on an application as one is more realistic than treating them independently. We compared the results before and after grouping vulnerabilities. It is obvious that the complexity of the attack graph is reduced significantly from Figure 7(a) to Figure 7(b). More importantly, the quantitative metrics indicating the likelihood that the server can be compromised through one of the client-side vulnerabilities drops from 0.71 to 0.45. This is a more realistic assessment, since the five client-side vulnerabilities are similar and should not significantly increase the attacker's success likelihood.

4 Related Work

Attack graphs have been developed for the purpose of automatically identifying multi-stage attack paths in an enterprise network [1–4, 8–13, 17–21, 23, 24, 26]. It has been observed that attack graphs are often too large to be easily understood by human observers, such as system administrators. In order to reduce the complexity of attack graphs to make them more accessible to use by system administrators, various approaches have been proposed to improve the visualization through abstraction, data reduction, and user interaction [7, 12, 13, 15, 30]. However, not much work has been done to study the effect of attack graph complexity on quantitative security assessment approaches based on attack graphs. Our study found that complexity caused by repetitive information commonly found in attack graphs not only increases the difficulty for the system administrator in digesting the information provided by the graph, but also distorts the risk picture by unrealistically casting the attack success likelihood for some privileges under probability-based security assessment. We show that such distortion can be avoided by abstracting the input to the attack-graph generator, i.e., the network model, so that such redundancy is removed a priori. By performing abstraction directly on the network model, the attack graph result can also be rendered on a higher level of system description which is easier to grasp by a human user.

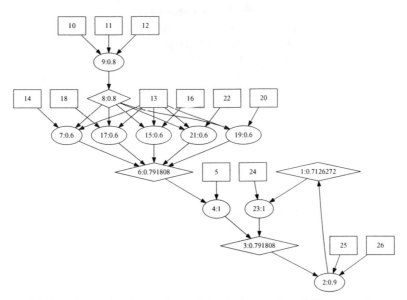

(a) Attack graph of a single machine before vulnerability grouping

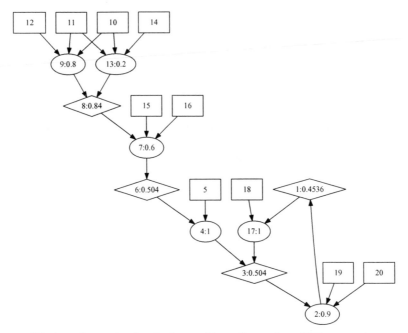

(b) Attack graph of a single machine after vulnerability grouping

Fig. 7. Effect of vulnerability grouping on a single host

Quantitative security assessment methods based on attack graphs have been proposed to indicate the severity levels of various vulnerabilities [5, 6, 16, 22, 25, 27–29]. Such methods typically utilize the dependency relations represented in an attack graph to aggregate individual vulnerability metrics to reflect their cumulative effects on an enterprise network. However, not all dependency relations are explicitly presented in an attack graph, particularly the similarities among large numbers of attack paths leading to the same privilege. Not accounting for the existence of this dependency on a large scale will significantly skew the analysis results. One method of dealing with such hidden dependency is to introduce additional nodes and arcs in the graph to model them, but this will make the visualization problem even more severe. We proposed a method based on model abstraction to remove the redundancy, and thus the hidden dependency resulted from it, so that it is no longer a problem for realistic risk assessment.

The size of enterprise networks could make vulnerability scanning prohibitively expensive [31]. Our abstraction technique provides a possible angle to address this problem. Prioritization can be applied based on the abstract model for identifying scanning which host can potentially provide critical information on the system's security. For example, if a host in the same abstract group has already been scanned, scanning one more host in the group may not provide the most useful information about the system's security vulnerabilities.

5   Conclusion and Future Work

We have presented an abstraction technique to aid in network security assessment based on attack graphs. We show that the large amount of repetitive information commonly found in attack graphs not only makes it hard to digest the security problems, but also distorts the risk picture by disproportionately amplifying the attack likelihood against privileges that have a large number of similar attack paths leading to them. We proposed an approach to abstract the network model so that such repetitive information is removed before an attack graph is generated. The abstraction happens at both the network and the host level, so that machines that have the same reachability relation and similar configurations with respect to vulnerability types are grouped together and represented as a single node in the abstracted model. Our experiments show that such abstraction not only effectively reduces the size and complexity of the attack graphs, but also makes the quantitative security assessment results more conforming to reality. This shows that appropriate abstraction on the input is a useful technique for attack graph-based analysis.

The abstraction techniques we have proposed are mostly suitable for risk assessment on the macroscopic level of an enterprise network. Abstraction unavoidably loses information and in reality no two hosts are completely identical. The abstracted network model can help in identifying security risks caused by the overall design and structure of the network, but may lose subtle security breaches that may occur due to, *e.g.* misconfiguration of a single host that is mistakenly deemed identical to a group of other hosts since the details of the differences may have been abstracted away. In general the more homogeneous the system is, the more pronounced the effect of abstraction will be. However, since no two hosts are really completely identical, the process is a balancing act. Being overly detailed about a host's configuration may lead to no possibility of abstraction and result in a huge attack graph where important security problems are buried. On the other hand, overly abstract models may lose the important information for subsequent analysis. More research is needed in identifying the most effective abstraction granularity for attack graph-based analysis.

Acknowledgment

This material is based upon work supported by U.S. National Science Foundation under grant no. 1038366 and 1018703, AFOSR under Award No. FA9550-09-1-0138, and HP Labs Innovation Research Program. Any opinions, findings and conclusions or recommendations expressed in this material are those of the authors and do not necessarily reflect the views of the National Science Foundation, AFOSR, or Hewlett-Packard Development Company, L.P.

References

1. Ammann, P., Wijesekera, D., Kaushik, S.: Scalable, graph-based network vulnerability analysis. In: Proceedings of 9th ACM Conference on Computer and Communications Security, Washington, DC (November 2002)
2. Dacier, M., Deswarte, Y., Kaâniche, M.: Models and tools for quantitative assessment of operational security. In: IFIP SEC (1996)
3. Dawkins, J., Hale, J.: A systematic approach to multi-stage network attack analysis. In: Proceedings of Second IEEE International Information Assurance Workshop, pp. 48–56 (April 2004)
4. Dewri, R., Poolsappasit, N., Ray, I., Whitley, D.: Optimal security hardening using multi-objective optimization on attack tree models of networks. In: 14th ACM Conference on Computer and Communications Security, CCS (2007)
5. Frigault, M., Wang, L., Singhal, A., Jajodia, S.: Measuring network security using dynamic Bayesian network. In: Proceedings of the 4th ACM Workshop on Quality of Protection (2008)
6. Homer, J., Ou, X., Schmidt, D.: A sound and practical approach to quantifying security risk in enterprise networks. Technical report, Kansas State University (2009)
7. Homer, J., Varikuti, A., Ou, X., McQueen, M.A.: Improving attack graph visualization through data reduction and attack grouping. In: Goodall, J.R., Conti, G., Ma, K.-L. (eds.) VizSec 2008. LNCS, vol. 5210, pp. 68–79. Springer, Heidelberg (2008)
8. Ingols, K., Lippmann, R., Piwowarski, K.: Practical attack graph generation for network defense. In: 22nd Annual Computer Security Applications Conference (ACSAC), Miami Beach, Florida (December 2006)
9. Jajodia, S., Noel Advanced, S.: cyber attack modeling analysis and visualization. Technical Report AFRL-RI-RS-TR-2010-078, Air Force Research Laboratory (March 2010)

10. Jajodia, S., Noel, S., O'Berry, B.: Topological analysis of network attack vulnerability. In: Kumar, V., Srivastava, J., Lazarevic, A. (eds.) Managing Cyber Threats: Issues, Approaches and Challenges, Massive Computing, vol. 5, pp. 247–266. Springer, Heidelberg (2005)
11. Li, W., Vaughn, R.B., Dandass, Y.S.: An approach to model network exploitations using exploitation graphs. SIMULATION 82(8), 523–541 (2006)
12. Lippmann, R.P., Ingols, K.W.: An annotated review of past papers on attack graphs. Technical report, MIT Lincoln Laboratory (March 2005)
13. Lippmann, R.P., Ingols, K.W., Scott, C., Piwowarski, K., Kratkiewicz, K., Artz, M., Cunningham, R.: Evaluating and strengthening enterprise network security using attack graphs. Technical Report ESC-TR-2005-064, MIT Lincoln Laboratory (October 2005)
14. Mell, P., Scarfone, K., Romanosky, S.: A Complete Guide to the Common Vulnerability Scoring System Version 2.0. In: Forum of Incident Response and Security Teams (FIRST) (June 2007)
15. Noel, S., Jajodia, S.: Managing attack graph complexity through visual hierarchical aggregation. In: VizSEC/DMSEC 2004: Proceedings of the 2004 ACM Workshop on Visualization and Data Mining for Computer Security, pp. 109–118. ACM Press, New York (2004)
16. Noel, S., Jajodia, S., Wang, L., Singhal, A.: Measuring security risk of networks using attack graphs. International Journal of Next-Generation Computing 1(1) (July 2010)
17. Ortalo, R., Deswarte, Y., Kaâniche Experimenting, M.: with quantitative evaluation tools for monitoring operational security. IEEE Transactions on Software Engineering 25(5) (1999)
18. Ou, X., Boyer, W.F., McQueen, M.A.: A scalable approach to attack graph generation. In: 13th ACM Conference on Computer and Communications Security (CCS), pp. 336–345 (2006)
19. Ou, X., Govindavajhala, S., Appel, A.W.: MulVAL: A logic-based network security analyzer. In: 14th USENIX Security Symposium (2005)
20. Phillips, C., Swiler, L.P.: A graph-based system for network-vulnerability analysis. In: NSPW 1998: Proceedings of the 1998 Workshop on New Security Paradigms, pp. 71–79. ACM Press, New York (1998)
21. Saha, D.: Extending logical attack graphs for efficient vulnerability analysis. In: Proceedings of the 15th ACM Conference on Computer and Communications Security, CCS (2008)
22. Sawilla, R.E., Ou, X.: Identifying critical attack assets in dependency attack graphs. In: Jajodia, S., Lopez, J. (eds.) ESORICS 2008. LNCS, vol. 5283, pp. 18–34. Springer, Heidelberg (2008)
23. Sheyner, O., Haines, J., Jha, S., Lippmann, R., Wing, J.M.: Automated generation and analysis of attack graphs. In: Proceedings of the 2002 IEEE Symposium on Security and Privacy, pp. 254–265 (2002)
24. Swiler, L.P., Phillips, C., Ellis, D., Chakerian, S.: Computer-attack graph generation tool. In: DARPA Information Survivability Conference and Exposition (DISCEX II 2001), vol. 2 (June 2001)
25. Ekstedt, M., Sommestad, T., Johnson, P.: A probabilistic relational model for security risk analysis. Computer & Security 29, 659–679 (2010)
26. Tidwell, T., Larson, R., Fitch, K., Hale, J.: Modeling Internet attacks. In: Proceedings of the 2001 IEEE Workshop on Information Assurance and Security, West Point, NY (June 2001)

27. Wang, L., Islam, T., Long, T., Singhal, A., Jajodia, S.: An attack graph-based probabilistic security metric. In: Proceedings of The 22nd Annual IFIP WG 11.3 Working Conference on Data and Applications Security, DBSEC 2008 (2008)
28. Wang, L., Singhal, A., Jajodia, S.: Measuring network security using attack graphs. In: Third Workshop on Quality of Protection, QoP (2007)
29. Wang, L., Singhal, A., Jajodia, S.: Measuring the overall security of network configurations using attack graphs. In: Proceedings of 21th IFIP WG 11.3 Working Conference on Data and Applications Security, DBSEC 2007 (2007)
30. Williams, L., Lippmann, R., Ingols, K.: An interactive attack graph cascade and reachability display. In: IEEE Workshop on Visualization for Computer Security, VizSEC 2007 (2007)
31. Xu, Y., Bailey, M., Vander Weele, E., Jahanian, F.: CANVuS: Context-aware network vulnerability scanning. In: Jha, S., Sommer, R., Kreibich, C. (eds.) RAID 2010. LNCS, vol. 6307, pp. 138–157. Springer, Heidelberg (2010)

Decoy Document Deployment for Effective Masquerade Attack Detection

Malek Ben Salem and Salvatore J. Stolfo

Computer Science Department
Columbia University
New York, New York 10027, USA
{malek,sal}@cs.columbia.edu

Abstract. Masquerade attacks pose a grave security problem that is a consequence of identity theft. Detecting masqueraders is very hard. Prior work has focused on profiling legitimate user behavior and detecting deviations from that normal behavior that could potentially signal an ongoing masquerade attack. Such approaches suffer from high false positive rates. Other work investigated the use of trap-based mechanisms as a means for detecting insider attacks in general. In this paper, we investigate the use of such trap-based mechanisms for the detection of masquerade attacks. We evaluate the desirable properties of decoys deployed within a user's file space for detection. We investigate the trade-offs between these properties through two user studies, and propose recommendations for effective masquerade detection using decoy documents based on findings from our user studies.

1 Introduction

The *masquerade attack* is a class of attacks, in which a user of a system illegitimately poses as, or assumes the identity of another legitimate user. Identity theft in financial transaction systems is perhaps the best known example of this type of attack.

Masquerade attacks can occur in different ways. A masquerader may get access to a legitimate user's account either by stealing a victim's credentials, or through a break-in and installation of a rootkit or key logger. A masquerade attack may also be caused by the laziness and misplaced trust of a user, such as the case when a user leaves his or her terminal or client open and logged in, allowing any nearby co-worker to pose as a masquerader. In most cases, the attacker's objective is to steal data that could be used for financial gains from home users or enterprise users, such as financial credentials or intellectual property. Masquerade attacks have been widespread. A Forbes report estimated that fraud incidents affected 11.2 million consumers in the United States in 2009, causing $54 billion in ID fraud costs [6]. In 2009, researchers who have monitored the Torpig botnet affirmed that, within the span of 10 days only, Torpig obtained the credentials of 8,310 accounts at 410 different institutions [15]. Enterprise users have also been targeted by different malware such as Confickr/Downadup [7].

T. Holz and H. Bos. (Eds.): DMIVA 2011, LNCS 6739, pp. 35–54, 2011.

The main approach for detecting masquerade attacks relies on computer user profiling and the modeling of statistical features, such as the frequency of certain events, such as issued user commands, the duration of certain events, the co-occurrence of multiple events combined through logical operators, and the sequence or transition of events. The focus of this line of work is primarily on accurately detecting change or unusual user command sequences [12,10,16]. These approaches suffered, like most anomaly detection-based approaches, from high false positive rates ranging between 1.3% and 7.7% [2].

Another approach for detecting masqueraders is the use of baits such as honeynets and honeypots. Honeypots are information system resources designed to attract malicious users. They have been widely deployed in De-Militarized Zones (DMZ) to trap attempts by external attackers to penetrate an organization's network. Some researchers proposed the use of honeyfiles, a type of honeypot, to detect malicious insider activity [4]. They introduced the concept of *perfectly believable decoys* and proposed several properties to guide the design and deployment of decoys, namely:

1. Believability: The attacker would not use the bait information if it did not appear authentic to the attacker.
2. Enticingness: No attack detection is possible if the attacker does not access the bait information because it does not look attractive enough.
3. Conspicuousness: Decoys should be easily located or retrieved in order to maximize the likelihood that an attacker takes the bait.
4. Detectability: If the access to the bait asset is not detectable than the deployment of the decoys is useless.
5. Variability: Decoys should not be easily identifiable to an attacker due to some shared invariant.
6. Non-interference: Decoys should not interfere with the legitimate user's normal activity. Non-interference has been defined as the likelihood that legitimate users access the real documents after decoys are introduced [4].
7. Differentiability: Legitimate users should be able to easily distinguish decoy documents from authentic documents, which has a direct affect on non-interference.
8. Shelf-life: Decoys may have a limited time period during which they are effective.

While all of the above are important decoy properties, it can be difficult to design and deploy decoy documents that would perfectly maximize the properties, which in turn would assure effective detection of a masquerade attack. One has to find the right trade-off between these properties in order to use them effectively. Such trade-offs may vary depending on the type of attack.

For example, while believability is a very important property of decoys when used for detecting insider attacks that aim to ex-filtrate sensitive information, it becomes of a lesser importance when the decoys are aimed at detecting masquerade attacks. In the case of an insider attack, the attacker already has legitimate access to the system where the sensitive information assets are located. Access to such assets does not necessarily constitute evidence of malicious intent or activity. However, subsequent ex-filtration and use of such information does. If the attacker identifies the decoy document as bogus, then they would not use the information contained in that document, which is why the *believability* of the decoy document is important. In the case of a masquerade attack, the mere access to the decoy document does constitute evidence of an attack as the masquerader is not a legitimate user of the system, and therefore should not be accessing any assets residing on that system. Whether the masquerader finds the decoy document believable or not, after having accessed it, is irrelevant to the detection of the attack, as evidence of the malicious activity has been already established.

In this paper, we attempt to investigate these trade-offs between decoy properties when applied to the masquerade detection problem through two user studies. The contributions of this work include:

- A host-sensor that detects access to decoy documents when loaded in memory using stealthy HMACs embedded in the decoy documents
- An investigation of the trade-offs between deployment properties of decoy documents when applied to the masquerade attack detection problem through two user studies
- A set of recommendations for the effective use of decoy documents for masquerade attack detection

The rest of this paper is organized as follows. In section 2, we briefly present the results of prior research work on masquerade detection. Section 3 expands on the threat model and presents the baiting technique used to detect masquerade attacks. In Sections 4 and 5, we describe two user studies to evaluate the different properties of the decoy documents and present the findings of these studies. Section 6 presents some recommendations for the effective use of decoy documents in masquerade attack detection in light of our findings. Finally, Section 7 concludes the paper by discussing directions for future work.

2   Related Work

Honeypots have been widely used in De-Militarized Zones (DMZ) to detect external attackers when attempting to penetrate an organization's network. Spitzner presented several ways to adapt the use of honeypots to the detection of insider attacks [13]. He introduced the notion of honeytokens, defined as 'information that the user is not authorized to have or information that is inappropriate' [13]. This information could then direct the attacker to the more advanced honeypot that could be used to discern whether the attacker's intention was malicious or not, a decision that may be determined by inspecting the attacker's interaction with the honeypot.

'Honeyfiles', or decoy files, were introduced by Yuill et al. [17].The authors proposed a system that allows users to turn files within the user space on a network file server into decoy files. A record that associates the filename with the userid is used to identify the honeyfiles

Bowen et al. extended the notion of a decoy document system, and developed an automated system for generating decoy files [4,3]. They also proposed several decoy properties as general guidelines for the design and deployment of decoys.

Honeyfiles suffer from some shortcomings. First, the attacker may not ever use or interact with the decoy file, especially if their identity is known to, or discovered by the attacker. Moreover, if an attacker discovers a honeyfile, they can potentially inject bogus or false information to complicate detection. In this paper, we investigate decoy deployment properties that should increase the likelihood of detecting a masquerade attacker.

3 Trap-Based Masquerader Detection Approach

3.1 Threat Model

Masqueraders impersonate legitimate users after stealing their credentials when they access a system. When presenting the stolen credentials, the masquerader is then a legitimate user with the same access rights as the victim user. To that extent, masquerade attacks represent one type of insider attacks. However, masquerade attacks can be characterized by the low amount of knowledge the attacker has about the system and policies in place. In this work, we focus on masqueraders and assume that the attacker has little knowledge about the system under attack. In particular, we assume that the attacker does not know whether the system is baited or not.

We have architected a Decoy Documents Access (DDA) sensor and designed decoy documents in such a way that a sophisticated attacker with more knowledge and higher capabilities, in particular an inside attacker, would not be able to escape detection if they touched a decoy document. Decoy documents have a HMAC tag computed over the document's contents as described in subsection 3.2. A sophisticated attacker with wide resources would not be able to distinguish the HMAC tags of decoy documents from random functions. Moreover, a highly privileged attacker would not be able to turn off the DDA sensor without getting detected. This is ensured through a self-monitoring mechanism as described in subsection 3.3. Both types of attackers would have to know that the system under attack is baited, and the detection of this class of attack is beyond the scope of this paper. Here, we devise user studies for attackers, who have no knowledge that the system is baited, with the objective of investigating the decoy deployment properties. The study of attacker behavior and their perception of risk and expected gain based on their knowledge of the existence of decoys on the system is beyond the scope of this paper, and will be the subject of a future user study.

3.2 Trap-Based Decoys

The trap-based technique used by our sensor relies on trap-based decoys [4] that contain 'bait information' such as online banking logins, social security numbers, and web-based email account credentials. Users of the DDA sensor can download such decoy files from the Decoy Document Distributor (D^3) [3], an automated service that offers several types of decoy documents such as tax return forms, medical records, credit card statements, e-bay receipts, etc..

The decoy documents carry a keyed-Hash Message Authentication Code (HMAC) [9] embedded in the header section of the document, and visible only if the document is opened using a hex editor. The HMAC is computed over a file's contents using a key unique to the user, and is hidden in the header section of the file. For instance, the use of the full version of the SHA1 cryptographic function in combination with a secret key to tag the decoy documents with an HMAC tag prevents the attacker from distinguishing the embedded HMAC from a random function [8]. An example of a decoy document with an embedded HMAC is shown in Figure 1. It is this marker or HMAC tag that our sensor uses to detect access to a decoy document. In the next section, we describe how our sensor makes use of this marker.

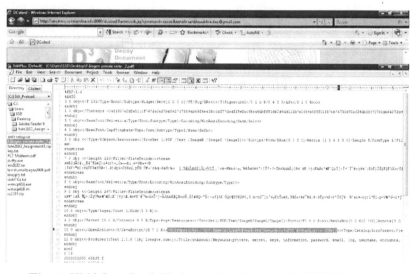

Fig. 1. HMAC in the OCP Properties Section of a PDF Document

3.3 Decoy Documents Access Sensor

The DDA sensor detects malicious activity by monitoring user actions directed at HMAC-embedded decoy documents, as any action directed toward a decoy document is suggestive of malicious activity [1]. When a decoy document is accessed by any application or process, the host sensor initiates a verification function. The verification function is responsible for distinguishing between decoys and normal documents by computing a HMAC as described in Section 3.2 for that document and comparing it to the one embedded within the document. If the two HMACs match, the document is deemed a decoy and an alert is triggered; otherwise, the document is deemed normal and no action is taken. The

DDA sensor detects when decoy documents are being read, copied, or zipped. The sensor was built for the Windows XP platform and relies on hooks placed in the Windows Service Table. The hooking is performed by injecting code into the address space of the processes, and by replacing the address of the *file open* system call which is present in the kernel (.dll) library of windows. This code injection guarantees that our code will be executed first, and post processing it will call the actual system call. This approach also enables the configuration of the list of processes that should be hooked into or should be excluded from hooking into.

In order to prevent the sensor from being shut down by the adversary, we used a random directed cycle of n monitors to protect the DDA sensor as proposed by Chinchani et al. [5] and Stolfo et al. [14]. One of the n monitors, call it m, monitors the critical processes of the sensor. If an attacker attempts to shut down any of the sensor processes, monitor m will issue an alert. Similarly, if m is shutdown, another monitor, as defined by the directed cycle of monitors, issues an alert. The directed cycle of monitors is created based on a seed known only to the owner of the system. It defines a unique shutdown sequence that must be followed in order to shut down the sensor without any alerts.

4   User Study 1

4.1   Experiment Design

Our first user study aims to measure decoy document accesses performed by the legitimate users of the system, which can be considered as false positives. We seek to answer two questions through this user study:

1. Does the number of decoy files planted in a file system have an impact on their non-interference with the legitimate user's normal activities?
2. What are the best locations for planting decoys on a file system, so as to minimize their non-interference?

To answer these questions, we designed an experiment where we controlled the number n of decoy documents planted in a file system. We postulate that non-interference is a variable that is dependent on the number of decoy documents n. We do not measure non-interference as a probability. However, we measure the average number of decoy accesses per one week of computer usage. To that extent, we asked four user groups of thirteen computer science students each, to plant ten, twenty, thirty, or forty decoy documents generated by D^3 on their own file systems. The 52 students downloaded a total of 1300 decoy documents from D^3. We encouraged the participants in the user study to carefully consider where to place the decoy files and how to name them by taking into account the desired properties of such documents, particularly enticingness, conspicuousness and non-interference [4]. The objective is to maximize the likelihood that a potential masquerader will get detected when they illegitimately access the victim's computer, while minimizing the likelihood that they (the legitimate user) accidentally accesses these documents due to confusion or interference with their normal activity. For instance, the user can choose file names that are easily recognizable as decoy by them, while remaining enticing to the adversary. The file name could, for example, include the name of a person who is outside the social network of the user. For instance, one participant renamed a decoy file to *TaxReturnSylvia.pdf*, while he did not file any tax returns jointly with *Sylvia*, nor did he know anyone with that name. Carefully selecting the file names would make the file easily recognizable as a decoy file by the legitimate user, but could make it intriguing for the attacker.

The participants in the user study, who installed our DDA sensor before downloading the decoy documents, agreed to share their data. The experiment lasted for about seven days on average, during which access to decoy files was monitored. The data collected by the DDA sensor was uploaded to a central server for analysis.

4.2   Experiment Findings

At the end of the user study, the participants reported the directories under which they placed the downloaded decoy files. We summarized the results of these reports and ranked the directories based on decreasing numbers of placed decoys. The top 42 directories are shown in Table 1. Subdirectories under the *My Documents* and *Desktop* directories seemed to be the most popular choices by the participants. In the following, we summarize the main findings of this user study.

Interference Increases With More Decoy Files: Recall that non-interference is defined as the likelihood of the legitimate user accessing the authentic files after installing the decoy files. Decoy files planted on a file system for masquerade detection are not supposed to be accessed by the legitimate user. They are placed there in order to entice attackers to open and use them. Any accidental accesses to decoy files by the legitimate users of the system, i.e. accesses that are not caused by an attacker gaining access to the file system, are considered as false positives. We have ignored all alerts issued within the first hour of the students installing the decoy documents on their systems, giving them an opportunity to decide where to place the decoy documents and how to rename them, based on the recommendations given to them in our user study description. Table 2 presents the number of false positives and shows that it grows super-linearly with the number of decoy files planted in the file system. The higher the number of decoy files placed in the file system, the higher the likelihood of a legitimate user accidentally accessing one of these decoy files, thus, the lower the non-interference of these decoy files with the normal activities of the legitimate user. While a more longitudinal study is needed to investigate the relationship between the number of decoys planted and their impact on non-interference, our preliminary results show that non-interference decreases with the number of decoys planted.

Table 1. Decoy Document Placement

Decoy File Number	Directory where Decoy was Placed
1	C:\Documents and Settings*username* \My Documents\Personal\Shopping\
2	C:\Documents and Settings*username*\My Documents\Taxes\
3	C:\
4	F:\
5	C:\Documents and Settings*username*\My Documents\Receipts\
6	C:\Documents and Settings*username*\Desktop\
7	C:\Documents and Settings*username*\My Documents\Financial\Bank Statements\
8	C:\Documents and Settings\Administrator\
9	C:\Documents and Settings*username*\My Documents\
10	C:\Documents and Settings*username*\My Documents\Financial\
11	C:\Documents and Settings*username*\My Documents\Private\
12	C:\Documents and Settings*username*\My Documents\Personal\
13	C:\Documents and Settings*username*\My Documents\Private\Medical
14	C:\Documents and Settings*username*\My Documents\Downloads\
15	C:\Documents and Settings*username*\My Documents\Financial\Lost Card\
16	C:\Documents and Settings*username*\My Documents\Financial\Disputes\
17	C:\Documents and Settings*username*\My Documents\onn\bills and all\eBay\
18	C:\Documents and Settings*username*\Desktop\Important\
19	C:\Program Files\License \
20	C:\Windows\Temp\
21	C:\Documents and Settings*username*\My Documents\Personal\Visa Applications\
22	C:\Documents and Settings*username*\My Documents\Private Vacation \
23	C:\Windows\
24	C:\Documents and Settings*username*\My Documents\Confidential\
25	C:\Documents and Settings*username*\Cookies\
26	C:\Documents and Settings*username*\Favorites\
27	C:\Documents and Settings*username*\workspace\
28	C:\Documents and Settings*username*\My Documents\Investments\
29	C:\Documents and Settings*username*\My Documents\Resume\
30	C:\Documents and Settings*username*\Desktop\My Journal\
31	C:\Backup\
32	C:\Documents and Settings*username*\My Pictures\
33	C:\Documents and Settings*username*\Desktop\Notes\
34	C:\Documents and Settings*username*\My Documents\Confidential\Employee Evaluations\
35	C:\Documents and Settings*username*\Recent\
36	C:\Documents and Settings*username*\Start Menu\
37	C:\Documents and Settings*username*\Desktop\Insurance\
38	C:\Documents and Settings*username*\Local Settings\
39	C:\Documents and Settings*username*\My Documents\401K\
40	C:\Documents and Settings*username*\My Documents\Mortgage\
41	C:\Documents and Settings*username*\My Music\
42	C:\Documents and Settings*username*\My Documents\Miscellaneous\

Table 2. Number of Decoys and Decoy Touches

Number of Placed Decoys	Number of Participants in Experiment	Number of Decoy Accesses
10	13	2
20	13	6
30	13	9
40	13	24

Distribution of False Positives: Figure 2 is a box-and-whisker plot of the decoy file accesses by the legitimate users for the four different values of decoys planted in the file system. The horizontal line in the middle of each of the boxes in these plots corresponds to the median value of decoy file accesses. Fifty per cent of the data falls within this box, while the top and bottom quartiles (25% of the data) of the data are represented by the whisker lines above and below this box. Data points whose value is above 1.5 times the upper quartile or lower than 1.5 times the lower quartiles are considered outliers, and are represented as small crosses. The short horizontal lines above and below the box represent the maximum and minimum data values excluding outliers.

The figure shows that for the case of ten decoys, only one false positive was recorded for any single user, whereas that number reaches up to nine false positives when 40 decoys are placed in the file system. Although the nine false positives is considered an outlier in this figure, more than 50% of the users who placed 40 decoy documents in their file systems did accidentally access at least one decoy file and experienced some level of interference with their normal activities. As the figure shows, not only does the likelihood of interference for each user grow with the number of decoy documents placed in the file system, but the amount of interference for each affected user increases non-linearly as well.

Placement of Decoy Files: Figure 3 shows the number of false positives by decoy location across the top 42 most popular locations as reported by the user study participants. The specific directory locations are listed in Table 1. The number of false positives varies widely by decoy document path or location. It is noteworthy that only fifteen of the top 40 decoy file locations were accidentally accessed by the legitimate users. Many decoy files were never accessed by these users demonstrating that non-interference of the decoy documents varies by the chosen decoy placement in the file system. While the ideal decoy placement that minimizes interference should be customized by the user based on their file system access habits, it seems that certain locations should be avoided such as the *high traffic* location or those locations that get automatically scanned by applications installed on the system.

The highest number of false positives are due to accesses to decoy files placed in location number 14, i.e. under the *Downloads* directory. While eight of the nine false positives in this location were triggered by a single user, the results show that decoy files in this location can introduce a high level of interference. This is not surprising knowing that most browsers save downloaded files in the

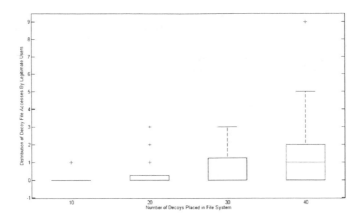

Fig. 2. Distribution of the Number of Decoy Document Accesses by Legitimate Users

Downloads directory by default, thus forcing a lot of user activity and *traffic* on files in this directory.

Differentiability to the User is Not Enough: The second decoy file location that exhibited a high number of false positives according to Figure 3 is the *My Music* directory. These false positives could be accidentally triggered by the legitimate users when manually browsing the directory, but they are more likely to be triggered by media player that are scanning the directory in order to discover recently added music files. Even though this scanning for media files is initiated by the user who knows exactly which files are decoy files, the media player or application performing a thorough scan cannot identify these decoy files, and therefore will access them in an attempt to identify whether these files are indeed music or video files.

We will further investigate the decoy placement strategies in the next section, where we will show that decoy placement, and therefore decoy conspicuousness, is also tightly linked with the ability to detect masqueraders.

5   User Study 2

5.1   Experiment Design

In this experiment, we investigate two decoy deployment-related properties, namely enticingness and conspicuousness. Evaluating the design-related properties such as believability, particularly as it pertains to the contents of the decoy document, is not very relevant to the masquerade attack problem. Recall that we detect access to the decoy files before the attacker sees the contents of the file. We ensure variability by tagging all files on the system with a pseudo-random HMAC tag. Detectability can be ensured through the use of the DDA

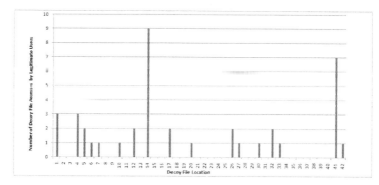

Fig. 3. Accidental False Positive Decoy Document Accesses by Legitimate Users

sensor and protecting the sensor, as well as protecting the key used to compute the HMAC tags of the decoy files. Note that any attempt to modify the HMAC tag by the attacker requires that the decoy file gets first accessed and loaded into memory, which would trigger an alert by the DDA sensor.

We seek to answer the following questions through this experiment:

1. How many decoy documents are needed to detect with a high probability masqueraders looking to steal information?
2. Where are decoy documents most likely to trap masquerade attackers, *i.e.* in which directories should one place the decoys in order to maximize the likelihood of catching a masquerader, while not interfering with the legitimate user's normal activities?
3. What is the number of decoy documents that leads to the best trade-off between masquerade detection while not interfering with the legitimate user's activities?
4. To what extent do decoy file accesses reveal a masquerader's *malicious* intent?

5.2 Experimental Set-Up

We conducted a set of experiments where we simulated masquerader attacks. While simulating masquerader attacks in the lab is not ideal, it was the best available option. We randomly selected 40 computer science students to participate in our user study and gave all participants a specific scenario that described the difficult financial situation that they were going through, and their need for additional financial resources. The participants were asked to perform a specific task, which consisted of stealing, from a coworker's desktop computer, any information that could be used for financial gain. They had access to the coworker's computer for 15 minutes while the coworker left for lunch. Besides their financial difficulties, the scenario also described the personal problems they were having with the coworker. In particular, they believed that their coworker had been undeservingly promoted instead of them, making any PII information theft or the cause of financial damage to their colleague, that they might engage in, justifiable to them. The task was goal-specific in order to capture the intent of the users. Although one may argue that simulating a masquerade attack is not appropriate, and that the participants may be constrained because of their ethical concerns. We claim that, with a well-written scenario and very clear instructions, the participants will act as masqueraders. To this extent, we refer the reader to the very well-known Milgram experiment [11]. Milgram showed that subjects would blindly follow clear instructions presented by an authority figure, even when they contradict their own values and ethics [11].

The participants in the user study knew that they were being monitored. They had unlimited access to a computer in our lab for 15 minutes using an administrator's account. So they had access to all the file systems mounted to that computer. None of the participants had access to this file system before, which was designed to look very realistic and to include potentially interesting patent applications, personally identifiable information, as well as account credentials. We installed the DDA sensor on this computer, and planted n decoy files in the file system. The goal was to monitor when and where the masqueraders accessed these decoy files. Table 3 shows how we varied the number of decoy documents n for each experiment, which involved ten participants acting as masqueraders.

In order to reduce experimenter bias when placing these decoy documents, we have surveyed 52 computer science students as to where they would place decoy documents on their file systems. The directory list shown in Table 1 indicate where we placed the decoy documents for each experiment (top 40, top 30, top 20, and top 10 directories respectively). Recall that these decoy locations have been selected based on the reports collected from the fifty-two student participants in our first user study.

The number of decoy documents n is the independent variable that we control in this user study. The number of decoy file touches is the dependent variable on the number of decoys n planted in the file system.

The file system used in our lab had more than 100,000 files indexed by desktop search tools installed on the system, and totaling a size of more than 70 GBytes. The file system included at least eighty files containing personal information that could be used for identity theft or financial gain. The contents of certain personal files were sanitized, so that no personal information was leaked.

Before conducting the experiments, we ensured that all non-decoy documents on the file system were tagged with a random tag, that is indistinguishable from the HMAC tag of the decoy documents. This was done so that a more

Table 3. Total Number of Decoy Alerts by Experiment

Experiment	Number of Placed Decoys	Number of Decoy Alerts
1	40	96
2	30	90
3	20	71
4	10	56

knowledgeable attacker cannot distinguish the decoy files from the normal files by editing them through a hex editor and looking for the HMAC tag within the document. This ensures the fifth desirable property of decoy documents, namely that they are not easily distinguishable as decoys to the attacker.

Besides tagging the real non-decoy files, we have indexed all the decoy files using the available desktop search tools on the system. Recall that the DDA sensor issues an alert if the contents of the decoy file are read or it gets loaded into memory. Thus, indexing the decoy files during the deployment phase can reduce potential false positive alerts that could be issued by the DDA sensor while conducting the experiments. The goal is to have more reliable and accurate results, where the sensor alerts are truly caused by the masquerader's activity, and not by desktop search tools suddenly scanning the decoy files.

5.3   Experiment Findings

In the following section, we list the major findings of this user study.

The Use of Decoys is Effective: The main purpose of our use of decoys is to detect masquerader attacks. While non-interference with legitimate users' activities is desirable, decoys would be useless if they fail to attract masqueraders by being enticing and conspicuous. The results displayed in Figure 4 suggest that at least one access to a decoy document was detected by the DDA sensor for every masquerader, regardless of the number of decoys planted in the file system. This finding shows that well-placed decoys can be very effective for masquerade detection. When combined with other intrusion detection techniques, they could potentially provide even more effective and accurate detectors.

Recommended Number of Decoys: Figure 4 shows the distribution of the number of decoy file accesses by attackers in the four experiments by the number of decoy files placed in the file system. One could clearly see that the average number of touched decoys (horizontal line within each box) is comparable in the case of 20, 30, and 40 decoys. Whereas it is slightly lower (5.6 touches) when 10 decoys are planted in the file system. Considering Figures 2 and 4 then, one can conclude that the use of twenty decoy documents provides the best trade-off between detection capability and non-interference. Although the minimum number of touched decoys jumps from 1 or 2 to 5 in the case of 40 planted decoys, this high number could be attributed to the location of the planted decoys and not merely to the higher number of decoys. This can be clearly seen in Figures 8 and 9 which show the conspicuousness of decoy files 33 and 37 for instance. We will elaborate on this point in the following discussion.

High Number of Decoy Accesses is Indicative of Attacker's Malicious Intent: The question is how many of these decoy file accesses are caused by the masquerader's malicious activity. To answer this question, we conducted an experiment with three groups of ten participants each. Each group was given a different scenario to execute: a 'malicious attacker' scenario which we described in subsection 5.2, a 'benign masquerader' scenario, or a 'neutral' scenario. In

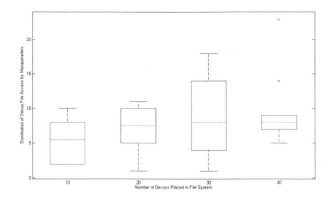

Fig. 4. Distribution of the Number of Decoy Document Accesses

the *benign* scenario, the participants in the experiment were allowed to access a coworker's computer for 15 minutes in order to accomplish a specific work-related task, after their own computer experienced a hard drive failure. In the *neutral* scenario, the participants were left to freely choose whether they wanted to access their coworker's desktop while the coworker left for 15 minutes. They had no specific motive to do so. In all three scenarios, we placed 30 decoys in the file system of the lab computer that served as the participant's coworker's computer. The benign and malicious scenarios can provide a baseline to compare the decoy touches of a malicious masquerader to. Figure 5 shows the distribution of decoy touches by scenario. One can clearly see that the number of decoy touches is very low in the benign and neutral scenarios when compared to the malicious scenario.

The Use of Decoys is Efficient: According to the results shown in Figure 6, 17 attackers were detected during the first minute of their masquerade activity, while another ten were detected during the second minute after accessing the victim's computer. All masqueraders were detected within ten minutes of their accessing the system under attack. Figure 6 also shows that for attackers 31-40, who participated in experiment 4 with only 10 planted decoy documents, the average period of undetected masquerader activity (3.6 minutes) is much longer, than for attackers 1-10 (1.3 minutes), 11-20 (1.6 minutes), and 21-30 (1.2 minutes).

Attackers 1 and 14 recorded the longest times of undetected masquerader activity. These attackers had a different strategy for finding personal information. One attacker was mostly after information related to the victim's online banking activity, rather than after information that existed locally on the file system. The attacker, therefore did not navigate or search the *My Documents* directory, where most decoys were located. Not surprisingly, the first decoy that they hit was decoy number 16. located under Internet Explorer's *Favorites* directory.

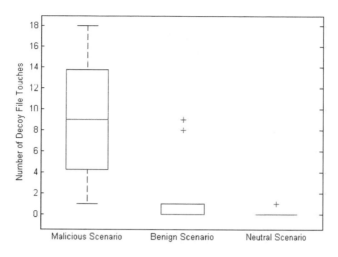

Fig. 5. Distribution of the Number of Decoy Document Accesses by Scenario

Attacker 14, on the other hand, suspected that no important information would be stored under the user's file system, but rather under the administrator's file system, which is why he only hit a single decoy document, namely decoy number 8 (see Table 1 for the exact decoy location). Note that attacker 1 took part in the first experiment where 40 decoys were planted, and attacker 14 participated in experiment 2, where 30 decoys were used. So even with a larger number of decoys, the attackers managed to escape detection for 10 minutes, which suggests we need a well thought-out placement of decoys, that covers all potential attacker strategies for locating and stealing information.

Consider the null hypothesis that a masquerader activity within a 10-minute time window gets missed with at least 10% probability in the presence of at least 40 decoy files. Based on the observed results, we can reject this hypothesis at the 2% significance level with a p-value=0.0148. In other words, we can claim that with a 98% probability, the probability of detecting a masquerader within 10 minutes of their activity on the victim's system is at least 90%.

Decoy Placement is Important: The objective is to identify the decoy document locations that would be less interfering with the normal activity of the legitimate user, while being conspicuous to potential attackers. While the experiments have not been conducted on the same system, and the decoy file locations vary by normal user (customized for their own non-interfering use of the system), we argue that the cumulative results do provide ground for comparison, as we have monitored the use for about 7 days on average for each user, for a total of 52 users.

Figure 8 shows the number of accesses to each decoy file by experiment. Note that the first ten decoy documents were present during all four experiments, whereas the decoys 31-40, for instance were in place only during the last

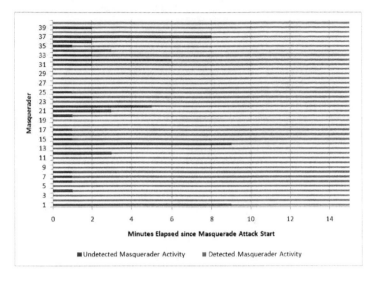

Fig. 6. Detection Time by User

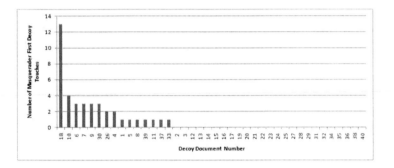

Fig. 7. Decoy File First Touches

experiment. This explains the falling line in Figure 8, which depicts the maximum number of potential attackers accessing these decoys, knowing that there were ten masqueraders in each experiment.

The number of decoy file accesses varies widely by file location. The locations are available in Table 1. Some files were accessed more than 25 times, while others, namely nine out of the forty decoy files, have never been touched by any attacker. This underlines the importance of decoy placement in highly conspicuous locations.

Considering figures 8 and 2 for instance, one can notice that the decoy placed in location 18 was touched by 28 masqueraders. Decoys placed in the same location by the participants in the first user study were not touched by the legitimate users and did not trigger any false positives. On the other hand,

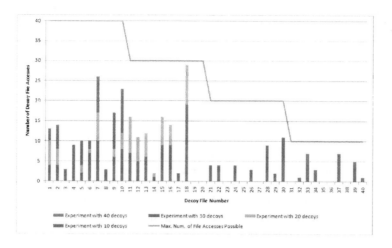

Fig. 8. Number of Decoy Document Accesses

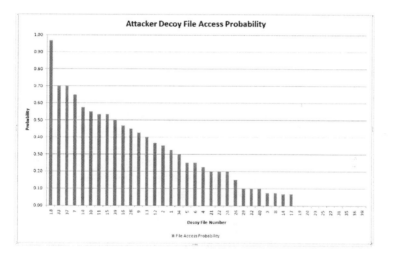

Fig. 9. Probability of an Attacker Opening the Decoy File

decoys placed in locations 19, 23, 25, and 31 for instance caused several false positives without catching any masquerader. The two figures clearly show that the location of the decoy document plays an important role in its detection capability and non-interference with normal user activities. While the locations that yield the least interference depend on the legitimate user's file system access patterns, there is clearly room for placing decoys under directories, so that high detection rates with very low interference rates.

Conspicuousness Comes First: In order to understand how effective each decoy file was in catching masqueraders, we have ranked the decoy files based on the probability of an attacker accessing them in Figure 9. Recall that an access in this case refers to viewing, editing, copying, zipping, or moving the decoy file. Considering Figure 9 and the table in Table 1, the top three decoy files that are most likely to be accessed by an attacker reside on the *Desktop*. These three files reside respectively in the *Important, Notes* and *Insurance* directories. The first file was a payment receipt. The second file included a budget plan, and the third file was a copy of test results from a medical lab. Other decoys with contents similar to the contents of decoy 18, such as decoys 4 and 5 which constituted payment receipts also, did not achieve the same detection capability as decoy 37. This leads us to the conclusion, that conspicuousness is more important than enticingness. Although the attackers were mostly after information with financial value, they were more likely to access files with health-related information that were highly conspicuous (located on the desktop), than other decoys with more relevant information to their objective, i.e. finance-related information.

6   Discussion and Recommendations

We list here a few recommendations related to the deployment of decoy documents for effective masquerade attack detection based on the findings of our user studies.

6.1   Recommendation 1

While, the detectability property of the decoy documents is the most important property, our second user study has shown how important the *conspicuousness* property is. The latter is even more important than the *enticingness* property, as revealed by the user study.

We recommend considering the following ranking of decoy properties when designing and deploying decoy documents for masquerade attack detection. The ranking is based on decreasing importance of the decoy properties.

1. Detectability
2. Conspicuousness
3. Enticingness
4. Non-Interference and Differentiability
5. Believability

The importance of the *variability* property varies by attacker sophistication. Similarly, the importance of the *decoy shelf-life* depends on the deployment environment.

6.2   Recommendation 2

While the number of false positives varies widely by user and by decoy document location, overall we averaged less than 1 false positive per user per week. This is a very encouraging number, but it could be even further reduced with more intelligent placement of the decoy documents. For example, the decoy files placed under the *My Pictures* and *My Music* directories could be accessed by applications scanning the file system for picture or music files respectively. Such accesses are not deliberate accesses by the legitimate user and could be avoided, if the decoy files are placed under directories that are not by default scanned by such applications. The user may choose to ignore decoy alerts triggered by these applications by configuring the sensor accordingly. Recall that, as described in section 3.3, the hooking mechanism used by the sensor enables the filtering of decoy alerts issued by user-defined processes.

7   Conclusion

In this paper, we presented an experimental evaluation of the different deployment-related properties of decoy documents. We also made a few recommendations based on the findings from our experiments. These recommendations should guide the deployment of decoy documents for effective masquerade detection.

In our future work, we will repeat the experiments in different environments, other than universities, to ascertain whether the results are broadly applicable. We will also evaluate other decoy document properties, including the *believability* of documents. Furthermore, we will investigate the decoy document properties for masquerade attacks perpetrated through the installation of rootkits and malware such as Torpig. Finally, we will study how attacker behavior changes based on their knowledge about the monitoring mechanisms running on the victim's system and their perception of risk and expected financial gain.

Acknowledgment. We thank Shlomo Hershkop and Brian Bowen for their work on D^3. We further thank Shlomo Hershkop for his support with the DDA sensor.

References

1. Ben-Salem, M.: DDA Sensor, http://www1.cs.columbia.edu/ids/ruu/data/
2. Ben-Salem, M., Hershkop, S., Stolfo, S.J.: A survey of insider attack detection research. In: Insider Attack and Cyber Security: Beyond the Hacker. Springer, Heidelberg (2008)
3. Bowen, B., and Hershkop, S. Decoy.: Document Distributor, http://sneakers.cs.columbia.edu/ids/ruu/dcubed/
4. Bowen, B.M., Hershkop, S., Keromytis, A.D., Stolfo, S.J.: Baiting inside attackers using decoy documents. In: SecureComm 2009: Proceedings of the 5th International ICST Conference on Security and Privacy in Communication Networks (2009)
5. Chinchani, R., Upadhyaya, S., Kwiat, K.: A tamper-resistant framework for unambiguous detection of attacks in user space using process monitors. In: Proceedings of First IEEE International Workshop on Information Assurance (IWIAS 2003), pp. 25–34 (2003)
6. Greenberg, A.: ID Theft: Don't Take it Personally (February 2010), http://www.forbes.com/2010/02/09/banks-consumers-fraud-technology-security-id-theft.html

7. Higgins, K. J.: Widespread Confickr/Downadup Worm Hard To Kill (January 2009), http://www.darkreading.com/security/attacks-breaches/212901489/index.html
8. Kim, J.-S., Biryukov, A., Preneel, B., Hong, S.H.: On the Security of HMAC and NMAC Based on HAVAL, MD4, MD5, SHA-0 and SHA-1 (Extended Abstract). In: De Prisco, R., Yung, M. (eds.) SCN 2006. LNCS, vol. 4116, pp. 242–256. Springer, Heidelberg (2006)
9. Krawczyk, H., Bellare, M., Canetti, R.: RFC2104, HMAC: Keyed-Hashing for Message Authentication. The Internet Engineering Task Force (IETF)
10. Maxion, R.A., Townsend, T.N.: Masquerade detection using truncated command lines. In: DSN 2002: Proceedings of the International Conference on Dependable Systems and Networks (2002)
11. Milgram, S.: Obedience to Authority: An Experimental View. Harpercollins, New York (1974)
12. Schonlau, M., Dumouchel, W., Ju, W., Karr, A.F., Theus, M., Vardi, Y.: Computer intrusion: Detecting masquerades. Statistical Science 16, 58–74 (2001)
13. Spitzner, L.: Honeypots: Catching the insider threat. In: Proceedings of the 19th Annual Computer Security Applications Conference, pp. 170–179 (December 2003)
14. Stolfo, S.J., Greenbaum, I., Sethumadhavan, S.: Self-monitoring monitors. In: Columbia University Computer Science Department, Technical Report # cucs-026-09 (2009)
15. Stone-Gross, B., Cova, M., Cavallaro, L., Gilbert, B., Szydlowski, M., Kemmerer, R., Kruegel, C., Vigna, G.: Your botnet is my botnet: analysis of a botnet takeover. In: CCS 2009: Proceedings of the 16th ACM conference on Computer and communications security, pp. 635–647. ACM Press, New York (2009)
16. Wang, K., Stolfo, S.J.: One-class training for masquerade detection. In: Proceedings of the 3rd IEEE Workshop on Data Mining for Computer Security (2003)
17. Yuill, J., Zappe, M., Denning, D., Feer, F.: Honeyfiles: deceptive files for intrusion detection. In: Proceedings from the Fifth Annual IEEE SMC Information Assurance Workshop, pp. 116–122 (June 2004)

Reverse Social Engineering Attacks in Online Social Networks

Danesh Irani[1], Marco Balduzzi[2], Davide Balzarotti[2],
Engin Kirda[3], and Calton Pu[1]

[1] College of Computing, Georgia Institute of Technology, Atlanta
[2] Institute Eurecom, Sophia Antipolis
[3] Northeastern University, Boston

Abstract. Social networks are some of the largest and fastest growing online services today. Facebook, for example, has been ranked as the second most visited site on the Internet, and has been reporting growth rates as high as 3% per week. One of the key features of social networks is the support they provide for finding new friends. For example, social network sites may try to automatically identify which users know each other in order to propose friendship recommendations.

Clearly, most social network sites are critical with respect to user's security and privacy due to the large amount of information available on them, as well as their very large user base. Previous research has shown that users of online social networks tend to exhibit a higher degree of trust in friend requests and messages sent by other users. Even though the problem of unsolicited messages in social networks (i.e., spam) has already been studied in detail, to date, reverse social engineering attacks in social networks have not received any attention. In a reverse social engineering attack, the attacker does not initiate contact with the victim. Rather, the victim is tricked into contacting the attacker herself. As a result, a high degree of trust is established between the victim and the attacker as the victim is the entity that established the relationship.

In this paper, we present the first user study on reverse social engineering attacks in social networks. That is, we discuss and show how attackers, in practice, can abuse some of the friend-finding features that online social networks provide with the aim of launching reverse social engineering attacks. Our results demonstrate that reverse social engineering attacks are feasible and effective in practice.

Keywords: social engineering, social networks, privacy.

1 Introduction

Social networking sites such as Facebook, LinkedIn, and Twitter are arguably the fastest growing web-based online services today. Facebook, for example, has been reporting growth rates as high as 3% per week, with more than 400 million registered users as of March 2010 [2]. Many users appreciate social networks because they make it easier to meet new people, find old friends, and share multimedia artifacts such as videos and photographs.

T. Holz and H. Bos. (Eds.): DMIVA 2011, LNCS 6739, pp. 55–74, 2011.

One of the key features of social networks is the support they provide for finding new friends. For example, a typical technique consists of automatically identifying common friends in cliques and then promoting new friendships with messages such as *"You have 4 mutual friends with John Doe. Would you like to add John Doe as a new friend?"*. Also, information on the activities of users are often collected, analyzed, and correlated to determine the probability that two users may know each other. If a potential acquaintance is detected, a new friendship recommendation might be displayed by the social network site when the user logs in.

Clearly, social networks are critical applications with respect to the security and privacy of their users. In fact, the large amount of information published, and often publicly shared, on the user profiles is increasingly attracting the attention of attackers. Attacks on social networks are usually variants of traditional security threats (such as malware, worms, spam, and phishing). However, these attacks are carried out in a different context by leveraging the social networks as a new medium to reach the victims. Moreover, adversaries can take advantage of the trust relationships between "friends" in social networks to craft more convincing attacks by exploiting personal information gleaned from victims' pages.

Past research has shown that users of online social networks tend to exhibit a higher degree of trust in friend requests and messages sent by other users (e.g., [1,5]). In addition, some forms of attacks on social networks, such as the problem of unsolicited messages, have already been studied in detail by the research community (e.g., [9,16]). However, to date, *reverse social engineering* attacks in social networks have not received any attention. Hence, no previous work exists on the topic.

In a reverse social engineering attack, the attacker does not initiate contact with the victim. Rather, the victim is tricked into contacting the attacker herself. As a result, a high degree of trust is established between the victim and the attacker as the victim is the entity that first wanted to establish a relationship. Once a reverse social engineering attack is successful (i.e., the attacker has established a friend relationship with the victim), she can then launch a wide range of attacks such as persuading victims to click on malicious links, blackmailing, identity theft, and phishing.

This paper presents the first user study on how attackers can abuse some of the features provided by online social networks with the aim of launching automated reverse social engineering attacks. We present three novel attacks, namely, recommendation-based, visitor tracking-based, and demographics-based reverse social engineering. Furthermore, using the popular social networks Facebook, Badoo, and Friendster, we discuss and measure the effectiveness of these attacks, and we show which social networking features make such attacks feasible in practice.

In the recommendation attack, the aim is to exploit the friend recommendations made by the social network to promote the fake profile of a fictitious user to the victim. The hope, from the attacker's point of view, is that the victim will be intrigued by the recommendation, and will attempt to contact the bogus profile that is under the attacker's control. In the visitor tracking attack, the aim is to trigger the target's curiosity by simply browsing her profile page. The notification that the page has been visited may be enough to attract the target to visit the attacker profile. Finally, in the demographic-based attack scenario, the attacker attempts to reach his victims by forging fake demographic or personal information with the aim of attracting the attention of users with similar preferences (e.g., similar musical tastes, similar interests, etc.).

Our findings suggest that, contrary to the common folk wisdom, only having an account with an attractive photograph may not be enough to recruit a high number of unsuspecting victims. Rather, the attacker needs to provide victims with a pretext and an incentive for establishing contact.

In this paper, we make the following contributions:

- We present the first user study on reverse social engineering in social networks and present three novel attacks. In particular, we discuss and measure how attackers can abuse some of the friend-finding features that online social networks provide with the aim of launching automated reverse social engineering attacks against victims.
- We measure how different user profile attributes and friend recommendation features affect the success of reverse social engineering attempts.
- We study the interactions of users with accounts that have been set up to perform reverse social engineering, and provide insights into why users fall victim to such attacks.
- We propose mitigation techniques to secure social networks against reverse social engineering attempts.

2   Reverse Social Engineering in Social Networks

Online social engineering attacks are easy to propagate, difficult to trace back to the attacker, and usually involves a low cost per targeted user. They are well-known threats in which the attacker aims at influencing the victims, and making them perform actions on her behalf. The attacker is typically interested in tricking the victims into revealing sensitive or important information. Examples of these attacks include traditional e-mail hoaxes and phishing, or their more advanced targeted forms, such as spear phishing.

Most online social engineering attacks rely on some form of "pretexting" [14]. That is, the attacker establishes contact with the target, and sends some initial request to bootstrap the attack. This approach, although effective because it can reach a large number of potential victims, has the downside that Internet users are becoming more and more suspicious about unsolicited contact requests. However, previous work has shown that it is possible to raise levels of trust by impersonating an existing friend of the target (e.g., [5,10]) or by injecting the attack into existing chat conversations [13].

Reverse Social Engineering (RSE) is a form of social engineering attack that has not yet been reported widely in an online context. RSE is a well-known

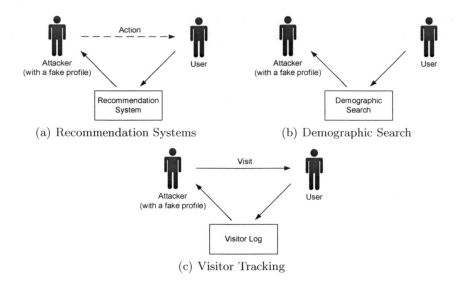

(a) Recommendation Systems   (b) Demographic Search

(c) Visitor Tracking

Fig. 1. Different types of Reverse Social Engineering attacks.

technique in the hacker community (e.g., [14]) for targeted phone attacks. The attack, in a first step, relies on some form of "baiting" to stimulate the victim's curiosity. In a second step, once the victim's interest is raised, the attacker waits for the victim to make the initial approach and initiate contact. An RSE attack usually requires the attacker to create a persona that would seem attractive to the victim and that would encourage the victim to establish contact. For example, directly calling users and asking them for their passwords on the phone might raise suspicion in some users. In the reverse social engineering version of the same attack, a phone number can be e-mailed to the targets a couple of days in advance by spoofing an e-mail from the system administrator. The e-mail may instruct the users to call this number in case of problems. In this example, any victim who calls the phone number would probably be less suspicious and more willing to share information as she has initiated the first contact.

RSE attacks are especially attractive for online social networks. First, from an attacker's point of view, there is a good potential to reach millions of registered users in this new social setting. Second, RSE has the advantage that it can bypass current behavioral and filter-based detection techniques that aim to prevent wide-spread unsolicited contact. Third, if the victim contacts the attacker, less suspicion is raised, and there is a higher probability that a social engineering attack (e.g., phishing, a financial scam, information theft, etc.) will be successful.

In general, Reverse Social Engineering attacks can be classified based on two main characteristics:

- *Targeted/Un-targeted*: In a targeted attack, the attacker focuses on a particular user. In contrast, in an un-targeted attack, the attacker is solely
  interested in reaching as many users as possible. Note that in order to

perform a targeted attack, the attacker has to know (or acquire) some previous information about the target (e.g., such as her username or e-mail address).

– *Direct/Mediated*: In a direct attack, the baiting action of the attacker is visible to the targeted users. For example, an attacker can post a message on a public forum, or publish some interesting picture on a website. Mediated attacks, in contrast, follow a two-step approach in which the baiting is collected by an intermediate agent that is then responsible for propagating it (often in a different form) to the targeted users.

In the following, we present three different combinations of RSE attacks within the context of online social networks.

Recommendation-Based RSE [Targeted, Mediated] Recommendation systems in social networks propose relationships between users based on background, or "secondary knowledge" on users. This knowledge derives from the interactions between registered users, the friend relationships between them, and other artifacts based on their interaction with the social network. For example, the social networking site might record the fact that a user has visited a certain profile, a page, a picture, and also log the search terms she has entered. Popular social networks (e.g., Facebook) often use this information to make recommendations to users (e.g., *"Visit page X"*, *"You might know person Y, click here to become her friends"*, etc.).

From an attacker's point of view, a recommendation system is an interesting target. If the attacker is able to influence the recommendation system and make the social network issue targeted recommendations, she may be able to trick victims into contacting her. Figure 1(a) demonstrates the recommendation system-based RSE attack scenario.

Demographic-Based RSE [Un-targeted, Mediated] Demographic-based systems in social networks allow establishing friendships based on the information in a person's profile. Some social networks, especially dating sites (e.g., Badoo), use this technique as the norm for connecting users in the same geographical location, in the same age group, or those who have expressed similar preferences.

Figure 1(b) demonstrates an RSE attack that uses demographic information. In the attack, the attacker simply creates a profile (or a number of profiles) that would have a high probability of appealing to certain users, and then waits for victims to initiate contact.

Visitor Tracking-Based RSE [Targeted, Direct] Visitor tracking is a feature provided by some social networks (e.g., Xing, Friendster) to allow users to track who has visited their online profiles.

The attack in this case involves exploiting the user's curiosity by visiting their profile page. The notification that the page has been visited might raise interest, baiting the user to view the attacker's profile and perhaps take some action. Figure 1(c) outlines this attack method.

Table 1. RSE attacks on three popular social networks. ✓ indicates that the attack is possible; ✠ indicates that we demonstrate and measure the effectiveness of this attack on the particular social network.

Type of Attack	Facebook	Badoo	Friendster
Recommendation-Based	✓✠	-	-
Demographic- Based	✓	✓✠	✓
Visitor Tracking-Based	-	✓	✓✠

3 RSE Attacks in the Real-World

In this section, we present three types of real-world RSE attacks that are possible on three different social network platforms: Facebook, Badoo, and Friendster. In particular, we describe a recommendation-based RSE attack on Facebook, a demographic-based RSE attack on Badoo, and a visitor tracking-based RSE attack on Friendster.

Table 1 shows the social networks that were used in our experiments, and also describes which kind of RSE attacks are possible against them. Note that not all the combinations are possible in practice. For example, Facebook does not provide any information about the users that visit a certain profile, thus making a visitor tracking attack infeasible. In the rest of this section, we describe the different steps that are required to automate the attacks, and the setup of the experiments we performed.

3.1 Ethical and Legal Considerations

Real-world experiments involving social networks may be considered an ethically sensitive area. Clearly, one question that arises is if it is ethically acceptable and justifiable to conduct experiments that involve real users. Similar to the experiments conducted by Jakobsson et al. [11,12] and our previous work [5], we believe that realistic experiments are the only way to reliably estimate success rates of attacks in the real-world.

Furthermore, during all the experiments we describe in the paper, we took into account the privacy of the users, and the sensitivity of the data that was collected. When the data was analyzed, identifiers (e.g., names) were anonymized, and no manual inspection of the collected data was performed.

Note that all the experiments described in the paper were performed in Europe. Hence, we consulted with the legal department of our institution (comparable to the Institute Review Board (IRB) in the US) and our handling and privacy precautions were deemed appropriate and consistent with the European legal position.

3.2 Influencing Friend Recommendations

A good example of a real recommendation system is Facebook's friend suggestions. During our tests with Facebook, we observed that Facebook promotes the connection of users by suggesting them friends that they probably know. The system computes these suggestions based on common information, such as mutual friends, schools, companies, and interests. This feature is well-known to many social network users. In fact, whenever a user is logged in, she is regularly notified of persons that she may know.

Previous work [4] has shown that Facebook also uses the e-mail addresses a user has queried to identify a possible friendship connection between two users. The premise is that if users know each other's e-mail addresses, they must be connected in some way. Therefore, if an attacker gains access to the e-mail address of a victim (e.g., a spammer who has a list of e-mails at her disposal), by searching for that address, she can have a fake attacker profile be recommended to the victims. In our experiments, we observed that this technique results in the attacker profile being the most highly recommended profile.

For the first experiment, we used the data collected for over a year in a previous study we performed on Facebook [4]. In the study, we registered a single account that we used to perform a large number of e-mail search queries, using an email list obtained from a dropzone on a machine compromised by attackers. Without our knowledge, our profile was later recommended to all the queried users as a potential friend. As a result, our test account received thousands of messages and friend requests.

3.3   Measuring RSE Effects by Creating Attack Profiles

In the second set of experiments, we created five different attack profiles in three social networks. The profiles were designed with different characteristics to enable us to observe and measure the effects that each characteristic had on the effectiveness of the RSE attacks. That is, we were interested in determining which features would attract the higher number of potential victims using the recommendation-based, demographic-based, and visitor tracking attacks.

The five attack profiles are shown in Table 3. For the profile pictures, we used popular photographs from Wikipedia, licensed under the Creative Commons

Table 2. Overview of OSNs as well as number of users targeted

Social Network	# of Targets	Total users	Alexia Rank
Badoo	-	73 million	143
Facebook	250,000	500 million	2
Friendster	42,000	8.2 million	643

Table 3. Characteristics of the dummy profiles used in the experiments. (* In Badoo, more popular in Europe, we replaced N.Y with London)

Attribute	Prof. 1	Prof. 2	Prof. 3	Prof. 4	Prof. 5
Age	23	23	23	35	23
Sex	Male	Female	Female	Female	Female
Location*	N.Y.	N.Y.	Paris	N.Y.	N.Y.
Real Picture	Yes	Yes	Yes	Yes	No

license. All photos represented an attractive male or female, with the exception of Profile 5 for which we used a synthetic cartoon picture.

Table 2 shows the number of users we targeted in the social networks we tested. For example, in the Facebook experiment, we targeted a total of 250,000 profiles, equally divided between the 5 attack profiles. In the demographic-based attack on Badoo, no action was required on behalf of the attacker. Hence, the number of targeted users is not given (i.e., all registered Badoo users could have found and contacted the attacker profile).

3.4 Automating the Measurement Process.

During our study we developed a number of scripts to automate the three attacks and the measurement process on the different social networks.

Recommendation-Based RSE on Facebook. As shown in Figure 1(a), the recommendation-based RSE attack against Facebook consisted of two parts: First, the target user's profile was probed using an e-mail lookup, and second, the attack accounts were automatically monitored for victims who contacted these accounts based on the friendship recommendation made by Facebook.

For the first part, we used the "contact import" functionality provided by Facebook and the API provided by Google Mail's address book to automatically search for users by their e-mail addresses. We broke the total set of users we wished to query into smaller sets, and sent multiple requests to Facebook, as they have limited the number of e-mail addresses that can be queried using a single request (because of recommendations made in previous work [4]).

In the second part of the experiments, we wrote an API that allowed us to interact with Facebook to accept friend requests, fetch user profiles, as well as fetch any private message that may have been sent to the attack profiles.

Note that CAPTCHAs in Facebook were only encountered if we were not careful about rate limiting.

Demographic-Based RSE on Badoo. We used Badoo to test the demographic-based RSE attack. Hence, we only had to create the attack profiles and automatically monitor incoming connections. Just like in the recommendation-based RSE attack, we automatically retrieved and collected any message sent to the attacker profiles. Furthermore, as Badoo allows to see which users have visited a profile, we also logged this information.

Visitor Tracking-Based RSE on Friendster. We used Friendster to perform the RSE attack based on visitor tracking. As shown in Figure 1(c), this attack consists of two parts: First, we visit the target user's profile and as a consequence, the system shows to the victim that someone has visited her profile. If the attacker profile is interesting, the victim may choose to contact the attacker. Hence, in a second step, the visits and the incoming messages to the attack profiles were automatically monitored to determine which of the victims came back and initiated contact.

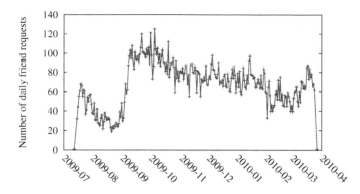

Fig. 2. Daily number of new friend requests in the initial Facebook experiment

4   Experimental Results

4.1   Recommendation-Based RSE Attack

Initial Experiment. During the study [4] we conducted, we observed that the test account we were using to query e-mail addresses were receiving a large number of friend requests. The profile used in this attack was similar to Profile 2 described in Table 3.

Figure 2 shows the number of daily friend requests received by the account used in this initial experiment. The graph shows that during the first two months, the account received an average of 45 requests per day, followed by an increase to an average of 75 requests per day for the next 6 months.

The rapid increase in the number of request is the consequence of the cascading effect that commenced when we started accepting the incoming invitations. The fact that the account had a large number of friends built up the "reputation" of our profile. In addition, we started being advertised by Facebook to new people with whom we shared common friends.

Of the over 500,000 e-mails queried by our decoy profile, we were contacted by over 17,000 users (i.e., 3.3% friend connect rate within 9 months and 0.37% friend connect rate per month). Note that our test account reached both the maximum number of active friend connections and the total number of pending friend requests allowed by Facebook.

Controlled, In-Depth Experiments. After the success of the initial experiment, we started a number of controlled, in-depth experiments to measure and determine which profile characteristics and social network features affect the success rates of RSE attacks.

To reach our goal, we created five attack profiles on Facebook. For each profile, we randomly selected 50,000 target users and looked up their e-mail addresses (hence, influencing the recommendations made by Facebook). We then measured the number of friend-requests, private messages, and other interaction sent to

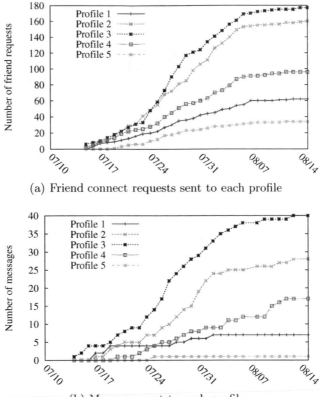

(a) Friend connect requests sent to each profile

(b) Messages sent to each profile

Fig. 3. Cumulative counts of interactions resulting from reverse social engineering on Facebook

each attack profile. Figure 3 depicts the result of this experiment. The y-axis represents the cumulative number of friend requests or messages for the period represented by the date on the x-axis.

Profiles 2 and 3 were the most successful in terms of the number of friend requests and messages that were received. Both profiles correspond to attractive females who are interested in friendship. Note that there was no correlation with the location of the attack profile (i.e., the location did not influence friend requests). Hence, an initial analysis seems to confirm the general intuition that an attractive female photograph will attract potential victims. In contrast to the other profiles, Profile 5 was the least effective. In this profile, a cartoon character was used as a photograph rather than a real picture. In comparison, Profile 1 performed only slightly better than Profile 5. This profile contained the photograph of an attractive male.

Over the entire month, the most effective profile had a friend connection rate of 0.35% (i.e., in line with the initial experimental profile). The least effective profile instead, had a friend connection rate of only 0.05%.

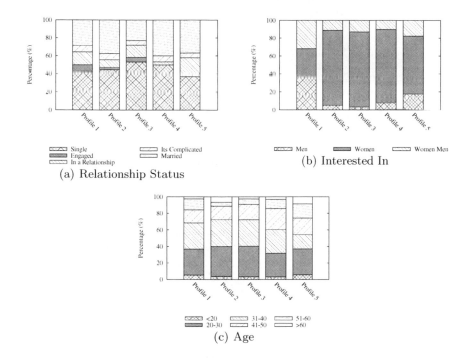

(a) Relationship Status

(b) Interested In

(c) Age

Fig. 4. Demographic breakdown by Relationship Status, Interested In, and Age for Friend Connect requests on Facebook

Although friend connection requests and private messages were the most common form of interaction with a decoy profile, we also received a large number of friend suggestions. Friend suggestions are suggestions made by the victim to other users. Such suggestions are important as they imply that a high level of trust has been achieved between the attacker and the victim. Also, note that over 94% of the messages to the attack profiles were sent after the friend connection requests.

By analyzing the demography of the users who contacted our attack profiles, we can identify potential characteristics that make a decoy profile appealing. In particular, we focused on three fields: relationship status, interested in, and age (Figure 4). The y-axis of the figure shows the percentage of friend connection requests that originated from a profile with the respective demographic value (empty values excluded) to the attack profile listed on the x-axis. Young, single users who have expressed interest in "Women" seem to be the easiest victims to attract. In comparison, Profile 1 (the only male profile) received a larger number of friend requests from users who had expressed interest in "Men".

Interestingly, the profile with a cartoon picture was the one to attract the largest number of requests coming from older users (i.e., those who were older than 40). Hence, the experiments show that by carefully tweaking the profile information, it is possible to obtain an higher success rate against a particular group of users.

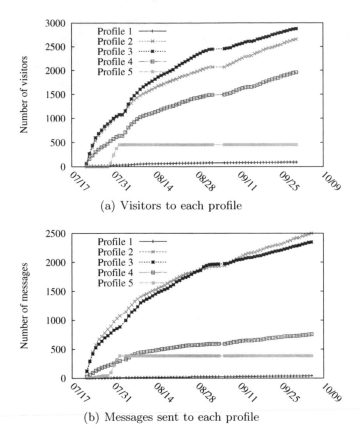

(a) Visitors to each profile

(b) Messages sent to each profile

Fig. 5. Cumulative counts of interactions resulting from reverse social engineering on Badoo

Finally, we analyzed the messages that were sent to the different attack profiles. To protect the privacy of individuals in the study, we first processed the messages and removed user identifiers. After anonymization, we only ran word-based statistical analyses on the message contents. That is, as a pre-processing step, we used Porter's stemming algorithm on the extracted tokens [15], followed by a count of n-grams (where a single gram is a stemmed token).

Around 10% of the messages mentioned the Facebook recommendation, including 3-grams such as "suggest you as" or "suggest I add". The analysis shows that some users used the recommendation made by the social network as a pretext to contact the attack profile.

4.2   Demographic-Based Experiment

For our demographic-based RSE attacks, we targeted Badoo, a dating oriented socializing system that allows users to meet new friends in a specific area. A registered user can list the people who have visited her profile and exchange

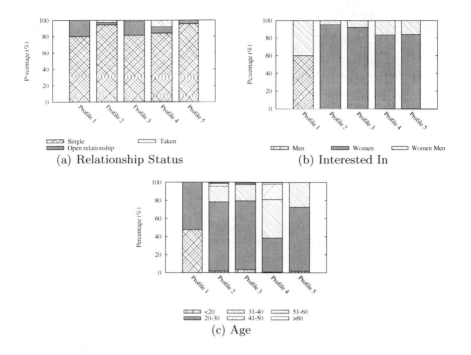

(a) Relationship Status   (b) Interested In

(c) Age

Fig. 6. Demographic breakdown by Relationship Status, Interested In, and Age for messages on Badoo

messages with other users. Figure 5 shows the cumulative number of visitors and messages received for each attack profile we created in the network.

Profiles 2 and 3 were again the most popular, and attracted the most visitors (over 2500 each). These profiles also received the largest number of messages (i.e., more than 2500 each). Because Profile 5 was not using a photograph of a person, it was removed by Badoo from the demographic search after it was visited by 451 users and it received 383 messages. Once again, Profile 1, the attack profile of a male user, received the fewest visits and friend requests.

Another measure of how successful an attack profile was is the percentage of users who decided to send a message after visiting a profile. These figures are over 50% for the two attractive female profiles (Profile 2 and 3), and 44% on average for all attack profiles.

We took a closer look at the demography of the users who contacted us. In the case of Badoo, sending a message is the most concrete form of interest, and one that can easily be exploited (e.g., [5]). Figure 6 shows a demographic breakdown by relationship status, what users were interested in, and age. Similar to Figure 4, the y-axis shows the percentage of users who sent messages that originated from a profile with the respective demographic value.

Note that Badoo is a site that is geared towards dating. Most of the users who initiate contact express that they are either single, or in an "open relationship". In general, the attack profiles only attracted users of the opposite gender. The age demographic shows that most of the victims belong to the same age group that the attack profile belongs to. In comparison, there was no correlation of age for contact requests on Facebook.

Another important difference with respect to Facebook was that the location was significant in Badoo. In fact, almost all the messages were sent by people living in the same country as the attack profile.

Finally, the 3-grams analysis for the messages received on Badoo showed that the most popular term was "how are you" occurring over 700 times. Other popular lines included "get to know" and "would you like", "you like" ... "chat" or "meet".

4.3 Visitor Tracking Experiment

In the visitor tracking RSE attack, we used each of the five attack profiles to visit 8,400 different user profiles in Friendster. As we have already previously

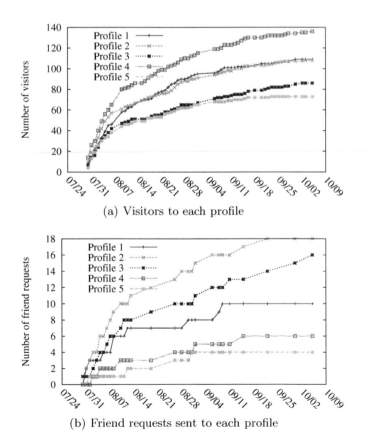

(a) Visitors to each profile

(b) Friend requests sent to each profile

Fig. 7. Cumulative counts of interactions resulting from reverse social engineering on Friendster

described, on Friendster a user can check which other users have visited her profile.

In our experiment, we tracked which victims visited our attack profiles, and then counted the number of users who sent us a friend request. The results of this experiment are shown in Figure 7 (the sub figure 7(a) and 7(b) represent the number of visitors and number of friend requests sent to the attack profiles).

The number of users who were curious about our visit, and visited us back was consistent with the results of the experiments we conducted on other social networks (i.e., between 0.25 and 1.2% per month). However, only a few users later sent a friend request or a message.

The demographic breakdown for Friendster is presented in Figure 8. The statistical distributions are similar to the ones obtained in the Facebook experiment, proving the difference in terms of characteristics between friend-oriented and dating-oriented social networks.

5 Discussion and Lessons Learned

In this section, based on the results of the empirical experiments, we distill some insights about the way RSE attacks work in social networks. We can summarize our findings in two main points: The importance of having the right profile, and the importance of providing a pretext to the victims.

The first, straightforward, factor we were able to measure is the impact of the profile characteristics on the overall effectiveness of an attack. The experiments confirm the folk wisdom that using an attractive female photograph is a good choice to attract victims. The success rate of the most successful female profile, in terms of both friend requests and number of received messages, is between 2 and 40 times higher than the worse performing profiles (i.e., the male profile and the profile without a photograph).

Note that if the objective of the attack is not simply to reach the highest number of users, but to target a specific person, or group, the success rate of the attack can be improved by carefully tuning the profile characteristics. For example, our experiments show that age and location information are decisive in dating sites, while this information is not as critical in more general, friend-oriented, social networks. Also, the results suggest that gender information is always very important. Hence, a successful reverse social engineering attack should use the opposite sex of the victims in the decoy profile.

The experiments show that the impact of the profile picture is quite uniform in different social networks. For example, we observe that young users are generally more intrigued by attractive photographs, while decoy profiles (e.g., Profile 5) that do not contain the photograph of a real person tend to attract more senior users.

Obviously, even though having a catchy, interesting profile is important, our research shows that there is a second, even more important factor that contributes to the success of the attack: the pretext. Our experiments indicate that users need an incentive and a good reason to engage in interaction with a person

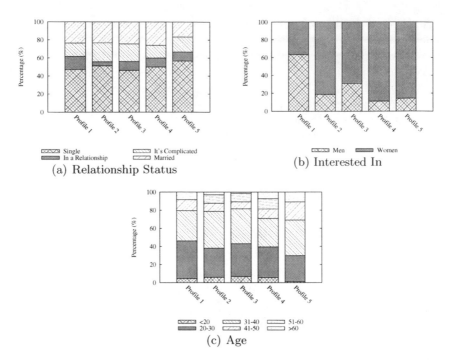

Fig. 8. Demographic breakdown by Relationship Status, Interested In, and Age for Friend Connect requests on Friendster

that they do not know. In other words, users need a good excuse to "break the ice" and motivate the first approach. The differences between the success rates of the attacks on Facebook and Friendster suggest that an incentive or a pretext is critical for reverse social engineering attacks to work in practice.

The analysis of the messages received on Facebook support the hypothesis that a recommendation system gives a reason to users to initiate contact. That is, a number of users referenced the Facebook recommendation as a motivation for their friend request. In contrast, on Friendster, even though the percentage of users that browsed our decoy profiles was consistent with the other social network experiments, very few people moved to the next step and sent a contact message. The reason is, in our opinion, that the visitor tracking attack failed to provide a good pretext to the victims.

Note that the demographic experiment on Badoo was also very effective. The reason for this success is that Badoo greatly relies on the demographic search functionality to allow users to find possible contacts. In the case of a dating site, the pretext for establishing contact was the fact itself of living in a close location, or being in the same age group of the victim.

Our experiments demonstrate that reverse social engineering attacks on social networks are feasible if they are properly designed and executed. However, contrary to the common folk wisdom, only having an account with an attractive photograph may not be enough to recruit a high number of unsuspecting victims.

Rather, the attacker needs to combine an attractive profile with a pretext and incentive for the victim to establish contact. Recommendation systems such as Facebook's friend suggestions are effective tools for creating such an incentive. Also, we see that profile attributes such as location and age may be the required incentives on dating networks such as Badoo.

6   RSE Countermeasures in OSN

Clearly, features that allow social network users to easily make new acquaintances are useful in practice. However, our paper demonstrates that such systems may also be abused to trick users on behalf of attackers. In this section, we list three countermeasures that would increase the difficulty of launching RSE attacks in online social networks.

First, while friend recommendation features are useful, our experiments show that they may pose a risk to users if the attackers are able to somehow influence the recommendation system. Hence, it is important for social network providers to show a potential connection between two users only if there is a strong connection between them. For example, in the case of Facebook, as our experiments show, a simple e-mail lookup does not necessarily indicate that the users know each other. Thus, one could check other information, such as the fact that the users already have some friends in common.

Second, we believe that it is important to closely monitor friendships that have been established in social networks. Benign user accounts will typically send and receive friend requests in both directions. That is, a user may be contacted by people she knows, but she will also actively search and add friends on the network. However, in contrast, a honeypot RSE account (as we describe in this paper) only receives friend requests from other users. Thus, it may be possible to identify such accounts automatically.

Third, we believe that CAPTCHA usage also needs to be extended to incoming friend requests. Today, because of the active threats of spamming and social engineering, social network providers may display CAPTCHAs when friend requests are sent to other users. However, no such precautions are taken for messages and friend requests that are received. By requiring to solve a CAPTCHA challenge before being able to accept suspicious incoming friend requests, we believe that RSE attacks would become more difficult. While CAPTCHAs are not the silver bullet in preventing and stopping malicious activity on social networks (e.g., as show in [1,5]), they do raise the difficulty bar for the attackers.

7   Related Work

Social engineering attacks are well-known in practice as well as in literature (e.g., [14,3,17,8,16]). Social engineering targets human weaknesses instead of vulnerabilities in technical systems. Automated Social Engineering (ASE) is the process of automatically executing social engineering attacks. For example, spamming and phishing can be seen as a very simple form of social engineering (i.e., making users click on links).

A general problem on social networks is that it is difficult for users to judge if a friend request is trustworthy or not. Thus, users are often quick in accepting invitations from people they do not know. For example, an experiment conducted by Sophos in 2007 showed that 41% of Facebook users acknowledged a friend request from a random person [1]. More cautions users can be tricked by requests from adversaries that impersonate friends [5]. Unfortunately, once a connection is established, the attacker typically has full access to all information on the victim's profile. Moreover, users who receive messages from alleged friends are much more likely to act upon such message, for example, by clicking on links. A similar result was reported by Jagatic et al. [10]. The authors found that phishing attempts are more likely to succeed if the attacker uses stolen information from victims' friends in social networks to craft their phishing e-mails.

In contrast to active social engineering that requires the attacker to establish contact with the victim, in a reverse social engineering attack, it is the victim that contacts the attacker. We are not aware of any previous reports or studies on reverse social engineering attacks in online social networks. The results of this paper demonstrate that automated reverse social engineering is a realistic threat, and that it is feasible in practice.

The most well-known attack to compromise the trust relationship in a social network that employs a reputation system is the *sybil attack* [6]. In this attack, the attacker creates multiple fake identities and use them to gain a disproportionately large influence on the reputation system. Note that the findings in this paper have implications for research that aims to defend social networks against sybil attacks (e.g., SybilGuard [18], SybilLimit [19]). SybilGuard and SybilLimit assume that real-world social networks are fast mixing [7] and this insight is used to distinguish the sybil nodes from normal nodes. Fast mixing means that subsets of honest nodes have good connectivity to the rest of the social network. Both SybilGuard and SybilLimit are good solutions for detecting Sybil nodes. However, the attacks we present in this paper result in legitimate friendship connections and, therefore, would not be detected by current sybil-detection approaches.

8   Conclusion

Hundreds of millions of users are registered to social networking sites and regularly use them features to stay in touch with friends, communicate, do online commerce, and share multimedia artifacts with other users.

To be able to make suggestions and to promote friendships, social networking sites often mine the data that has been collected about the registered users. For example, the fact that a user looks up an e-mail address might be assumed to indicate that the user knows the person who owns that e-mail account. Unfortunately, such assumptions can also be abused by attackers to influence recommendations, or to increase the chance that the victim's interest is intrigued by a fake honey-account.

Although social engineering attacks in social networks have been well-studied to date, *reverse social engineering* (RSE) attacks have not received any attention.

This paper presents the first user study on how attackers can abuse some of the features provided by online social networks with the aim of launching automated reverse social engineering attacks. We present and study the effectiveness and feasibility of three novel attacks: Recommendation-based, visitor tracking-based, and demographic-based reverse social engineering.

Our results show that RSE attacks are a feasible threat in real-life, and that attackers may be able to attract a large numbers of legitimate users *without* actively sending any friend request. The experiments we have conducted demonstrate that suggestions and friend-finding features (e.g., demographic-based searches) made by social networking sites may provide an incentive for the victims to contact a user if the right setting is created (e.g., an attractive photograph, an attack profile with similar interests, etc.).

We hope that this paper will raise awareness about the real-world threat of reverse social engineering in social networks and will encourage social network providers to adopt some countermeasures.

Acknowledgments. The research leading to these results has received funding from the European Union Seventh Framework Programme (FP7/2007-2013) under grant agreement n° 257007. This research has been partially funded by National Science Foundation by IUCRC, CyberTrust, CISE/CRI, and NetSE programs, National Center for Research Resources, and gifts, grants, or contracts from Wipro Technologies, Fujitsu Labs, Amazon Web Services in Education program, and Georgia Tech Foundation through the John P. Imlay, Jr. Chair endowment. Any opinions, findings, and conclusions or recommendations expressed in this material are those of the author(s) and do not necessarily reflect the views of the National Science Foundation or other funding agencies and companies mentioned above.

References

1. Sophos Facebook ID Probe (2008), http://www.sophos.com/pressoffice/news/articles/2007/08/facebook.html
2. Facebook Statistics (2010), http://www.facebook.com/press/info.php?statistics
3. Sophos Security Threat 2010 (2010), http://www.sophos.com/sophos/docs/eng/papers/sophos-security-threat-report-jan-2010-wpna.pdf
4. Balduzzi, M., Platzer, C., Holz, T., Kirda, E., Balzarotti, D., Kruegel, C.: Abusing Social Networks for Automated User Profiling. In: Jha, S., Sommer, R., Kreibich, C. (eds.) RAID 2010. LNCS, vol. 6307, pp. 422–441. Springer, Heidelberg (2010)
5. Bilge, L., Strufe, T., Balzarotti, D., Kirda, E.: All Your Contacts Are Belong to Us: Automated Identity Theft Attacks on Social Networks. In: 18th International Conference on World Wide Web, WWW (2009)
6. Douceur, J.R.: The sybil attack. In: Druschel, P., Kaashoek, M.F., Rowstron, A. (eds.) IPTPS 2002. LNCS, vol. 2429, p. 251. Springer, Heidelberg (2002)

7. Flaxman, A.: Expansion and lack thereof in randomly perturbed graphs. Internet Mathematics 4(2), 131–147 (2007)
8. Irani, D., Webb, S., Giffin, J., Pu, C.: Evolutionary study of phishing. In: eCrime Researchers Summit, pp. 1–10. IEEE, Los Alamitos (2008)
9. Irani, D., Webb, S., Pu, C., Li, K.: Study of Trend-Stuffing on Twitter through Text Classification. In: Collaboration, Electronic messaging, Anti-Abuse and Spam Conference, CEAS (2010)
10. Jagatic, T.N., Johnson, N.A., Jakobsson, M., Menczer, F.: Social phishing. Commun. ACM 50(10), 94–100 (2007)
11. Jakobsson, M., Finn, P., Johnson, N.: Why and How to Perform Fraud Experiments. IEEE Security & Privacy 6(2), 66–68 (2008)
12. Jakobsson, M., Ratkiewicz, J.: Designing ethical phishing experiments: a study of (ROT13) rOnl query features. In: 15th International Conference on World Wide Web, WWW (2006)
13. Lauinger, T., Pankakoski, V., Balzarotti, D., Kirda, E.: Honeybot, your man in the middle for automated social engineering. In: LEET 2010, 3rd USENIX Workshop on Large-Scale Exploits and Emergent Threats, San Jose (2010)
14. Mitnick, K., Simon, W.L., Wozniak, S.: The Art of Deception: Controlling the Human Element of Security. Wiley, Chichester (2002)
15. Porter, M.: An algorithm for suffix stripping. Program 14(3), 130–137 (1980)
16. Stringhini, G., Kruegel, C., Vigna, G.: Detecting Spammers on Social Networks. In: Annual Computer Security Applications Conference, ACSAC (2010)
17. Webb, S., Caverlee, J., Pu, C.: Social Honeypots: Making Friends with a Spammer Near You. In: Conference on Email and Anti-Spam, CEAS (2008)
18. Yu, H., Kaminsky, M., Gibbons, P., F.: Sybilguard: defending against sybil attacks via social networks. In: Proceedings of the 2006 Conference on Applications, Technologies, Architectures, and Protocols for Computer Communications, pp. 267–278. ACM, New York (2006)
19. Yu, H., Kaminsky, M., Gibbons, P. B., Flaxman, A.: SybilLimit: A Near-Optimal Social Network Defense against Sybil Attacks. In: IEEE Symposium on Security and Privacy (2008)

Timing Attacks on PIN Input in VoIP Networks (Short Paper)

Ge Zhang and Simone Fischer-Hübner

Karlstad University
{ge.zhang,simone.fischer-huebner}@kau.se

Abstract. To access automated voice services, Voice over IP (VoIP) users sometimes are required to provide their Personal Identification Numbers (PIN) for authentication. Therefore when they enter PINs, their user-agents generate packets for each key pressed and send them immediately over the networks. This paper shows that a malicious intermediary can recover the inter-keystroke time delay for each PIN input even if the standard encryption mechanism has been applied. The inter-keystroke delay can leak information of what has been typed: Our experiments show that the average search space of a brute force attack on PIN can be reduced by around 80%.

1 Introduction

An Interactive Voice Response (IVR) system enables interactions between telephone users and an automated voice server: After the conversation has been established, users listen prerecorded announcements and then react by pressing the buttons on their telephone keypads. Their telephones generate Dual-Tone Multi-Frequency (DTMF) [12] signals to the server for each button pressed. The server decodes the received DTMF signals to understand the feedback from users. There are some popular IVR applications, one of which is the authentication. For example, users are required to give their Personal Identification Numbers (PIN) to configure their setups or to access a third party voice mail. In many cases, a PIN is a 4-digital secret number, which should only be shared between a user and his/her service provider for authentication.

Nowadays the deployment of IP telephony, also called Voice over IP (VoIP), is experiencing a phenomenal growth. It was mainly designed for voice communications over packet switched networks. Besides voice communications, it also inherits most features from traditional telephony services including IVR [10]: a particular packet payload format is used to indicate each button has been pressed. It is functionally equivalent with DTMF signals.

However, unlike traditional telephone networks, a large packet-switched network (e.g., the Internet) usually contains a number of intermediaries which cannot be trusted. These intermediaries can easily wiretap communication channels and eavesdrop their contents. To prevent this, IETF working group [4] standardized a mechanism to encrypt packet payload. It has been widely supported in the SIP

T. Holz and H. Bos. (Eds.): DMIVA 2011, LNCS 6739, pp. 75–84, 2011.

community. Unfortunately, this mechanism does not provide protection for packet header fields, which are then available to intermediaries. In this paper, we introduce a method which enable an intermediary to recover the inter-keystroke delay for each PIN input repetition using the header fields and the arrival time of packets. We further apply the timing attack proposed by Song et al. [11] using a Hidden Markov Model. The attack does not directly disclose what a victim typed, but can significantly reduce the search space of it (80% in this paper).

The rest of the paper is organized as follows. Section 2 describes the background of VoIP protocols. Section 3 elaborates our methods for detecting inter-keystroke delays and for reducing PIN search space. Section 4 reports and illustrates our experimental study. We present related work in Section 5. Section 6 concludes the paper and plans for future work.

2   Background in VoIP

The Realtime Transport Protocol (RTP) [9] standardizes the packet format for VoIP conversations. It provides end-to-end delivery schemes for data with real-time features in the Internet and supports different payload types, including

- Voice payload: It is the most frequently used payload format, mainly for voice communication. In a conversation, a user-agent constantly encodes voice signal into digital data and generates RTP packets with the encoded digital data as payloads. The user-agent on the other side recovers the voice signal by decoding the payloads from the received RTP packets. We name the packets with this kind of RTP payloads as *RTP voice packets*.
- Event payload [10]: It was designed to achieve the DTMF signal function. When a user presses a phone key in a conversation, the user-agent generates event payloads to indicate which key has been pressed. The RTP packets with event payloads are called *RTP event packets*.

In most cases, a VoIP user-agent continuously generates RTP packets at a constant time interval (e.g., 20 ms) during the whole conversation. Each RTP packet only contains one type of payload. Given both a voice payload and an event payload at the same time, the event payload will be taken as higher priority and the voice payload will be neglected. The Secure Realtime Transport Protocol (SRTP) [4] has been widely applied to encrypt RTP payloads for confidentiality and integrity. Nevertheless, as stated in the specification, SRTP only protect RTP payloads instead of the whole packet[1]. This means that the RTP header fields are still available to be eavesdropped despite of the protection. Some RTP header types are introduced as follows:

- Payload type: It identifies the type of the included RTP payload. e.g., a voice payload or a event payload.

---

[1] RTP headers should be clear text for billing purposes and header compression.

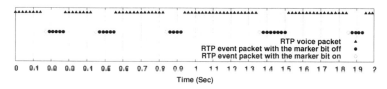

Fig. 1. A example RTP flow with voice and event packets

- Marker bit: It indicates the beginning of a new keystroke event. A user pressing a key may span a series of RTP event packets depending on how long the key being pressed, but only the first packet has the marker bit set on.
- Sequence number: The RTP sequence number is incremented by one in each successive RTP packet sent. It is mainly due to that the transmission of RTP packets is based on UDP, an unreliable transport protocol. Therefore, the sequence numbers allow the receiver to restore the original sequence.

Figure 1 plots a typical RTP flow including both event and voice packets. The packet inter-arrival time is equally around 20 ms. It can be predicted that 5 events are represented in this flow by five groups of RTP event packets.

3   Attacks

Image the following scenario: A victim VoIP user provides a PIN (a 4-digital number) to an automated voice server for authentication. To do so, the user clicks the keys on the soft keypad of a user-agent to generate RTP event packets. The layout of its virtual keypad is illustrated in Figure 2(a). An attacker is a malicious intermediary which can eavesdrop the communications in the network. The attacker aims to find out the user's PIN. However, SRTP [4] has been applied so that the PIN is not directly readable from the packets. The attacker can mount a brute force attack by guessing all the possible PINs. With limited prior knowledge (e.g., only knowing the length of PIN), the attacker needs to search $10^4/2$ different PINs to hit the correct one on average. Nevertheless, previous work [11] shows that keystroke delays may partly disclose the information of typed content. This section states how to recover keystroke delays from RTP flows and how to reduce the search space using the delays in detail.

3.1   Recover Inter-Keystroke Delays

Since only RTP event packets represent keystroke events, the attacker needs to select RTP event packets from a given RTP flow. Actually it is rather simple: Despite of the protection by SRTP, the RTP headers are still in plain text. Thus, the attacker can easily distinguish packet types by reading the "Payload-Type" header field. After picking RTP event packets from a flow, the next step is to recover the inter-keystroke delay. Let y to be an actual inter-keystroke delay and $\hat{y}$ to be the corresponding one recovered from the network flow. The attacker can only detect $\hat{y}$, which ideally should be close to y. We assume that the attacker

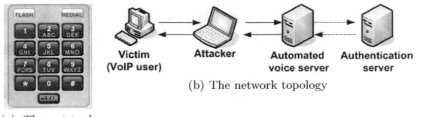

(a) The virtual keypad

(b) The network topology

Fig. 2. The environment of attacks

also knows the length of a PIN and knows that users will enter a "#" to indicate the end of input. Similarly, the attacker can find the packet representing the start of an event with its "marker bit" header field is set on. To the attacker, a $\hat{y}$ is represented by the arrival time difference between the first packet of an event (with the "marker bit" on) and the last packet of its previous event. If we take Figure 1 as an example, the four inter-keystroke delays are: (1) 0.18 s (0.45-0.27 s), (2) 0.29 s (0.84-0.55 s), (3) 0.44 s (1.36-0.92 s), and (4) 0.35 s (1.85-1.5 s).

3.2 The Impact of Networking Conditions

The conditions of connections in a packet-switched network vary. It affects the packets arrival time and may make the attack inaccurate. In this section, we discuss the impacts by taking latency, jitter and packet loss into account.

Latency: It is the time cost to transmit a packet from the sender to the receiver. If latency is constant, it does not affect this attack since attackers are only interested in inter-keystroke delays.

Jitter: If latency is not constant, we need to take jitter into account. It is the latency variations for different packets in a flow. For instance, a packet sent earlier may arrive later due to network congestion. It makes the inter-keystroke delays recovering unreliable. However, attackers can restore the original sequence of the packets using the "sequence number" header information. Moreover, attackers can know what the fixed time interval between two successive packets should be (e.g., 20 ms in our examples). In this way, the impact of jitter is not vital to the attackers.

Packet loss: It is the amount of packets which are accidentally dropped in the transmission. To achieve a fair conversation quality, the packet loss rate should be less than 1% [8]. Although attackers can detect packet loss by reading "sequence number", they do not know the type of the lost packet. The attackers may heuristically guess the type of the lost packet by those of its neighbor packets.

Jitter and packet loss make similar attacks on SSH [11] unpractical [5]. However, this is not the case for VoIP, as they can be detected and eliminated using header information.

3.3 Reducing the Search Space

We apply the method developed by Song et al. [11] for inter-keystroke timing attacks based on a Hidden Markov Model [7], which describes a finite stochastic process with unobserved states. However, the outputs of these states are observable and thus can be used to predict the existence of these states. A HMM requires two assumptions: (1) Only the current state decides the next available states to the system, and (2) The outputs of a state only depends on the state. The previous paper [11] proposed the timing attack to infer the typing content using a HMM: For a pair of continuous keystroke, the key pair is taken as a state and its inter-keystroke delay is the output of the state. It basically satisfies the two assumptions: (1) the key pairs available on the next states depends on the current states. For instance, if the key pair in current state is {2,8}, the next possible key pair must begins with "8". It might be {8,0}, but cannot be {9,1}. (2) Previous tests showed that an inter-keystroke delay is empirically dependent on the distance between the keys on a keypad [6]. For example, the distance between key pair {1,2} is shorter than {1,9} according to the keypad in Figure 2(a). Then the delays between {1,2} is expected to be smaller than those between {1,9}.

The HMM in our case is illustrated in Figure 3. Let $\overrightarrow{PIN} = \{k_0, \cdots, k_4\}$ be a candidate PIN to try, and q_i to be a sequence of states representing the keystroke pair (k_i, k_{i+1}). In addition, $\overrightarrow{y} = \{\hat{y}_0, \cdots, \hat{y}_3\}$ indicates the observed inter-keystroke delays. Thus, the probability that the candidate $\overrightarrow{PIN}$ is what the user inputs can be calculated as:

$$Pr[\overrightarrow{PIN}] = \prod_{i=0}^{3} Pr[q_i|\hat{y}_i] \prod_{j=0}^{2} Pr[q_{j+1}|q_j]$$

For a given $\hat{y}_x$, the probability of its corresponding keystroke pair as q_i is:

$$Pr[q_i|\hat{y}_x] = \frac{Pr[\hat{y}_x|q_i]Pr[q_i]}{\sum_{q \in Q} Pr[\hat{y}_x|q]Pr[q]}$$

Where Q indicates all possible keystroke pairs. Previous research found that the inter-keystroke delay for a given keystroke pair roughly follows the Gaussian-like distribution [11,13]. Our experiments described below also confirmed this. Thus,

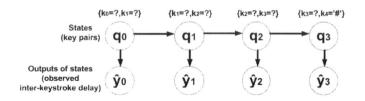

Fig. 3. A Hidden Markov Model used in our case

$Pr[\hat{y}|q]$ is priori knowledge computed using the Gaussian distribution based on previous observations, using

$$Pr[\hat{y}|q] = \frac{1}{\sqrt{2\pi}\sigma_q}e^{-\frac{(\hat{y}-\mu_q)^2}{2\sigma_q{}^2}}$$

Where μ_q is the mean value of the inter-keystroke delay for q and σ_q is its standard deviation.

4   Experiments

To test the performance of this attack, we did experiments in two steps: We empirically collected inter-keystroke delays for 92 different keystroke pairs from 35 students at Karlstad University as the training dataset. We then observed the inter-keystroke delays done by other students as the testing dataset and quantified how much information will be disclosed using the attack.

4.1   Priori-Knowledge Preparation

To build the training dataset, we asked each participate to input two randomly selected 4-digit PINs on X-lite [3] by mouse clicking. They were requested to type in the same PIN for 30-50 repetitions and to enter a "#" to indicate the end of a PIN input for each repetition. We run a TCPDump [2] on a intermediary machine to intercept all packets and recover the inter-keystroke delay of each keystroke pair for all repetitions using the method mentioned in Section 3.1 and Section 3.2. In total, we collected inter-keystroke delays for 92 different keystroke pairs. We confirmed that the inter-keystroke delay of a given pair forms a Gaussian-like distribution. For example, Figure 4 plots the delay histogram of two sample keystroke pairs: {3,6} and {9,4}. Both of them follow a basic Gaussian-like distribution. In addition, the average delay of {3,6} is clearly less than that of {9,4}.

We further calculated the mean value and the standard deviation for each keystroke pair. Figure 5 plots the results ordered by the mean values. Due to the

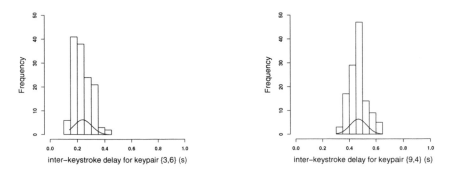

Fig. 4. Histogram and distribution of observed inter-keystroke delays (2 examples)

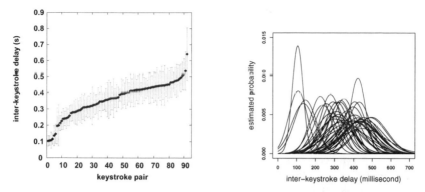

Fig. 5. Mean value with standard deviation of observed inter-keystroke delay for each pair

Fig. 6. Estimated distribution of observed inter-keystroke delay for each pair

page limitation, we list the details in Appendix A, from which we found that the average delays of keystroke pairs roughly depends on the distances between the keys. Moreover, we curve the Gaussian distribution of the inter-keystroke delay for each pair based on the mean value and the standard deviation in Figure 6. We can observe that most of the delays lie between 100 to 600 milliseconds and the distributions of them heavily overlap.

4.2   Results for PIN Inference

We invited another 5 students and let them input 20 different PINs, with 30-50 repetitions for each PIN. We recovered the traffic and recovered the inter-keystroke delays. We applied the timing attacks (Section 3.3) with the training dataset on the delays: For a brute-force attack on cracking a PIN, we ranked all possible candidate PINs (from 0000 to 9999) according to their probabilities and ordered them descendingly. The position of the real PIN on the list indicates the search space that a brute force attacker has to explore. For instance, an attacker only has to try the 499 attempts to hit the real one when the real PIN is located at the 499th position on the list. Figure 7 plots the Empirical Cumulative

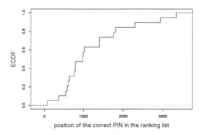

Fig. 7. The ECDF of the position of the real PIN on the ranking list

Distribution (ECDF) of the positions hit: Most of them are around 800-1000. Considering the theoretical average attempts without this attack (5000), the search space has been considerably reduced.

5   Related work

Song et al. [11] noticed that every individual keystroke was sent in a separate IP packet when a user entered a password to login to a remote SSH server. This enables an eavesdropper to learn inter-keystroke delay of users' typing from the arrival times of packets. They further observed that the inter-keystroke delay of a key pair follows a Gaussian-like distribution. Therefore, the attacker can calculate the probability of whether a given password had been typed from the observed inter-keystroke delay using a Hidden Markov Model. Promising as it seems, Hogye et al. [5] discussed the practical issues of [11]. They argued that unstable network conditions (e.g., jitter, packet loss) can make the observations inaccurate. Since it is not easy to eliminate the impact in the SSH scenario, the attack on SSH [11] is not practical.

The method also has been extended to other applications. For example, keypad acoustic emanations [6] can leak out information of a user's keystrokes. Many keypads provide an audio feedback to the user for each key pressed. An attacker in a reasonable distance can record the acoustic signals and thus can easily observe the inter-keystroke delay. Therefore, the attacker can apply the Song's attack [11] to reduce the PIN search space. Zhang et al. [13] proposed how to observe the inter-keystroke delay of other users on a multi-user system. A keystroke event triggers specific system calls. Thus, a keystroke event can be identified from the changing of CPU register variables. Similarly, a HMM can be applied to infer the content of typing. These two attacks do not require observations on networks so the network conditions impact less on the accuracy.

Different to the previous research, our timing attack is for VoIP applications by recovering inter-keystroke delay from RTP packets arrival time and their header information. Although the observation is on networks, the impact from network conditions can be detected and minimized by reading the packet header information.

6   Conclusion and Future Work

Despite of the protection of the SRTP scheme, RTP packet header fields are still readable to networking intermediaries. Based on arrival time and header fields information of observed RTP packets, a malicious intermediary can easily recover the inter-keystroke delays when a victim VoIP user enters his/her PIN to a remote server. The varying network conditions (jitter and packet loss) affect little on the accuracy of the measurement as they can be detected and minimized using packet headers information. A HMM can be applied to calculate the probability of whether a candidate PIN is the typed one using the inter-keystroke delays. The result can be used to considerably reduce the PIN search space for a brute force attack on PIN cracking. Our experiments show that an attacker only needs to try on average 1000 attempts for cracking a 4-digital PIN by this attack instead of 5000 attempts.

We only consider 4 digital PINs in this paper. Future work can be extended to further applications. For example, some IVR offers credit card payment. In this way, users give their credit cards by clicking phone keys in IVR conversations [1]. A credit card number contains more digits than a PIN. On the other hand, as many different devices support VoIP, we will consider investigating the keystroke patterns of users when they employ other input interfaces, including standard keyboards and smart phone keypads.

Acknowledgement. This work is partly supported by the EU C-BIC 2 project. The authors also would like to thank the anonymous reviewers for their valuable comments.

References

1. Automated Telephone Payments. visited at 15th-Nov-2010, http://www.elmbridge.gov.uk/online/atp.htm
2. TCPDump. visited at 20th-July-2010, http://www.tcpdump.org/
3. X-Lite. visited at 18th-July-2010, http://www.counterpath.com/x-lite.html
4. Baugher, M., McGrew, D., Naslund, M., Carrara, E., Norrman, K.: The Secure Real-time Transport Protocol (SRTP). RFC 3711 (2004)
5. Hogye, M.A., Hughes, C.T., Sarfaty, J.M., Wolf, J.D.: Analysis of the feasibility of keystroke timing attacks over ssh connections, technical report (2001)
6. Foo Kune, D., Kim, Y.: Timing attacks on pin input devices. In: Proceedings of CCS 2010, USA, pp. 678–680. ACM Press, New York (2010)
7. Rabiner, L.R.: Readings in speech recognition. In: Chapter A Tutorial on Hidden Markov Models and Selected Applications in Speech Recognition, pp. 267–296. Morgan Kaufmann Publishers Inc. San Francisco (1990)
8. Reynolds, R.J.B., Rix, A.W.: Quality voip: An engineering challenge. BT Technology Journal 19, 23–32 (2001)
9. Schulzrinne, H., Casner, S., Frederick, R., Jacobson, V.: RTP: A transport protocol for real-time applications. RFC 3550 (2003)
10. Schulzrinne, H., Taylor, T.: RTP Payload for DTMF Digits, Telephony Tones, and Telephony Signals. RFC 4733 (2006)
11. Song, D.X., Wagner, D., Tian, X.: Timing analysis of keystrokes and timing attacks on ssh. In: Proceedings of SSYM 2001. USENIX Association, Berkeley (2001)
12. International Telecommunication Union. Technical features of push-button telephone sets. ITU-T Recommendation Q.24 (1988)
13. Zhang, K., Wang, X.: Peeping tom in the neighborhood: keystroke eavesdropping on multi-user systems. In: Proceedings of SSYM 2009, Berkeley, CA, pp. 17–32. USENIX Association (2009)

A   Appendix: Inter-stroke delay of key pairs

The table lists the average delays with standard deviations of 92 keystroke pairs.

No	Key-pair	Avg(s)	Sd	No	Key-pair	Avg(s)	Sd	No	Key-pair	Avg(s)	Sd
1	{6,6}	0.104	0.031	32	{6,2}	0.328	0.060	63	{6,#}	0.423	0.088
2	{1,1}	0.105	0.029	33	{4,5}	0.331	0.058	64	{3,4}	0.425	0.071
3	{5,5}	0.107	0.049	34	{5,7}	0.336	0.098	65	{0,4}	0.428	0.060
4	{4,4}	0.114	0.031	35	{4,3}	0.346	0.055	66	{0,7}	0.429	0.048
5	{2,2}	0.135	0.061	36	{3,2}	0.347	0.092	67	{3,8}	0.432	0.097
6	{3,3}	0.146	0.057	37	{4,2}	0.347	0.056	68	{4,7}	0.433	0.095
7	{8,8}	0.195	0.110	38	{8,0}	0.352	0.056	69	{6,8}	0.436	0.068
8	{9,6}	0.198	0.126	39	{7,1}	0.356	0.070	70	{3,1}	0.437	0.094
9	{9,8}	0.212	0.045	40	{1,4}	0.358	0.105	71	{4,9}	0.440	0.090
10	{0,8}	0.225	0.054	41	{6,5}	0.361	0.118	72	{1,#}	0.442	0.116
11	{3,6}	0.238	0.063	42	{2,6}	0.364	0.101	73	{5,#}	0.443	0.075
12	{8,6}	0.240	0.045	43	{5,1}	0.367	0.072	74	{1,5}	0.445	0.090
13	{0,#}	0.242	0.063	44	{5,4}	0.367	0.119	75	{9,1}	0.446	0.121
14	{6,3}	0.247	0.052	45	{8,1}	0.368	0.060	76	{6,7}	0.447	0.088
15	{2,5}	0.257	0.062	46	{9,5}	0.369	0.082	77	{1,9}	0.447	0.123
16	{7,5}	0.274	0.050	47	{8,2}	0.373	0.063	78	{8,3}	0.450	0.073
17	{5,9}	0.279	0.052	48	{9,7}	0.387	0.037	79	{7,6}	0.452	0.101
18	{8,9}	0.280	0.070	49	{5,3}	0.393	0.093	80	{5,0}	0.453	0.085
19	{5,8}	0.282	0.076	50	{9,2}	0.394	0.087	81	{3,#}	0.462	0.093
20	{6,9}	0.287	0.087	51	{3,5}	0.395	0.066	82	{4,6}	0.466	0.093
21	{2,4}	0.291	0.059	52	{0,5}	0.400	0.095	83	{9,4}	0.468	0.062
22	{9,#}	0.294	0.075	53	{4,0}	0.404	0.080	84	{2,#}	0.473	0.086
23	{1,2}	0.301	0.089	54	{4,8}	0.404	0.059	85	{8,#}	0.476	0.102
24	{5,6}	0.310	0.073	55	{2,0}	0.413	0.099	86	{9,0}	0.478	0.098
25	{2,1}	0.311	0.082	56	{0,2}	0.414	0.073	87	{3,7}	0.487	0.086
26	{2,3}	0.312	0.060	57	{8,4}	0.415	0.099	88	{3,0}	0.495	0.085
27	{0,9}	0.314	0.067	58	{6,4}	0.418	0.103	89	{7,9}	0.506	0.086
28	{7,4}	0.315	0.064	59	{1,0}	0.419	0.065	90	{7,#}	0.515	0.097
29	{5,2}	0.318	0.078	60	{2,7}	0.420	0.086	91	{7,2}	0.537	0.118
30	{7,0}	0.320	0.117	61	{4,#}	0.420	0.090	92	{7,3}	0.640	0.164
31	{7,8}	0.325	0.075	62	{3,9}	0.421	0.041				

Biting the Hand That Serves You: A Closer Look at Client-Side Flash Proxies for Cross-Domain Requests

Martin Johns and Sebastian Lekies*

SAP Research Karlsruhe
{martin.johns,sebastian.lekies}@sap.com

Abstract. Client-side Flash proxies provide an interface for JavaScript applications to utilize Flash's cross-domain HTTP capabilities. However, the subtle differences in the respective implementations of the same-origin policy and the insufficient security architecture of the JavaScript-to-Flash interface lead to potential security problems. We comprehensively explore these problems and conduct a survey of five existing proxy implementation. Furthermore, we propose techniques to avoid the identified security pitfalls and to overcome the untrustworthy interface between the two technologies.

1 Introduction

Over the period of the last decade, Web applications have exposed an ever growing emphasis on sophisticated client-side functionality. In many places, the request-response-render Web of the early days has made way for rich JavaScript clients that utilize AJAX-driven communication and dynamic user interfaces. However, as the evolution of the Web browser's native capabilities did not always kept pace with the rapid innovation of the application's demands, plug-in technologies, such as Adobe Flash [1] filled the gap and provided advanced features which were missing in the browsers.

However, the security policy implemented by browser plug-ins does not always exactly match the security model of the Web browser. In certain areas, already subtle deviations can lead to security implications which are hard to handle.

In this paper we examine how the difference in handling the same-origin policy in respect to cross-domain JavaScript and cross-domain Flash lead to unexpected consequences. For this purpose, we explore the field of client-side Flash proxies for cross-domain requests. After covering the technological basis of client-side HTTP requests (Sec. 2), we explore a little known security flaw that can occur when cross-domain Flash applets interact with adversary controlled JavaScript (Sec. 3). To substantiate our observation, we examine five publicly available client-side Flash proxies (see Sec. 3.3). Furthermore, we show how to overcome

---

* This work was in parts supported by the EU Project WebSand (FP7-256964), http://www.websand.eu

T. Holz and H. Bos. (Eds.): DMIVA 2011, LNCS 6739, pp. 85–103, 2011.

the identified issues. First, we solve the specific problem of providing a secure and flexible client-side Flash proxy (Sec. 4). Secondly, we tackle the general problem of implementing Flash-based functionality that reliably makes origin-based security decisions even when interacting with untrustworthy JavaScript (Sec. 5). After discussing related work (Sec. 6) we finish with a conclusion (Sec. 7).

2   Client-Side Cross-Domain HTTP Requests

2.1   Technical Background

In general, the same-origin policy (SOP) [26] is the main security policy for all active content that is executed in a Web browser within the context of a Web page. This policy restricts all client-side interactions to objects which share the same origin. In this context, an object's origin is defined by the URL, port, and protocol, which were utilized to obtain the object. While this general principle applies to all active client-side technologies (e.g., JavaScript, Java applets, Flash, or Silverlight), slight variations in the implementation details exist. Please refer to [35] for further reference.

Based on the SOP, the initiation of network connections from active content in the browser is restricted to targets that are located within the origin of the requesting object[1]. This means, a JavaScript that is executed in the browser in the context of the origin http://www.example.org is only permitted to generate HTTP requests (via the XMLHttpRequest-object [31]) to URLs that match this origin. The same general rule exist for Flash, Silverlight, and Java.

However, in the light of increasing popularity of multi-domain, multi-vendor application scenarios and ever growing emphasis on client-side functionality, a demand for browser-based *cross-domain* HTTP requests arose (e.g., in the field of Web2.0 Mashups), as such request have the ability to mix data and code from more then one authorization/authentication context (see Sec. 2.2).

Following this demand, the ability to create cross-domain HTTP requests from within the browser has been introduced by Adobe Flash [1]. To avoid potential security implication (see Sec. 2.5), the designated receiver of the HTTP request has to explicitly allow such requests. This is done through providing a crossdomain.xml-policy file [2] which whitelists all domains that are allowed to send browser-based cross-domain HTTP request.

Following Flash's example, Silverlight and Java have also introduced capabilities for browser-based cross-domain HTTP requests. To enforce similar 'recipient-opt-in' policies as in Flash's model, Silverlight and Java imitate the crossdomain.xml mechanism of requiring policy files.

2.2   Use Cases for Client-Side Cross-Domain HTTP Requests

The need for client-side cross-domain requests is not immediately obvious. Alternatively, the Web application could offer a server-side proxying service that

---

[1] NB: This restriction only applies to HTTP requests that are created by active code. HTML elements, such as IMG or IFrame are unaffected and can reference cross-domain objects.

fetches the cross-domain content on the server-side, instead of requiring the client-side browser to issue the cross-domain requests. Such a service can be accessed by the client-side code via standard, SOP-compliant methods. This technique is offered for example by Google's Gadget API [11].

However, this technique is only applicable in cases in which the Web application's server-side code is able to access the requested content, e.g, when requesting publicly available internet resources.

Server-side proxies might not be applicable whenever the access to the requested content is restricted. Examples for such scenarios include situations in which the requested content is unavailable to the server because of network barriers (e.g., an internet Web application interacting with intranet data) or cases in which the demanded information is only available in the current authentication context of the user's Web browser (e.g., based on session cookies, see Sec. 2.5 for details). Such use cases can only be realized with client-side cross-domain capabilities.

2.3   The Current Move towards Native Browser Capabilities

After a period of perceived stagnation of Web browser development and innovation, the recent years have shown rapid progression of browser technologies. This movement was initially lead by the Web Hypertext Application Technology Working Group (WHATWG [33]) and has now been picked up by the W3C and IETF.

A significant part of the work of these groups (and associated Web browser vendors) is the adoption of capabilities, that have successfully been introduced by browser plug-in, and their addition to the browser's native HTML/JavaScript functionality. Examples for such capabilities include audio/video playback and expanded networking capabilities.

This development leads to the prediction that in the future such native capabilities will reduce the current dependency on browser plug-ins. First indicators of this trend are the mobile Web browsers of the iOS and Windows Phone Seven platforms that completely rely on native technologies and do not provide support for browser plug-ins.

In the course of expanding JavaScript's networking stack, the ability to create cross-domain HTTP requests have been added. JavaScript's native implementation is called Cross-origin Resource Sharing (CORS) [32]. CORS utilizes JavaScript's XMLHttpRequest-object for this purpose. Instead of following Flash's example of utilizing policy files, CORS utilizes HTTP response headers to allow or deny the requests. Only if the HTTP response carries an allowing HTTP header, the received data is passed on to the calling script. This behavior allows much more fine-grained access control compared to the established policy-based mechanisms.

2.4   Client-Side Cross-Domain Flash-Proxies for Legacy Browsers

Given the move towards native JavaScript capabilities in modern browsers and the expected fading importance of browser plug-ins (see above), it becomes

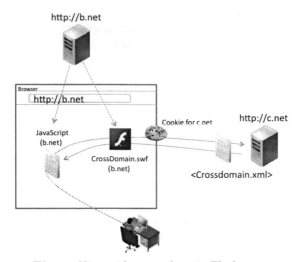

Fig. 1. Client-side cross-domain Flash proxy

increasingly important for Web applications to support CORS for scenarios which utilize client-side cross-domain requests. As a consequence, for the time being developers will have to implement two variants of the same cross-domain request functionality in parallel: A version that utilizes Flash or Silverlight for legacy browsers that do not yet provide CORS and a CORS version for modern browsers that either do not support plug-ins, such as most mobile browsers, and for browsers in which plug-ins have been disabled (e.g., for security reasons). Based on experiences with the longevity of old browser variants, such as Internet Explorer 6, it can be expected that this transitional phase will last a considerable amount of time.

To ease this development, client-side Flash-proxies have been introduced which export Flash's cross-domain capabilities to JavaScript (see Fig. 1). These proxies are small, single-purpose Flash applets combined with a small JavaScript library that together provide an interface to the enclosing page's JavaScript for initiating HTTP requests to cross-domain targets and passing the corresponding HTTP response back to the calling script. Figure 2 shows the interaction pattern between the JavaScript library and the Flash applet.

To further ease the use of these proxy libraries, extensions for popular JavaScript frameworks, such as JQuery or Dojo, are provided that import the functionality into the respective framework. In most cases this is done in a fashion that makes its usage almost transparent to the developer, i.e., through exchanging the framework's networking methods with the corresponding functions of the proxy library.

In a survey we were able to identify five different published Flash proxy libraries which provide the described functionality. See Table 1 for a brief overview.

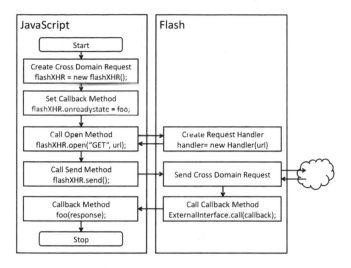

Fig. 2. Interaction between JavaScript and the Flash proxy

2.5   Security Implications of Client-Side Cross-Domain HTTP Requests

Before we discuss the potential security problems introduced by client-side Flash proxies in Section 3, we briefly revisit the general potential security problem that can arise in connection with client-side cross-domain HTTP requests.

Attacker model: From now on, we consider the following scenario: The victim visits a Web site a.net, which is under the control of the attacker. This Web site is granted the right to create cross-domain requests to a second Web site b.net, for instance because b.net has an over-allowing crossdomain.xml policy file that whitelists ("*") all foreign domains. Furthermore, the victim currently possesses an authenticated session state with b.net, i.e., in the victim's browser a session cookie for this domain exists.

This setting allows the attacker to create arbitrary HTTP requests to b.net from within the victim's browser and read the corresponding HTTP responses. The victim's cookies for b.net, including the authenticated session cookies, are attached to these requests automatically by the browser, as the cookies' domain matches the target domain of the outgoing HTTP request. These requests are received and handled by b.net in the same fashion as regular requests coming from the victim, hence, they are interpreted in the victim's current authentication context.

Resulting malicious capabilities: We can deduct the several potential attack vectors, based on the scenario discussed above.

Leakage of sensitive information [13]: The adversary can obtain all information served by b.net which the victim is authorized to access by simply requesting the information via HTTP and forwarding the corresponding HTTP responses to the attacker's server.

Circumvention of Cross-site Request Forgery protection [27]: The security guarantee of nonce-based Cross-site Request Forgery (CSRF) protection [7] is based on the assumption that the attacker is not able to obtain the secret nonce which is required for the server to accept the request. These nonces are included in the HTML of b.net. As the adversary is able to read HTTP responses from b.net, he can request the page from b.net that contains the nonce, extracting the nonce from the page's source code, and using it for the subsequent HTTP request.

Session hijacking [23]: As discussed, the adversary has the ability to create arbitrary HTTP requests that carry the victim's authentication credentials and read the corresponding HTTP responses. In consequence, this enables him to conduct attacks that are, for most purposes, as powerful as session hijacking attacks which are conducted via cookie stealing: As long as the targeted application logic remains in the realm of the accessible domain (in our case b.net), the attacker can chain a series of HTTP requests to execute complex actions on the application under the identity of the user, regardless of CSRF protection or other roadblocks. This can happen either in a fully automatic fashion, as for instance XSS worms [18,21] function, or interactive to allow the attacker to fill out HTML forms or provide other input to his attacks. Frameworks such as BeEF [5] or MalaRIA [23] can be leveraged for the interactive case.

3   Abusing Client-Site Cross-Domain Flash Proxies

In this section, we explore a little known[2] security problem that is caused by the way Web browsers handle the SOP in respect to cross-domain Flash applets. Hence, from now on, we limit the scope of the discussion to JavaScript and Flash.

3.1   Subtle Differences in the SOP

Both JavaScript files and Flash applets can be included in foreign Web pages of arbitrary origin due to the HTML's transparent handling of cross-domain locations in tags, such as `script`, `object`, or `embed` (see Listing 1). However, the specifics how the SOP is applied to such cross-domain active content differs [35]:

Cross-domain JavaScript code inherits the origin of the enclosing domain. It is handled as if it was a native component of the enclosing Web page and looses all ties to its original origin.

Opposed to this, cross-domain Flash applets keep the origin from which the Flash's swf-file was retrieved. As a consequence, all security relevant actions are restricted or granted in the context of the Flash's original origin. In particular, this means that a browser's decision if an outgoing HTTP request will be

---

[2] During investigating the topic, we only encountered one single blog post discussing the issue [29]. Besides that, there appears to be no awareness.

Listing 1. Cross-domain inclusion of script and Flash code

```
<!-- HTML source of a Web page served by a.net -->
[...]
<!-- cross-domain JavaScript -->
<script src="http://b.net/somescript.js" />

<!-- cross-domain Flash -->
<object [...]>
  <param name="movie" value="http://b.net/flash_proxy.swf" />
  <param name="quality" value="high" />
  <embed src="http://b.net/flash_proxy.swf" [...]></embed>
</object>
```

permitted, is made based on checking the destination URL of the request against the original origin of the Flash and **not** based on the origin of the enclosing Web page.

Consequently, in cases in which a Flash applet provides a public JavaScript interface, this interface can be used by scripts running in the context of the enclosing Web page to cause actions which are executed under the cross-domain origin of the Flash applet.

Please note: To provide a public JavaScript interface which can be abused in the outlined fashion, the Flash applet has to release the exported methods for external domains using the `allowDomain()`-directive [4]. The value of this directive is a list of domains which are permitted to access the declared interface. However, in the case of general purpose Flash libraries it is common practice to whitelist all domains (using the wildcard mechanism `allowDomain("*")`), as at the time of development the programmer cannot know on which domains the library will be used (see also Sec. 3.4).

In the remainder of this section we explore attack vectors that result from the consequences of the mismatching SOP implementations in the context of client-side Flash proxies.

3.2   Attack Vectors

Scenario: In this section we consider a scenario that is similar to the general misuse case which was discussed in Section 2.5. The victim accesses a Web page from the domain `a.net` which is under the control of the attacker. Hence, the adversary is able to execute JavaScript in the context of `a.net` and import content from other domains via HTML tags, including cross-domain Flash applets.

In addition to `a.net`, two more domains exist: `b.net` and `c.net` (see Fig. 3). The application hosted on `c.net` exports cross-domain services to `b.net` and, hence, provides a `crossdomain.xml` policy file that allows requests coming from `b.net`. To access these services, the application running on `b.net` utilizes a client-side Flash proxy, as described in Section 2.4.

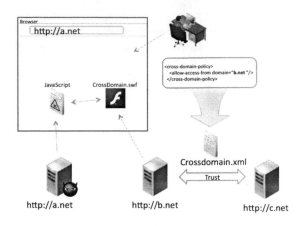

Fig. 3. Scenario

Attack variant 1 - **Transitivity of trust:** The adversary's script on a.net can utilize b.net's Flash proxy to create HTTP requests. Requests to locations that whitelist b.net in their crossdomain.xml policy are permitted, as the browser's security decision is made in respect to the origin of the Flash. This way, the attacker can conduct the attacks outlined in Section 2.5 targeting c.net, even though he has no direct control over the domain b.net (see Fig.4).

Attack variant 2 - **Return to sender:** In addition to creating requests to all domains that list b.net in their crossdomain.xml policies, the adversary is also

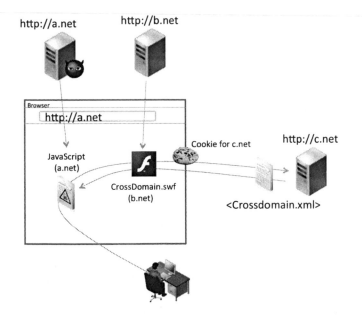

Fig. 4. Attack variant 1 - Transitivity of trust

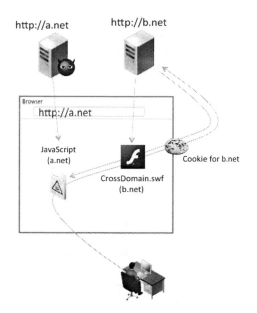

Fig. 5. Attack variant 2 - Return to sender

able to make requests from a.net to b.net itself, even in cases in which b.net does not provide a crossdomain.xml policy at all (see Fig.5). The reason again is the fact that the Flash applet's actions are permitted on the basis of its own origin (b.net) and not on the actual origin of requests (a.net).

Summary: In consequence, through merely hosting a susceptible client-side Flash proxy, a Web application can undermine both its own security as well as the security of all Web applications that express trust in this application's domain via their crossdomain.xml policy.

3.3 Survey of Published Flash Proxies

In order to assess how wide spread the issues are, we conducted a survey to identify readymade client-side Flash proxies. We were able to identify five different publicly available implementations: flXHR [30],SWFHttpRequest [34], FlashXMLHttpRequest [8], CrossXHR [24], and F4A[3].

Experimental setup: To check wether the found proxies expose the suspected vulnerability, we set up the network layout that is shown in Figure 3. The attacking JavaScript and its enclosing Web page were hosted on the domain a.net. The domain b.net hosted the five swf-files and on c.net a crossdomain.xml policy was set, which whitelisted only b.net. After writing code to connect the attacker script with the proxies for the five individual interfaces, we tested

---

[3] The development of F4A seems to have ended. We included it in this survey, as it is still in productive use, e.g., by sites such as nike.com

if a script executed under the origin of a.net is able to access text-files which are hosted on the other two domains.

Results: Out of the five examined implementation, three were vulnerable (see Table 1). For the two proxies which were not vulnerable the attack didn't work out, because these two libraries do not utilize the allowDomain(*) directive, which is needed to expose the SWF's interface to JavaScript originating from different domains. Two of the three vulnerable proxies (CrossXHR and F4A) were exploitable on the first try. The case of flXHR was more interesting, as the author of the proxy apparently was aware of the security problem and took measures to mitigate it (he even wrote a blog post about the problem [29]).

Case study - the flXHR proxy: flXHR is the only implementation that attempts to defend directly against the in Section 3.2 identified attack vectors. Before initiating a request, a flXHR proxy tries to compare its own origin with the origin of the interfacing JavaScript. If these two origin values do not match, flXHR checks the crossdomain.xml file of the request's target domain manually, if the origin of the JavaScript is whitelisted in the policy. This is even done, when the target of the request matches the origin of the Flash itself.

The problem that arises from this solution is how the origin-value of the interfacing JavaScript is obtained: As Flash does not provide such a mechanism natively, the only possibility to accomplish this task is to use the ExternalInterface API [3] to call a JavaScript function. In the examined case, flXHR obtains the value through calling the function window.location.href.toString().

However, the JavaScript of the enclosing Web page is completely controlled by the adversary and, thus, all public JavaScript functions can be overwritten with function wrappers [22]. With the method presented in Listing 2, an attacker can fake the location of his page and make flXHR believe that the enclosing origin matches its own.

As we will discuss further in Section 5.1, with the ExternalInterface API it is not possible to fix this problem, because it only allows to call public JavaScript functions by name and not by reference. Therefore, it is not possible to call a function which cannot be overwritten by an adversary. In Section 5.2 we describe our approach towards ensuring that the received location value has not been tampered with.

Table 1. List of existing proxies

Name	Year	Source	JS-libs	Vulnerable
flXHR [30]	2010	No	1,2,3,4	Yes, despite of countermeasures
SWFHttpRequest [34]	2007	Yes	1,2,3	No
FlashXMLHttpRequest [8]	2007	No	3	No
CrossXHR [24]	2010	Yes	1,2	Yes
F4A	unknown	No	-	Yes

Legend:
Year: Year of last recorded activity
Source: Is source code available?
JS-libs: Available plug-in for popular JavaScript frameworks: 1) JQuery, 2) Prototype, 3) Dojo, 4) Mootools

Listing 2. Subverting flXHR's protective measures

```
self = new function(){}
self.location = new function(){};
self.location.href = new function() {
    this.toString = function(){
        return "http://b.net";
    };
};
```

3.4   Analysis

After conducting the practical vulnerability testing, we further investigated the cause of the problem via analysis of the source code (when available) or via decompilation of the binaries.

In all three vulnerable cases, the cause of the exposed insecurity is an over-allowing internal policy in respect to interaction with external JavaScript: All three vulnerable applets used the directive `allowDomain("*")` within their code (see Sec. 3.1). Even the author of the flXHR proxy decided to do so, although he was aware of the resulting potential security problems.

The reason for this design decision is inherent in the purpose of the applets: They are built to function as pre-built, drop-in solutions which can be used without modifications, following the design of general purpose programming libraries.

Without an `allowdomain()` directive, the Flash would only function with JavaScript of an origin that exactly matches the origin of the Flash file. This behavior is bound to cause problems with Web application configurations that utilize more than one (sub-)domain. Already enabling the Web application to be accessed using both the plain domain (e.g., `http://example.org`) and the www-subdomain (`http://www.example.org`) potentially breaks the proxy's functionality for one of the two alternatives.

4   Methods to Provide Secure Client-Side Flash Proxy Functionality

In this section we explore the safe inclusion of a client-side Flash proxy in a Web application. For this, we propose two approaches: First, we discuss how to apply the general method of CSRF protection to securely include a prefabricated, potentially vulnerable Flash proxy (see Sec. 4.1). Secondly, we show how to build a custom proxy that is safe against the attack without giving up to much of the flexibility of the existing solutions (see Sec. 4.2).

4.1   Secure Inclusion via CSRF Protection

Some of the already existing Flash proxies (e.g. flXHR) are matured software and provide well tested support code, such as plug-ins for popular JavaScript frameworks. For this reason it might be desirable to use them regardless of the identified security issues.

To do so securely, the application has to ensure that the proxy is only used within its foreseen environment, i.e., the proxy is indeed included in a Web page that belongs to the application. This can be done by adapting the nonce-based schema of CSRF-protection [7]: Instead of serving the applet's swf-file as a static binary, the code is delivered by a server-side script. This script verifies that the requesting URL contains a secret nonce which is tied to the requesting browser's session cookie, e.g., in the form of a URL parameter (see Listing 3 for an example). Only if the received nonce matches the expected value, the SWF is delivered to the browser. As the adversary cannot obtain such a nonce for the victim's current browser context, he is not able to create the attacking page and, hence, is unable to execute the attack.

Listing 3. CSRF protected delivery of Flash code (PHP example)

```php
<?php
if ($_GET["anti_csrf_nonce"] == $_SESSION["nonce"]){
    $swf = [...]    // binary data of the .swf file
    header("Content-type: application/x-shockwave-flash");
    echo $swf;
} else {
    ... // Generate 500 internal server error
}
?>
```

4.2 Flexibly Restricting the Flash-to-JavaScript Interface

In order to enable HTML-to-SWF communication, Flash uses the External-Interface API to expose functionality to JavaScript. Cross-domain scripting from JavaScript to Flash, however, is forbidden by default. In cases where cross-domain communication is needed the directive flash.system.Security.allowDomain("http://c.net") can be used inside an SWF to grant scripting access from c.net.

As explained in Section 3.4 this fact causes problems for general purpose, pre-built solutions which are supposed to be usable without modifications. Thus, these libraries often use allowDomain('*'), which grants cross domain scripting access from all domains to the SWF. However, using this directive has severe security implications as the SWF is now vulnerable to the attack vectors described in Section 3.2.

As it is not feasible to disable cross-domain scripting on SWF files for general purpose libraries, we see two possibilities on how to avoid the use of allowDomain("*"): Hardcode the set of trusted domains or dynamically parametrize allowDomain-based on a separate configuration file.

The first solution requires the user to hardcode all domains he would like to grant cross-domain access to in the source code of the swf-file. This solution has two major shortcomings. For one, the user needs to have the ability to compile the source code into a working swf-file. Furthermore, he needs to do this each time he wants to update his access grants.

Therefore, we propose an alternative solution which uses a separate configuration file and dynamically grants access to all domains specified in this file. With the help of this file a user can change his configuration at any time without the need of recompiling the SWF. As this solution provides the needed flexibility and does only grant cross-domain access to trusted domains and not to the general public it is well suited for general purpose libraries.

Implementation: To examine the feasibility of this approach, we successfully created a slightly modified version of the open source crossXHR [24] proxy. On instantiation, the modified proxy now requests an `alloweddomains.xml` file from the proxy's original host (this location information can be obtained without requiring interaction with the potentially untrustworthy interfacing JavaScript). The set of domain-values contained in the received file are passed to the `allowDomain` call.

5   Securely Offering Public Flash Interfaces

The methods described in Section 4 are sufficient to securely provide a Web application with a client-side Flash proxy. However, the underlying problem remains unsolved: How can we publicly provide a general purpose Flash applet that reliably enforces security restrictions based on the origin of the JavaScript which the applet interacts with?

5.1   Problem: An Untrustworthy Interface

Flash's provided option to interact with it's surrounding container is via the `ExternalInterface.call()` method [3]. This method takes the name of one public function and an arbitrary number of arguments as parameters. If the surrounding container is an HTML page, this method invokes a JavaScript function and returns the value provided by the function.

As all public JavaScript functions can be overwritten [22], an adversary is able to manipulate any value `call()` could receive, even if the called method is a native JavaScript method such as `eval()` or `window.location.href.toString()` (see Sec. 3.3). Thus, data which is received by ExternalInterface.call cannot be trusted. As discussed in [22], in most browsers a wrapped JavaScript function can be restored to its original state by calling a `delete` on the function. Hence, in theory it should be possible to circumvent all actions an adversary has taken by calling `delete` before each usage of a native function. But unfortunately, as `delete` is a JavaScript keyword and not a function, it cannot be used as a parameter for `ExternalInterface.call()`, rendering this potential solution infeasible.

5.2   Solution: Redirection to Fragment Identifier

As discussed above, a Flash applet's capabilities to interact with the enclosing HTML/JavaScript environment are severely limited and for most parts not outfitted to counter JavaScript wrappers which have been set up by the adversary. Hence, data retrieved from JavaScript cannot be trusted. Nevertheless, Flash needs to rely on JavaScript to obtain the URL of the enclosing page, in order to make certain security sensitive decisions.

The idea of the proposed countermeasure is to utilize redirects to fragment identifiers: If a browser window redirects itself to a URL containing a fragment identifier (also know as a local anchor), the browser automatically scrolls to the corresponding location in the displayed document after the page-loading process has terminated. However, if the URL of the currently displayed Web page already equals the target of the redirect, the page-loading step is skipped and the local anchor is accessed directly. This behavior can be utilized for validating the correctness of an URL which was retrieved by Flash's external interface mechanism:

After receiving the supposed URL of the enclosing page, the flash applet appends a fragment identifier to the URL and instructs the browser to redirected to the resulting location.

If the originally received URL was correct, i.e., it is indeed the URL of the enclosing Web page, this redirect does not cause the browser to do an actual reload. Instead, only the scroll position of the page is changed to the location of the local anchor, if a matching anchor exists in the page. If no matching anchor exist, the redirect causes no effects at all[4]. In any case, the Flash remains active in the page and can conduct the initiated action (e.g., initiating the cross-domain request).

However, if the URL received from JavaScript was manipulated, it differs from the correct URL. Thus, the browser will redirect the user to the page the attacker's JavaScript claims to have as an origin and the Flash applet stops executing. E.g., in the attack scenario described in Section 3.3, the redirect would cause the browser window to navigate away from a.net towards b.net.

One remaining weakness of this scheme is, that the attacker could stop the browser from redirecting, using JavaScript event handlers, such as window.onbeforeunload. Such an action is not directly noticeable by the Flash applet and, hence, is indistinguishable from the browser's behavior in the correct case.

In order to prevent such attempts, we include a random nonce (large and unguessable) into the fragment identifier (see Listing 4). Before executing the security sensitive action the Flash applet requests the enclosing URL from JavaScript for a second time and compares the received URL to the URL saved by the Flash applet (includes the nonce) before. If the redirect was prevented, the attacker is not able to identify the random number and, thus, Flash can detect that the redirect was stopped and reject the call. If the redirect was successful

---

[4] We tested this behavior with the following browsers: Firefox, Internet Explorer, Google Chrome, Opera, Safari

and the URL was not tampered with, Flash is able to verify that the two nonces and the URLs are equal and, thus, can conclude that the first URL received from JavaScript was indeed correct (see Listing 5).

Listing 4. Redirect to fragment (sketch)

```
var location: String =
        ExternalInterface.call("self.location.href.toString");
var rand = String(Math.floor(Math.random()*RANDOM_MAX_SIZE));
this.newLocation = location + "#nonce" + rand";
var request: URLRequest = new URLRequest(this.newLocation);
navigateToURL(request,"_self");
```

Listing 5 Verifying the fragment identifier after the redirect (sketch)

```
var location: String =
    ExternalInterface.call("self.location.href.toString");

if(this.newLocation = location){
    newLocation = null;
    objects[id].send(content);
}else{
    newLocation = null; //invalidate to prevent brute forcing
    [...]                // die
}
```

Implementation: To verify our hypothesis, we implemented the outlined protection mechanism, again using the open source proxy crossXHR [24] as the basis of our implementation. Please refer to Figure 6 for further details on the modified interaction pattern between the Flash applet and surrounding JavaScript. Our implementation successfully defied both the general attacks (see Sec. 3.2) as well as the function wrapper trick (see Sec. 3.3 and Listing 2) while continuing to provide its designated functionality in legitimate use cases.

Limitation: The proposed countermeasure might cause problems with Web applications that utilize fragment identifiers to reflect their current application-state in the URL. Web applications that rely heavily on AJAX-driven interaction with their server-side, traditionally expose problems when it comes to creating hyperlinks which directly lead to specific parts of the application. For this reason, such applications occasionally append the identifier of the currently displayed application unit in the form of a fragment identifier to the URL (e.g. http://twitter.com/#!/datenkeller). If such applications do not foresee that the proposed countermeasure extends the window's URL (including the current fragment identifier) with the random nonce, erroneous behavior might result.

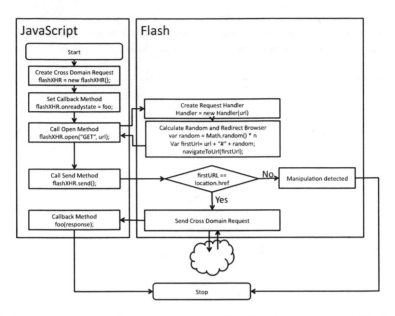

Fig. 6. Interaction pattern between untrusted JavaScript and a secured Flash applet

However, this problem is easily avoided by the application. The appended nonce is clearly marked. Thus, removing it before processing the application's own fragment identifier is straight forward.

6   Related Work

The recent history has shown that the evolution of the browser's client-side capabilities is often accompanied by the introduction of new security problems. In this section we list documented cases that relate to the issues discussed in this paper.

Issues with Flash's cross-domain request mechanism: The potential security issues with Flash's cross-domain capabilities have received some attention from the applied security community [28,10]. To assess the potential attack surface, Grossman examined in 2008 the policy files of the Alexa 500 and Fortune 500 websites [12]. He found that at this point in time 7% of the examined websites had a policy that granted every domain full access via the *-wildcard. Public documentation of real issues were given by, e.g., Rios [25] who compromised Google's mail service GMail by attaching a forged crossdomain.xml to an email, and by Grossman [13] who accessed private information on youtube.com by uploading a swf-file to a host which was whitelisted in YouTube's policy. In 2010, the tool MalaRIA (short for 'Malicious Rich Internet Application') [23] was released. The tool provides a graphical user interface to interactively conduct session hijacking attacks, as outlined in Section 2.5.

Further flaws of Flash's client-side networking: Besides cross-domain aspects, Flash's handling of client-side HTTP requests exposed further security short-comings (which have been resolved in the meantime): For one, Flash allowed in the past to add arbitrary HTTP headers to outgoing requests, leading to issues such as referrer spoofing or cross-site scripting [20]. Furthermore, it was shown that Flash's handling of client-side networking was susceptible to DNS rebinding attacks [19,17].

Security problems with modern browser features: The introduction of client-side cross-domain requests is not the only modern browser feature that was the cause of security problems. Huang et al. [16] recently discovered that the current de-sign of the Web socket protocol [15] in the presence of transparent Web proxies can be abused to conduct DNS cache poisoning attacks. Furthermore, Barth et al. [6] exposed a shortcoming in the `postMessage`-API [9] for asynchronous communication between frames which allowed, under certain circumstances, to compromise the confidentiality of the inter-frame message exchange. Finally, Heyes et al. [14] demonstrated how advanced features of cascading style sheets (CSS) can be utilized to create various information leaks.

7 Conclusion

As we have shown in this paper, the current movement to drop reliance on browser plug-ins in favor of applications that take full advantage of modern browser features might expose unexpected security pitfalls. There is a high probability that for practical reasons, in this transition phase, Web applica-tions might utilize a hybrid model for client-side code, which is mainly based on native JavaScript code and uses Flash (or other plug-in technologies) solely for fallback solutions on legacy browsers. However, the subtle difference in the respective implementations of the same-origin policy together with the insuffi-cient security architecture of the interfaces between the two technologies lead to complex security issues.

In this paper, we have demonstrated how the class of client-side Flash proxies for cross-domain HTTP requests is affected by this general problem. Further-more, we proposed two separate countermeasures that allow the specific case of Flash HTTP proxies to be handled. These protective measures are not limited to the explored application scenario but can be applied to securely handle the gen-eral case – whenever Flash functionality is exposed to potentially untrustworthy JavaScript. Thus, the discussed techniques can be used to provide generic drop-in components for legacy browsers to securely support the transitional hybrid model.

Acknowledgments

We would like to thank Kyle Simpson for feedback and valuable insight in the development of flXHR.

References

1. Adobe Coperation. Adobe flash,
   `http://www.adobe.com/products/flash/flashpro/`
2. Adobe Systems Inc. Cross-domain policy file specification (January 2010), `http://www.adobe.com/devnet/articles/crossdomain_policy_file_spec.html`
3. Adobe Systems Incorporated. flash.external ExternalInterface . ActionScript 3.0 Reference for the Adobe Flash Platform (December 2010), `http://help.adobe.com/en_US/FlashPlatform/reference/actionscript/3/flash/external/ExternalInterface.html` (accessed in January 2011)
4. Adobe Systems Incorporated. flash.system Security. ActionScript 3.0 Reference for the Adobe Flash Platform (December 2010), `http://help.adobe.com/en_US/FlashPlatform/reference/actionscript/3/flash/system/Security.html` (accessed in January 2011)
5. Alcorn, W., et al.: Browser Exploitation Framework BeEF (2011) software, `http://code.google.com/p/beef/` (accessed in January 2011)
6. Barth, A., Jackson, C., Mitchel, J.C.: Securing Frame Communication in Browsers. In: USENIX Security, pp. 17–30 (2008)
7. Burns, J.: Cross Site Request Forgery - An introduction to a common web application weakness. Whitepaper (2005), `https://www.isecpartners.com/documents/XSRF_Paper.pdf`
8. Couvreur, J.: FlashXMLHttpRequest: cross-domain requests (2007) software, `http://blog.monstuff.com/archives/000294.html` (accessed in January 2011)
9. IanHickson, I. (ed.).: HTML - Living Standard. WHATWG working draft (2010), `http://www.whatwg.org/specs/web-apps/current-work/`
10. Esser, S.: Poking new holes with Flash Crossdomain Policy Files (October 2006), `http://www.hardenedphp.net/library/poking_new_holes_with_flash_crossdomain_policy_files.html` (accessed in January 2011)
11. Google inc. Google Gadgets API: Working with Remote Content, `http://code.google.com/apis/gadgets/docs/remote-content.html` (accessed in January 2011)
12. Grossman, J.: Crossdomain.xml Invites Cross-site Mayhem (May 2008), `http://jeremiahgrossman.blogspot.com/2008/05/crossdomainxml-invites-cross-site.html` (accessed in January 2011)
13. Grossman, J.: I used to know what you watched, on YouTube (September 2008), `http://jeremiahgrossman.blogspot.com/2008/09/i-used-to-know-what-you-watched-on.html` (accessed in January 2011)
14. Heyes, G., Nava, E.V., Lindsay, D.: CSS: The Sexy Assassin. In: Talk at the Microsoft Blue Hat conference (October 2008), `http://technet.microsoft.com/en-us/security/cc748656`
15. Hickson, I.: The Web Sockets API. W3C Working Draft WD-websockets-20091222 (December 2009), `http://www.w3.org/TR/2009/WD-websockets-20091222/`
16. Huang, L.-S., Chen, E.Y., Barth, A., Rescorla, E., Jackson, C.: Transparent Proxies: Threat or Menace? Whitepaper (2010), `http://www.adambarth.com/experimental/websocket.pdf`
17. Jackson, C., Barth, A., Bortz, A., Shao, W., Boneh, D.: Protecting Browsers from DNS Rebinding Attack. In: Proceedings of the 14th ACM Conference on Computer and Communication Security, CCS 2007 (October 2007)
18. Kamkar, S.: Technical explanation of the MySpace worm (October 2005), `http://namb.la/popular/tech.html` (accessed in January 2011)

19. Kanatoko. Anti-DNS Pinning + Socket in Flash (January 19, 2007), http://www.jumperz.net/index.php?i=2&a=3&b=3
20. Klein, A.: Forging HTTP Request Headers with Flash ActionScript. Whitepaper (July 2006), http://www.securiteam.com/securityreviews/5KP0M1FJ5E.html
21. Livshits, B., Cui, W.: Spectator: Detection and Containment of JavaScript Worms. In: Usenix Annual Technical Conference (June 2008)
22. Magazinius, J., Phung, P.H., Sands, D.: Safe wrappers and sane policies for self protecting JavaScript. In: Aura, T. (ed.) The 15th Nordic Conference in Secure IT Systems. LNCS, Springer, Heidelberg (October 2010); (Selected papers from AppSec 2010)
23. Oftedal, E.: Malicious rich internet application (malaria) (April 2010) software, http://erlend.oftedal.no/blog/?blogid=107 (accessed in January 2011)
24. Reitman, B.: CrossXHR - a Cross-Domain XmlHttpRequest drop-in-replacement (Feburary 2010) software, http://code.google.com/p/crossxhr/wiki/CrossXhr (accessed in January 2011)
25. Rios, B.: Cross Domain Hole Caused By Google Docs (2007), http://xs-sniper.com/blog/Google-Docs-Cross-Domain-Hole/ (accessed in January 2011)
26. Ruderman, J.: The Same Origin Policy (August 2001), http://www.mozilla.org/projects/security/components/same-origin.html (October 1, 2006)
27. Shiflett, C.: Cross-Domain Ajax Insecurity (August 2006), http://shiflett.org/blog/2006/aug/cross-domain-ajax-insecurity (accessed in January 2011)
28. Shiflett, C.: The Dangers of Cross-Domain Ajax with Flash (September 2006), http://shiflett.org/blog/2006/sep/the-dangers-of-cross-domain-ajax-with-flash (accessed in January 2011)
29. Simpson, K.: (new) Adobe Flash Player security hole found, flXHRs response (August 2008), http://www.flensed.com/fresh/2008/08/adobe-flash-player-security-hole/ (accessed in January 2011)
30. Simpson, K.: flXHR - Cross-Domain Ajax with Flash (2010) software, http://flxhr.flensed.com/ (accessed in January 2011)
31. van Kesteren, A.: The XMLHttpRequest Object. W3C Working Draft (April 2008), http://www.w3.org/TR/XMLHttpRequest
32. van Kesteren, A.(ed.).: Cross-Origin Resource Sharing. W3C Working Draft, Version WD-cors-20100727 (July 2010), http://www.w3.org/TR/cors/
33. Web Hypertext Application Technology Working Group (WHATWG). Welcome to the WHATWG community (2011), http://www.whatwg.org/ (accessed in January 2011)
34. Wilson, J.R.: SWFHttpRequest Flash/Ajax Utility (December 2007) software, http://jimbojw.com/wiki/index.php?title=SWFHttpRequest_Flash/Ajax_Utility (accessed in January 2011)
35. Zalewski, M.: Browser Security Handbook. Whitepaper, Google Inc. (2008), http://code.google.com/p/browsersec/wiki/Main (January 13, 2009)

Mitigating Cross-Site Form History Spamming Attacks with Domain-Based Ranking

Chuan Yue

University of Colorado at Colorado Springs
Department of Computer Science, Colorado Springs, CO 80918, USA
cyue@eas.uccs.edu

Abstract. Modern Web browsers often provide a very useful form autocomplete feature to help users conveniently speed up their form filling process. However, browsers are generally too permissive in both saving form history data and suggesting them to users. Attackers can take advantage of this permissiveness and use malicious webpages to inject a large amount of junk or spam data into the form history database of a browser, performing invasive advertising or simply making this useful form autocomplete feature almost useless to users. In this paper, we illustrate that this type of *cross-site form history spamming attacks* can be feasibly achieved at least on the recent versions of Mozilla Firefox and Google Chrome browsers. We inspect the autocomplete feature implementations in open source Firefox and Chromium browsers to analyze how basic and advanced cross-site form history spamming attacks can be successful. Browser vendors are apparently taking active measures to protect against these attacks, but we explore a different approach and propose a domain-based ranking mechanism to address the problem. Our mechanism is simple, transparent to users, and easily adoptable by different browsers to complement their existing protection mechanisms. We have implemented this mechanism in Firefox 3 and verified its effectiveness. We make our Firefox 3 build available for download and verification.

1 Introduction

Modern Web browsers often provide a very useful form autocomplete feature to help users speed up their form filling process. This feature keeps remembering a user's form filling history, predicts what a user wants to type in a new form field, and pops up a list of candidate history input values for a user to reuse. By directly selecting a matching history input value, a user can effectively reduce the keyboard typing time and effort.

However, browsers are generally too permissive in both saving form history data and suggesting them to users. When browsers save form history data, they disregard the origin of the form data. No matter on which website the form is submitted, the form field data are simply saved to the history database as name-value pairs. When browsers suggest a list of candidate history input values to a user, they again disregard the origins of both the current Web form and the

T. Holz and H. Bos. (Eds.): DMIVA 2011, LNCS 6739, pp. 104–123, 2011.

history data. Normally, all the form field history values that have the matching field name and matching field value pattern with the current input field will be selected from the history database and displayed in the form autocomplete dropdown list. Such a permissive behavior is common to the three most popular browsers Internet Explorer, Mozilla Firefox, and Google Chrome.

A direct consequence of this permissiveness is that attackers can use malicious webpages to inject a large amount of junk or spam data into the form history database of a browser. These data may contain advertisement words used for getting financial or political benefits, or they are simply meaningless words used for nullifying the form autocomplete feature. The malicious webpages can trigger automatic form submissions, can inject all kinds of name-value combinations into the form history database of a browser, and can use different tricks to have their submitted field values ranked as top candidates by browsers. Later on, when users need to fill out forms on other legitimate websites, a large number of spam input values will be prompted by browsers as top form autocomplete candidates. This result may force users to read advertisement spams, may force them to spend more time and effort in choosing the desired reusable input value, and may also confuse them by suggesting many irrelevant junk input values. We call this type of attacks *cross-site form history spamming attacks*, and we illustrate in Section 3 that these attacks can be feasibly achieved at least on the recent versions of two popular browsers Firefox and Google Chrome.

Generally speaking, there could be two approaches to defending against cross-site form history spamming attacks. The first approach is to prevent the insertion of automatically submitted spam data into the form history database; the second approach is to prevent the suggestion of spam data values to a user. The former restricts the permissiveness of browsers in saving form history data, and the latter restricts the permissiveness of browsers in suggesting candidate form data. Both approaches have their own merits, and ideally browsers should leverage the advantages of both approaches to provide a strong protection against cross-site form history spamming attacks.

Browser vendors such as Google and Microsoft are apparently taking active measures to protect against cross-site form history spamming attacks [12,13]. However, they mainly took the first approach to fix the form autocomplete bugs in their browsers. Their efforts reduced the chances for attackers to inject junk form data, but still any spam that does make it into the form history database is persistent and stays until the user cleans it up. Moreover, the *cross-site autocomplete* phenomenon (Section 3) still exists in the latest versions of the three most popular browsers Internet Explorer 8.0.7600.16385, Google Chrome 8.0.552.237, and Firefox 3.6.13. Therefore, the form autocomplete feature in those browsers may still not able to ensure the availability of the most relevant form history data to a user (Section 4).

In this paper, we take the second approach and propose a domain-based ranking mechanism to restrict the suggestion of irrelevant form history field values to a user. We choose to take the second approach because no serious attention has been given to it yet, and we believe a solution with this approach could be beneficial to all popular browsers. We choose to explore the domain-based ranking mechanism because it is simple, transparent to users, and easily adoptable by different browsers. Meanwhile, our domain-based design philosophy is consistent with those of other efforts in securing browsers [1,3,5,6,10,14].

The basic idea of our domain-based ranking mechanism is to first ask a browser to also remember the origin domain of the form data when it saves a new name-value pair into the form history database. Later on, whenever a user needs to fill out a form on a webpage, the domain of the current website will also be inspected so that matching form history data with the matching domain will always be ranked higher than other matching form history data without the matching domain. This mechanism always allows users to conveniently select the most relevant form history data, thus rendering the cross-site form history spamming effort of attackers futile. We have implemented this defense mechanism in Firefox 3 and verified its effectiveness (Section 5). We make our Firefox 3 build on openSUSE Linux accessible to researchers for verifying its correctness and usefulness. Our source code is also available upon request.

The main contributions of this paper are as follows: (1) We illustrate that cross-site form history spamming attacks are feasible and can make the very useful form autocomplete feature almost useless to users. (2) We inspect the autocomplete feature implementations in open source Firefox and Chromium browsers to analyze how basic and advanced cross-site form history spamming attacks can be successful. (3) We propose a domain-based ranking mechanism for protecting browsers from those attacks. This mechanism is simple, so its correct implementation can be ensured with high confidence. It is completely transparent to users, so they need not to be trained or informed of its use. It is not bound to browsers' any specific support of DOM, event model, and JavaScript, so it can be easily adopted by different browsers as a defense-in-depth mechanism to complement their existing protections to the autocomplete feature.

2   Background

The form autocomplete feature is supported by the four most popular browsers: Internet Explorer, Firefox, Google Chrome, and Safari. Another popular browser Opera does not have a form autocomplete feature. The basic functioning of the form autocomplete feature is simple: it saves what a user has previously submitted in the *text* type input fields of a form into a history database, and makes the saved history data available to reuse to help speed up a user's future form filling tasks. A user is allowed to turn on or off this feature by configuring a preference option in the browser.

Some browsers also support another related feature called form autofill. Strictly speaking, form autofill is different from form autocomplete. Form autofill requires a user to explicitly save personal information such as name and address through the browser's form autofill user preference interface, and then allows the user to reuse the saved information to fill the corresponding forms. Table 1 lists the support of the form autocomplete and form autofill features in the recent versions of different browsers; it also lists the locations for configuring these two features.

Table 1. The support of form autocomplete and form autofill features in browsers

Browser	Auto-complete	Auto-fill	Configuration Location
Internet Explorer (8.0.7600.16385)	Yes	No	Tools → Internet Options → Content → AutoComplete → Settings
Firefox (3.6.10 to 3.6.13)	Yes	No	Tools → Options → Privacy → History → Remember search and form history
Google Chrome (6.0.472.63, 7.0.517.41, 8.0.552.237)	Yes	Yes	Options → Personal Stuff → Autofill options → Enable Autofill to fill out web forms in a single click
Safari (5.0.1 7533.17.8, 5.0.2 7533.18.5)	Yes	Yes	Preferences → AutoFill → AutoFill web forms
Opera (10.62, 10.63)	No	Yes	Settings → Preferences → Forms

From this table, we can see that the feature support, feature configuration locations, and even the usage of terms are inconsistent among different browsers. For one example, Internet Explorer and Firefox only have the form autocomplete feature. For another example, Google Chrome uses the same term autofill to represent both the autocomplete and autofill features, although internally they have different interfaces and implementations. Therefore, we want to make it clear that our work only focuses on the form autocomplete feature. The key reason is because attackers can simply use malicious webpages to abuse this feature (next section), but it is much harder for them to directly inject junk form data through a browser's form autofill user preference interface.

Two more autocomplete related features in modern browsers are also out of the scope of this paper. One is the website password remembering feature. This feature is normally controlled by the password manager of a browser, and similarly it is very difficult for attackers to directly manipulate it via malicious webpages. The other feature is the location bar autocomplete. This feature guesses what a URL address a user wants to type in the address bar based on what websites the user has visited before. Attackers can also inject junk data to a browser's URL location history database, but the severity of such attacks is limited. This is because browsers such as Firefox and Google Chrome do not save URLs with invalid domains and meanwhile it is difficult to load a large number of URLs from the address bar without being perceived by a user.

3   Attacks

In this section, we illustrate and analyze the cross-site form history spamming attacks. First, we use some concrete examples to show that modern browsers are generally too permissive in both saving form history data and suggesting them to users. Second, we construct basic attacks to demonstrate that cross-site form history spamming is feasible. Third, we construct advanced attacks by inspecting the implementation of the form autocomplete feature in open source Firefox and Chromium (which provides source code for Google Chrome) Web browsers; we illustrate that such advanced attacks can make the very useful form autocomplete feature almost useless to users.

3.1   The Permissiveness in Autocomplete

First, let us open either a Firefox or a Google Chrome browser window, and make sure its form autocomplete feature is not turned off (Table 1 has the configuration location information). Then, we visit the following three groups of example websites listed in Table 2 and submit forms on them.

Table 2. Three groups of example websites

Website	Webpage Form	Field Label / Name
login.yahoo.com	Sign in to Yahoo!	Yahoo! ID / login
login.live.com	sign in	Window Live ID / login
amazon.com	Sign in	My e-mail address is / email
facebook.com	login	Email / email
usps.com	Search USPS.com	*empty* / q
flickr.com	SEARCH	*empty* / q

For the first group, we submit the "sign in" form on either login.yahoo.com or login.live.com. We can randomly type in some dummy ID and password combinations in our login attempts, and we do not need to ensure those attempts to be successful. It is easy for us to observe that a submitted Yahoo! ID on login.yahoo.com will appear in the autocomplete dropdown list when we plan to type in a Windows Live ID on login.live.com as shown in Figure 1. Similarly, a submitted Windows Live ID on login.live.com will also appear in the autocomplete dropdown list when we plan to type in a Yahoo! ID on login.yahoo.com. We refer to this phenomenon as *cross-site autocomplete*.

We can observe the same phenomenon between the login forms of the two websites listed in the second group of Table 2. We can also observe this phenomenon on many other types of form submissions. For example, in the third group, the search data submitted on usps.com will be suggested to us in the autocomplete dropdown list when we plan to type in the search form on flickr.com, and vice versa. All these observations are common to the latest versions of Google Chrome (6.0.472.63 to 8.0.552.237) and Firefox (3.6.10 to 3.6.13).

We also observed the cross-site autocomplete phenomenon on these three groups of websites in Internet Explorer 8 before a security update was automatically applied on October 12, 2010 [13]. With that update, Internet Explorer 8.0.7600.16385 disables its form autocomplete feature on https webpages. However, the cross-site autocomplete phenomenon still exists in Internet Explorer on http webpages such as the ones listed in the third group of Table 2. We did not observe the cross-site autocomplete phenomenon on the Safari Web browser. Indeed, we found that the autocomplete feature on Safari 5.0.1 7533.17.8 and the latest version 5.0.2 7533.18.5 does not work at all, and form data are not saved even for the same form of the same website.

The key reason why such a cross-site autocomplete phenomenon occurs is because modern browsers are generally too permissive in both saving form history

Fig. 1. The cross-site autocomplete phenomenon

data and suggesting them to users. Modern browsers simply disregard the important origin domain information in their autocomplete feature design. When browsers save form data, they save the form field name-value pairs without saving the corresponding domain information. When browsers suggest a list of candidate form history input values to a user, they select values that have the matching field name and matching field value pattern[1] with the current input field regardless of the current domain name. For example, the two input fields Yahoo! ID and Windows Live ID in the first group have the same input field *name= "login"*, the two input fields in the second group have the same input field *name= "email"*, and the two input fields in the third group have the same input field *name= "q"*. This is why the cross-site autocomplete phenomenon can be observed between the two websites in each group.

It is reasonable to assume that the original autocomplete feature designers had the intentions to promote cross-site autocomplete so that form data submitted from different websites can be ubiquitously reused. However, considering the widespread growth of Web-based threats in recent years [7,17], we believe it is time now to revise the design of this feature to restrict its permissiveness. Otherwise, as we show below, attackers can launch cross-site form history spamming attacks to perform invasive advertising or simply make the very useful form autocomplete feature almost useless to users.

3.2   Basic Spamming Attacks

Cross-site form history spamming attacks take advantage of browsers' permissiveness in autocomplete to inject a large amount of junk or spam data into the form history database of a browser. They may force users to read advertisement spams, may force them to spend more time and effort in choosing the desired reusable input value, and may also confuse them by suggesting many irrelevant junk input values. To be successful, such an attack needs to satisfy two basic conditions: the first condition is to attract a user to visit a malicious webpage,

---

[1] The field name is used to select the initial candidate list; the field value pattern is used to refine that initial list once a user begins to type something in the input field.

and the second one is to trigger automatic form submissions on the malicious webpage to spam the form history database.

There is no silver bullet for preventing the satisfaction of the first condition. For example, attackers can host malicious webpages on their own websites, or they can inject malicious scripts to compromise webpages hosted on legitimate websites. They can also use phishing attacks or malicious advertisements to further allure users to visit malicious webpages.

```html
<html>
<head>
<script language="javascript" type="text/javascript">
function submitJunkData() {
  var charSet = "ABCDEFGHIJKLMNOPQRSTUVWXTZabcdefghiklmnopqrstuvwxyz0123456789._";
  var newValue = "";
  for (var i=0; i<8; i++) {
    var index = Math.floor(Math.random() * charSet.length);
    newValue += charSet.charAt(index);
  }
  document.getElementById('fieldID').value = newValue;
  document.getElementById('formID').submit();
}
</script>
</head>

<body onload="setInterval('submitJunkData()', 300)">
<p>Contents that attract a user to stay on this webpage.</p>
<form id="formID" method="post" action="" target="iframe-hole" style="visibility:hidden">
<input type="text" name="login" id="fieldID" value="" size=100>
</form>
<iframe name="iframe-hole" width=0 height=0 style="visibility:hidden"></iframe>
<input type="text" name="somethingelse" value="" size=100>
</body>
</html>
```

Fig. 2. Malicious example one (attack1.htm)

Now, we focus on illustrating that the second condition for a successful cross-site form history spamming attack can be feasibly achieved at least on the recent versions of two popular browsers Mozilla Firefox (3.6.10 to 3.6.13) and Google Chrome (6.0.472.63). Figure 2 illustrates one malicious webpage example attack1.htm. Basically, once this page is loaded on a user's browser, it will automatically trigger the form submission action every 300 milliseconds. In each form submission, a randomly generated junk value for the input field *name= "login"* will be submitted, and that value will be saved by the browser to its form history database. Later on, when a user fills an input form field with *name= "login"* such as the Yahoo! ID field or the Windows Live ID field listed in Table 2, those saved junk data will be suggested to the user in the browser's autocomplete dropdown list.

Looking at the content of this webpage, we can identify that it uses the JavaScript setInterval function to periodically call the submitJunkData function to submit a special form. The form itself is invisible and it employs a "hole in the page" technique [16] to set its *target* attribute pointing to an invisible iframe. Using these techniques, the malicious webpage can submit the form in a hidden manner without reloading the page, so that a user's interactions with other

```
<html>
<head>
<script language="javascript" type="text/javascript">
function submitJunkData() {
  //This function is the same as that in attack1.htm
}
</script>
</head>

<body onload="setInterval('submitJunkData()', 300)">
<p>Contents that attract a user to stay on this webpage.</p>
<form id="formID" method="post" action="" target="_self" style="visibility:hidden">
<input type="text" name="login" id="fieldID" value="" size=100>
</form>
</body>
</html>
```

Fig. 3. Malicious example two (attack2.htm)

```
<html>
<head>
</head>
<frameset cols="1%,*" name="frameset_01">
  <frame src="attack2.htm" name="frame_01" noresize>
  <frame src="http://www.amazon.com" name="frame_02" noresize>
</frameset>
</html>
```

Fig. 4. Malicious example two (frameset.htm)

elements such as the "somethingelse" input field will not be affected. Therefore, it is hard for a user to notice the behind the scenes automatic form submissions.

Even without using the "hole in the page" technique, a malicious webpage that reloads itself can also be very stealthy. Figure 3 and Figure 4 illustrate such an example. The malicious webpage attack2.htm is almost identical to attack1.htm, except for (1) removing the hidden iframe and the "somethingelse" input field, and (2) setting the form *target= "_self"* to reload the page itself. To hide the automatic form submissions from users, an attacker can use a framed webpage frameset.htm to include attack2.htm as a frame element. Therefore, when a user interacts with other frame pages of frameset.htm such as amazon.com, attack2.htm can continuously inject junk data to the browser's form history database.

In both attack1.htm and attack2.htm example webpages, the *target* attribute of the form is used to specify where to open the URL once the form is submitted. The *target* attribute of *<form>* is deprecated in HTML 4.01, but it is still supported by all the five popular browsers (Table 1) to maintain backward compatibility. However, attack2.htm can also be successful without using the deprecated *target* attribute. In such a case, attack2.htm can be modified by removing *target= "_self"* and setting *action= "attack2.htm"*. In these two example webpages, the intervals on how often to submit the form can also be dynamically adjusted by changing the setInterval function call. In addition, the *<body>* onload event handler in attack2.htm can be optionally changed from setInterval to setTimeout.

Last but not least, what we have introduced so far are just two examples of basic cross-site form history spamming attacks. We verified these attacks on the recent versions of Mozilla Firefox (3.6.10 to 3.6.13) and Google Chrome (6.0.472.63). There could exist many other techniques for performing the same or similar spamming attacks; however, the objective of our work is not to enumerate all the attacking techniques, but to protect the form autocomplete feature of browsers no matter what techniques are used by attackers to inject junk data into browsers' form history database. We also verified that these two example malicious webpages cannot successfully attack Internet Explorer 8 even before applying its security update [13]. They can still trigger periodical form submissions, but the submitted form data are not saved by Internet Explorer to its form history database. It seems that Internet Explorer 8 and the latest versions of Google Chrome (7.0.517.41 to 8.0.552.237) require a user initiated action to enter data into the autocomplete database, thus mitigating the attacks.

3.3   Advanced Spamming Attacks

Advanced cross-site form history spamming attacks improve over basic spamming attacks to make them more effective. Here, from different perspectives, we illustrate three types of techniques that could be used in advanced spamming attacks: the first one is *target selection techniques* that can increase the possibility for a browser to select junk data from its form history database to the autocomplete dropdown list, the second one is *ranking promotion techniques* that can improve the ranking of junk data in a browser's autocomplete dropdown list, and the third one is *value generation techniques* that can help keep junk data in the autocomplete dropdown list even when a user begins to type something in an input field.

Target selection techniques. focus on properly choosing form input field names to increase the possibility for a browser to select the submitted junk data. Recall that when browsers suggest a list of candidate history input values to a user, they will first check the *name* property of the *text* type input field and will only select history input data that have the matching field name with the current input field. This practice is common to the three most popular browsers Internet Explorer, Firefox, and Google Chrome[2]. Therefore, to make their attacks effective, attackers can select certain targeted field names that may match the field names in users' potential future form filling activities.

The targeted field names can be selected from different sources. To attack popular websites such as the ones listed in Table 2, attackers can visit those sites and directly extract their form input field names. To attack as many websites as possible, attackers can use tools to crawl the Web and identify those most commonly used form input field names. After selecting the targeted field names, attackers can use those names on a malicious webpage in different ways. For one example, they can simply put a list of *text* type input fields with different

---

[2] A small difference: Firefox and Google Chrome perform case sensitive field name comparison, but Internet Explorer performs case insensitive field name comparison.

```
<script language="javascript" type="text/javascript">
function submitJunkData() {
  //The code that constructs new newName and newValue
  //......
  document.getElementById('fieldID').name = newName;
  document.getElementById('fieldID').value = newValue;
  document.getElementById('formID').submit();
}
</script>
```

Fig. 5. Example JavaScript code that dynamically changes the name of a *text* type input field

names inside of a single form. Note that browsers often set an upper limit on the maximum number of input field values that can be saved to the history database in a single form submission. This limit is 100 in Firefox and 256 in Chromium. For another example, attackers can also dynamically change the names of existing input fields using JavaScript as shown in Figure 5. These techniques work on recent versions of Firefox and Google Chrome as listed in Table 1.

Ranking promotion techniques. focus on improving the ranking of junk data in a browser's autocomplete dropdown list. Normally, after selecting the initial candidate form history values based on the current input field name, browsers will rank those values with the expectation that one of the top-ranked values could be a user's desired input value. Browsers often only show those top-ranked values in the autocomplete dropdown list. For example, both Firefox and Google Chrome limit that at any time at most six suggested values can appear in the autocomplete dropdown list window for a *text* type input field. Firefox enables a scrollbar for the dropdown list to allow a user to view more suggested values, but Google Chrome does not enable a scrollbar for its autocomplete dropdown list. Therefore, to make their junk data occupy the limited positions in the auto-complete dropdown list and out-compete a user's desired history data, attackers have to raise the ranking of their junk data.

By inspecting the source code of Firefox and Chromium, we can identify exactly how these two browsers rank matching input field values. In Firefox, three main factors are considered and values that are used more times, used more recently, or used more frequently over a long period of time will be ranked higher based on a complex formula. In Chromium, the main factor is the total number of times used, and the larger this number the higher the ranking of a value. While there are some differences between these two browsers in ranking form history values, a common and reasonable criterion is the number of times that a value is used. Indeed, in the form history databases of both browsers, such a timesUsed number is associated with each unique *text* type name-value pair. When a form is submitted and if a submitted name-value pair already exists in the form history database, both browsers will simply increase the timesUsed number of this existing record by one.

Based on these analyses, we can see that attackers may raise the ranking of their injected junk form data by submitting the same name-value pairs multiple times. We provide such an example in Figure 6. Basically, in a malicious

```
<script language="javascript" type="text/javascript">
var months=['January','February','March','April','May','June',
            'July','August','September','October','November','December'];

function submitJunkData() {
  var index = Math.floor(Math.random() * 12);
  var newValue = months[index];
  document.getElementById('fieldID').value = newValue;
  document.getElementById('formID').submit();
}
</script>
```

Fig. 6. Example JavaScript code that repeatedly submits some name-value pairs in a form

webpage such as attack1.htm or attack2.htm, the submitJunkData function will be periodically invoked to repeatedly submit the names of the twelve months as junk data. If their numbers of submitted times become much larger than those of a user's desired values, these junk data can occupy the limited positions in the autocomplete dropdown list for a long time. We have also verified this example on recent versions of Firefox and Google Chrome as listed in Table 1.

Value generation techniques. can help keep junk data in the autocomplete dropdown list even when a user begins to type something in an input field. Normally, once a user begins to type something in an input field, browsers will immediately refine the values suggested in the dropdown list. Internet Explorer and Google Chrome only use prefix matching, i.e., those suggested values must begin with what a user has typed into the input field. Firefox uses both prefix matching and substring matching at the same time. When a user has typed more than one character into the input field, substring matching will include those values that contain (not necessarily prefix) this partial input into the suggested list. In all these three browsers, case insensitive comparison is used to match input field values.

Based on these practices in browsers, attackers may want to generate junk values that start with a user's partial input. While it is very difficult to predict a user's input, attackers can simply generate junk values that start with the permutation of two alphabets or other unique characters according to the purpose of an input field such as a username field or a zip code field. Therefore, the junk data could still be selected into the autocomplete dropdown list even after a user types in two characters. We should note that with each keystroke the user is willing to type, the attack work required increases exponentially. Another important consideration in value generation is that attackers may put advertisement words in junk values to get financial or political benefits. This could be the strongest incentive for attackers to perform the cross-site form history spamming attacks.

4   Defenses

In general, there could be two approaches to defending against cross-site form history spamming attacks. The first approach is to prevent the insertion of automatically submitted junk or spam data into the form history database. The second approach is to prevent the suggestion of spam data values to a user. Some efforts have been made very recently in browsers such as Google Chrome [12] and Internet Explorer [13] to protect the form autocomplete feature, and actually those efforts followed the first approach by requiring a user initiated action to enter data into the autocomplete database. However, taking the first approach alone does not necessarily solve the whole problem. On the one hand, security bugs and flaws in modern browsers are inevitable [2,3,8,9,11]; therefore, attackers may still able to inject junk data to the form history database by exploiting some vulnerabilities in browsers. Any spam that does make it into the form history database is persistent and stays until the user cleans it up. On the other hand, the cross-site autocomplete phenomenon illustrated in the last section still exists in all the three most popular browsers; therefore, the most relevant site-specific form history data may still not be selected as top autocomplete candidates.

Therefore, we argue that modern browsers should also take the second approach to better protect the autocomplete feature. We explore this second approach by proposing a domain-based ranking mechanism. This mechanism is simple, transparent to users, and easily adoptable by different browsers as a defense-in-depth mechanism to complement their existing protection mechanisms. In this section, we present and analyze our domain-based ranking mechanism.

4.1   The Domain-Based Ranking Mechanism

The key idea of this mechanism is very simple. When a browser saves a new name-value pair into the form history database, it will also remember the corresponding origin domain of the submitted form data. Later on, when the browser selects candidate form history values, it will inspect the domain of the current website and will always rank matching values that have the corresponding domain higher than other matching values that do not have the corresponding domain. For example, a user has submitted the "sign in" forms before on login.yahoo.com (see Table 2) using the *login* value "yahoo2010" and on login.live.com using the *login* value "live2010". When the user visits login.yahoo.com again, the value "yahoo2010" will always be ranked higher than the value "live2010" and any *login* values submitted from other (potentially malicious) domains.

To integrate such a domain-based ranking mechanism into a browser's form autocomplete feature, we need to make three modifications: updating the form history database, updating the form data saving functionality, and updating the autocomplete suggestion functionality. Using our implementation of this mechanism in Firefox 3 as the example, we present the details of these modifications.

Form history database:Browsers usually save form history data into a database. For example, both Firefox and Chromium use a zero-configuration transactional SQLite [15] database engine to store all the form history data. In the SQLite database of Firefox 3, the original form history table consists of six columns as shown in Table 3.

To save the origin domain information of a fieldname-value pair, we need to add one new column to this form history table. We name this new column as *baseDomain* and specify its data type as TEXT. Adding this new column to the

Table 3. Form history table modification in Firefox

The original version with the six columns						
id	fieldname	value	timesUsed	firstUsed	lastUsed	–
The new version with an added column baseDomain						
id	fieldname	value	timesUsed	firstUsed	lastUsed	**baseDomain**

form history table is straightforward and we simply modified the table creation SQL statement. However, considering the scenario that a *.sqlite* database file with the old version database schema may exist when a browser is upgraded to include our domain-based ranking mechanism, we also need to instruct the browser to perform a database migration to migrate old data records to the new form history table. In such a case, a default domain name will be used to indicate that those records came from the old version of browser. Actually in Firefox 3, timesUsed, firstUsed, and lastUsed were new columns added to the database schema version one. We strictly followed their migration steps to ensure the correctness of our migration implementation.

We should also note that originally, each record in the form history table is uniquely identified by a fieldname-value pair, and a unique id is generated to represent that pair. This practice is common to both Firefox and Chromium. With our modification to the form history table, each record is now uniquely identified by a triplet (fieldname, value, baseDomain), and a unique id is generated to represent that triplet. Thus, baseDomain will be taken into account in all the related database operations such as insertion and updating.

Form data saving: When a form is submitted and its data need to be saved to the form history database, a browser will notify its autocomplete feature to perform the task. We need to make modifications to this form data saving functionality so that the domain name information of the corresponding form data will also be saved.

To extract the domain name information, we consider two main factors: the source of the domain name and the parts of the domain name. In terms of the source, we extract the domain name of a form's owner document. In other words, we are interested in where exactly a form comes from, instead of what is the domain name of the top-level document. This design choice is reasonable because the owner document contains the most relevant information of a form. For example, on mashup websites, if a form is submitted from a sub-frame document, the domain name of the sub-frame document will be extracted and used by our mechanism. Therefore, the saved form history data can always be available no matter a owner document (e.g., www.flickr.com) is included in mashup websites as a sub-frame document (Figure 7(a)) or is directly loaded as a top-level document (Figure 7(b)) from a browser's URL address bar.

In terms of the parts of the domain name, we extract the base domain name and save it as baseDomain into the form history database (Table 3). For example, if a form's owner document domain name is login.yahoo.com, the extracted base domain name will be yahoo.com; if a form's owner document domain name is www.bbc.co.uk, the extracted base domain name will be bbc.co.uk. Once the

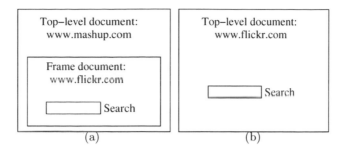

Fig. 7. Flickr.com (a) as a sub-frame document, (b) as a top-level document

base domain name is extracted, it will be used in the triplet (fieldname, value, baseDomain) for inserting or updating each unique form history record.

Autocomplete suggestion: When a user plans to fill out a form, a browser will search its form history database to check if any previously submitted *text* type input field values can be suggested to the user. In our mechanism, the initial search criterion is unchanged, i.e., all the records that have the matching field name with the current input field will be selected. However, with our modification, the values of the new added baseDomain column will also be retrieved for all the selected form history records. Then, our mechanism will mainly focus on adjusting the ranking of these selected records based on the domain name.

The first step is to extract the domain name of the current input form. Similar to what we modified in the form data saving functionality, here we also extract and use the domain name of the form's owner document. The second step is to compare the domain names. If the extracted owner document domain name contains the baseDomain of a selected form history record as the suffix, this record will be identified as a domain-matching record; otherwise, this record will be identified as a domain-mismatching record. For example, if the extracted owner document domain name is news.bbc.co.uk and a selected form history record has the baseDomain bbc.co.uk, this record will be identified as a domain-matching record. The way we use baseDomain and suffix matching in our mechanism is reasonable and it is consistent with the way HTTP cookie service of Firefox 3 checks whether a domain is a foreign domain for a cookie.

The ranking adjustment is purely based on the final ranking result of a browser's original algorithm. In other words, our mechanism does not manipulate the original formula used by a browser for ranking matching input field values; it simply adds one more adjustment step just before a browser suggests the ranked input field values to a user. In this final adjustment step, all the values of the domain-matching records will be moved ahead of all the values of domain-mismatching records. However, the relative ranking relations within the values of the domain-matching records will be preserved, and the relative ranking relations within the values of the domain-mismatching records will also be preserved. Meanwhile, if a value has appeared in a domain-matching record, that value will no longer be selected from any domain-mismatching record. Therefore, no duplicate values will be suggested to a user.

Table 4. An original ranking of "login" values

Rank	value	baseDomain
1	Eve	malicious.com
2	Chuck	malicious.com
3	Dave	yahoo.com
4	Carol	live.com
5	Fran	live.com
6	Bob	yahoo.com
7	Fran	yahoo.com
8	Alice	live.com

Table 5. The adjusted ranking on *.yahoo.com

Rank	value
1	Dave
2	Bob
3	Fran
4	Eve
5	Chuck
6	Carol
7	Alice

Table 6. The adjusted ranking on *.live.com

Rank	value
1	Carol
2	Fran
3	Alice
4	Eve
5	Chuck
6	Dave
7	Bob

For example, we assume that eight input values for the input field *name= "login"* are currently stored in our modified form history database. Two values were submitted from attack.malicious.com, and three values were submitted from login.yahoo.com, and another three values were submitted from login.live.com. Table 4 lists these eight values and their ranking calculated by a browser's original algorithm. Our domain-based ranking adjustment is based on this original ranking. If a user plans to fill a "login" form field on any yahoo.com webpage, the three history values submitted from yahoo.com will be ranked higher than any other values as shown in Table 5. Similarly, if a user plans to fill a "login" form field on any live.com webpage, the three history values submitted from live.com will be ranked higher than any other values as shown in Table 6.

As we discussed in the last section, when a user begins to type something in an input field, browsers will immediately refine the values suggested in the dropdown list. In such partial input cases, our mechanism still simply performs the same domain-based ranking adjustment step based on the original ranking calculated by a browser's original algorithm. Finally, the adjusted ranking results will be suggested to a user in the autocomplete dropdown list.

4.2   Security and Usability Analysis

The design philosophy of our domain-based ranking mechanism is consistent with those of other domain-based efforts in securing Web browsers [1,3,5,6,10,14].

In general, no matter attackers use what types of basic or advanced attacking techniques presented in Section 3, our domain-based ranking mechanism can always ensure that form history data previously submitted on the same domain can have the highest ranking in the autocomplete dropdown list. Note that newly visited websites will still be subject to the attack because there will be no previously submitted data to serve as good suggestions in this case. By ensuring the availability of those previously submitted most relevant form history data, our mechanism can prevent attackers from using junk data to make the autocomplete feature completely useless to users.

One rare exception is that attackers directly compromise the webpages of a vulnerable legitimate website to inject junk form data. In such a case, injected junk data may still be ranked higher than the form history data submitted by a user. However, compromising a legitimate website especially a high-security website is much more difficult than setting up a malicious website. Moreover, our mechanism can still successfully limit the influence of those junk data to the compromised website, and form autocomplete on other legitimate websites are still protected. On the other hand, we demonstrated in the last section that cross-site form history spamming attacks work in the absence of any vulnerability in websites; therefore, our mechanism is especially valuable in more general cases. As emphasized at the beginning of this section, the objective of our mechanism is not to replace browser vendors' efforts in securing the form autocomplete feature, but to complement those efforts to better protect this useful feature.

Even if spamming attacks do not happen and there is no junk data injected into the form history database, our domain-based ranking mechanism can still provide usability advantages over existing methods used in browsers. For example, a user may have visited a few other legitimate websites that have the "login" form field (Table 4), and may have multiple "login" IDs on each website. Even without injected junk data, current browsers cannot guarantee that the relevant "login" values on a legitimate website can be ranked high and directly suggested in the autocomplete dropdown list. This usability problem could be further aggravated considering that browsers such as Firefox and Google Chrome only allow at most six suggested values to appear at the same time in the autocomplete dropdown list. Integrating our domain-based ranking mechanism into the autocomplete feature of a browser can definitely help increase the relevancy of this feature's suggestions and improve its usability.

There is another usability consideration. In the current design, our domain-based ranking mechanism simply adjusts the ranking of all the selected values that have the matching field name. It moves the values of the domain-matching records ahead of the values of domain-mismatching records, but it does not remove those values of domain-mismatching records. We made such a design decision because sometimes users may want to reuse the values submitted from other domains. With such a design choice, injected junk data will still stay in the autocomplete dropdown list as shown in Table 5 and Table 6. If necessary, one potential enhancement is to further rank those values of domain-mismatching records. We leave this topic to our future research. One caveat is that if a user enters a typo on one website, the typo will be ranked above frequently used values entered on other websites. Enabling a user to easily remove a typo data record is desirable in general cases, and we expect browser vendors to provide such a user interface in the future.

4.3   Deployment Analysis

Our domain-based ranking mechanism can be easily deployed in popular browsers. First, the mechanism itself is very simple. It does not mandate underlying logic or algorithm changes to the autocomplete feature of browsers. Thus, the correct implementation of this mechanism can be ensured with high confidence.

Second, this mechanism is not bound to browsers' any specific support of DOM, event model, and JavaScript. We mentioned at the beginning of this section that some efforts have been made recently in Internet Explorer and Google Chrome to restrict the permissiveness of browsers in saving form history data. Normally, those efforts are quite browser-specific and they have to deal with the low-level details of how the form autocomplete feature is supported by browsers' specific DOM, event model, and JavaScript implementations. Our mechanism simply focuses on the upper-level form history data suggestion, so it can be easily adopted by different browsers to complement their existing protection mechanisms.

Finally, our mechanism is completely transparent to users. There is no need to train users, and there is no need to inform them of the deployment of this mechanism. Indeed, a user may not even notice the integration of our mechanism into a browser because nothing will be disabled by our mechanism.

5   Implementation and Evaluation

We have implemented our domain-based ranking mechanism in Firefox 3.6.10. The form autocomplete feature in Firefox 3 includes both C++ components and JavaScript components. The C++ components are responsible for the form filling control, form history database maintenance, as well as form data inserting, updating, and retrieving. The JavaScript components are responsible for preparing SQL search statements and ranking calculation. Overall, our modifications in the C++ and JavaScript components are within 180 lines of code. Our mechanism is easily implemented in Firefox, and we believe this simple mechanism can also be easily implemented in other modern browsers.

We have built the modified Firefox 3.6.10 on an openSUSE 11.3 (x86_64) Linux system and performed different types of experiments on it. We verified the correctness of our implementation and its integration with the browser. Basically, our implementation does not cause any runtime error or logic problem. We verified the effectiveness of our mechanism in ranking adjustment on over 30 various legitimate websites. Basically, the ranking adjustment step presented in the last section was properly executed; for example, all the values of the domain-matching records were moved ahead of all the values of domain-mismatching

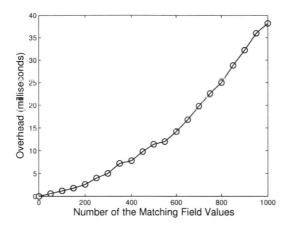

Fig. 8. Overhead of the ranking adjustment

records. We also used attack examples presented in Section 3 to inject a large amount of junk data and verified the usefulness of our protection mechanism. Basically, whenever a legitimate website was visited, junk data injected from an attack website were always ranked behind the data previously submitted on that legitimate website. We make our Firefox 3.6.10 openSUSE build available http://www.cs.uccs.edu/~cyue/auto/ff3 for download and verification. Our source code is also available upon request.

We also measured the performance overhead of our mechanism in the Firefox 3.6.10 Linux build on a laptop with a 2.67GHz CPU. Our modifications made in the C++ components cause negligible overhead on data inserting, updating, and retrieving because they do not introduce new database operations. The ranking adjustment implemented in the JavaScript components can incur some overhead, but the overhead is very low. Figure 8 presents the ranking adjustment overhead (in milliseconds) versus the total number of the selected matching values, i.e., those values with the matching field name. We can see that the overhead increases approximately linearly with the increasing number of the matching values. The overhead is still less than 40 milliseconds even when the ranking of 1,000 matching values needs to be adjusted. These overhead results are averaged over five times of execution. If necessary, we can further reduce the overhead by implementing the ranking adjustment into an XPCOM (Cross-Platform Component Object Mode) C++ component in Firefox.

6   Related Work

In the BlackHat USA 2010 conference, Grossman [4] presented a few autocomplete and autofill vulnerabilities in popular browsers. One of the vulnerabilities reported in Grossman's talk is that attackers can automatically inject junk data into the form history database of a browser. Grossman described that automatically injected form data could be annoying, and perhaps browser vendors should fix that bug. However, we analyzed that injected junk data can make the useful autocomplete feature almost useless. Moreover, the problem is not just about fixing a bug in specific browsers; it is also about introducing new defense-in-depth mechanisms to the autocomplete feature. The *cross-site autocomplete* phenomenon is also what we need to pay attention to. Our domain-based ranking mechanism is a solution that can restrict the permissiveness of cross-site autocomplete, but still preserve its potential usability benefits.

Browser vendors are apparently taking active measures to protect against the cross-site form history spamming attacks. Just very recently, when we were finalizing this paper, we observed that Google Chrome 7.0.517.41 released on October 19, 2010 [12] has a security fix for its form autocomplete feature. Starting from this Google Chrome 7, the two malicious examples (attack1.htm and attack2.htm) presented in Section 3 are no longer successful. Security update for Internet Explorer released on October 12, 2010 also has a fix for the form autocomplete feature [13]. With that security update, Internet Explorer 8.0.7600.16385 disables its form autocomplete feature on https webpages. Firefox 3.6.11, 3.6.12, 3.6.13 were released on October 19, 2010, October 27, 2010, and December 09, 2010 respectively, but we verified that all the attacks presented in Section 3 can still be successful. The key point is that the *cross-site autocomplete* phenomenon still exists in the latest versions of the three most popular browsers. For Google Chrome and Firefox, this phenomenon exists on both http and https webpages. For Internet Explorer, it still exists on http webpages. So far, the security fixes made to these browsers focus on restricting the permissiveness of browsers in saving form history data. Our domain-based ranking mechanism complements browser vendors' efforts by focusing on restricting the permissiveness of browsers in suggesting candidate form history data. Such a domain-based design philosophy is also consistent with those of other efforts in securing Web browsers.

7   Conclusion

In this paper, we illustrated that modern browsers are generally too permissive in both saving form history data and suggesting them to users. A direct consequence of this permissiveness is that attackers can inject a large amount of junk or spam data into the form history database of a browser. These data may contain advertisement words used for getting financial or political benefits, or they are simply meaningless words used for nullifying the form autocomplete feature. We exemplified that both basic and advanced cross-site form history spamming attacks can be constructed by attackers. Browser vendors are apparently taking active measures to fix the security bugs in their browsers' form autocomplete feature, but we emphasized that they should also pay attention to the *cross-site autocomplete* phenomenon itself. Based on our analysis, we explored a different approach and proposed a domain-based ranking mechanism for protecting browsers from cross-site form history spamming attacks. Our mechanism restricts the permissiveness of cross-site autocomplete but still preserves its potential usability benefits. This mechanism is simple, transparent to users, and easily adoptable by different browsers as an in-depth defense to complement their existing protection mechanisms. We implemented our mechanism in Firefox 3.6.10 and verified its effectiveness. We believe that this simple mechanism can also be easily implemented in other popular browoors.

References

1. Barth, A., Jackson, C., Mitchell, J.C.: Robust defenses for cross-site request forgery. In: Proc. of the CCS, pp. 75–88 (2008)
2. Chen, S., Meseguer, J., Sasse, R., Wang, H.J., Wang, Y.-M.: A systematic approach to uncover security flaws in gui logic. In: Proc. of the IEEE Symposium on Security and Privacy, pp. 71–85 (2007)
3. Chen, S., Ross, D., Wang, Y.-M.: An analysis of browser domain-isolation bugs and a light-weight transparent defense mechanism. In: Proc. of the CCS (2007)
4. Grossman, J.: Breaking Browsers: Hacking Auto-Complete. In: Proc. of the BlackHat USA Technical Security Conference (2010), http://jeremiahgrossman. blogspot.com/2010/08/breaking-browsers-hacking-auto-complete.html
5. Jackson, C., Barth, A.: Beware of finer-grained origins. In: Proc. of the Web 2.0 Security and Privacy, W2SP (2008)
6. Jackson, C., Bortz, A., Boneh, D., Mitchell, J.C.: Protecting browser state from web privacy attacks. In: Proc. of the WWW, pp. 737–744 (2006)
7. Provos, N., Rajab, M.A., Mavrommatis, P.: Cybercrime 2.0: when the cloud turns dark. Commun. ACM 52(4), 42–47 (2009)
8. Reis, C., Barth, A., Pizano, C.: Browser security: lessons from google chrome. Commun. ACM 52(8), 45–49 (2009)
9. Reis, C., Dunagan, J., Wang, H.J., Dubrovsky, O., Esmeir, S.: Browsershield: vulnerability-driven filtering of dynamic html. In: Proc. of the OSDI (2006)
10. Ross, B., Jackson, C., Miyake, N., Boneh, D., Mitchell, J.C.: Stronger password authentication using browser extensions. In: Proc. of the USENIX Security Symposium, pp. 17–32 (2005)
11. Singh, K., Moshchuk, A., Wang, H.J., Lee, W.: On the incoherencies in web browser access control policies. In: Proc. of the IEEE Symposium on Security and Privacy, pp. 463–478 (2010)
12. Google Chrome Releases: Stable Channel Update, http://googlechromereleases.blogspot.com/2010/10/ stable-channel-update.html
13. Microsoft Security Bulletin MS10-071 - Critical, http://www.microsoft.com/ technet/security/bulletin/ms10-071.mspx
14. Same origin policy, http://en.wikipedia.org/wiki/Same_origin_policy
15. SQLite Home Page, http://www.sqlite.org
16. Submit form without reloading page, http://codingforums.com/showthread. php?t=61444.
17. Symantec Internet Security Threat Report Volume XV (April 2010), http://www. symantec.com/business/theme.jsp?themeid=threatreport

Escape from Monkey Island:
Evading High-Interaction Honeyclients*

Alexandros Kapravelos[1], Marco Cova[2], Christopher Kruegel[1], and Giovanni Vigna[1]

[1] UC Santa Barbara
{kapravel,chris,vigna}@cs.ucsb.edu
[2] University of Birmingham, UK
{m.cova}@cs.bham.ac.uk

Abstract. High-interaction honeyclients are the tools of choice to detect malicious web pages that launch drive-by-download attacks. Unfortunately, the approach used by these tools, which, in most cases, is to identify the side-effects of a successful attack rather than the attack itself, leaves open the possibility for malicious pages to perform evasion techniques that allow one to execute an attack without detection or to behave in a benign way when being analyzed. In this paper, we examine the security model that high-interaction honeyclients use and evaluate their weaknesses in practice. We introduce and discuss a number of possible attacks, and we test them against several popular, well-known high-interaction honeyclients. Our attacks evade the detection of these tools, while successfully attacking regular visitors of malicious web pages.

1 Introduction

In a drive-by-download attack, a user is lured into visiting a malicious web page, which contains code that exploits vulnerabilities in the user's browser and/or its environment. If successful, the exploits can execute arbitrary code on the victim's machine [33]. This ability is typically used to automatically download and run malware programs on the compromised machine, which, as a consequence, often becomes part of a botnet [31].

Drive-by-download attacks are one of the most pervasive threats on the web, and past measurements have found millions of malicious web pages [3, 32]. In addition, studies have shown that a large portion of the online population uses software that is vulnerable to the exploits used in drive-by-download attacks [12].

A primary line of defense against drive-by-download attacks consists of detecting web pages that perform such attacks and publishing their addresses on blacklists. Then, browsers can consult these blacklists and block requests to pages that are known to be malicious. This mechanism is currently used in all major browsers, typically by querying Google's Safe Browsing API or Microsoft's SmartScreen Filter [14, 23].

The creation of comprehensive lists of malicious web pages requires mechanisms to detect drive-by-download attacks. The current state-of-the-art for the detection of

---

* The title is a pun that uses the name of a famous LucasArts computer adventure game to describe the purpose of our attacks, which is to evade high-interaction honeyclients such as *HoneyMonkey* [46].

T. Holz and H. Bos. (Eds.): DMIVA 2011, LNCS 6739, pp. 124–143, 2011.

these attacks is high-interaction honeyclients. High-interaction honeyclients are systems where a vulnerable browser is used to visit potentially malicious web sites. During the visit of a web page, the system (typically, an instrumented virtual machine) is monitored so that all changes to the underlying file system, configuration settings, and running processes are recorded. If any unexpected modification occurs, this is considered the manifestation of a successful attack, and the corresponding web page is flagged as malicious [25, 26, 32, 40, 46].

The approach used in high-interaction honeyclients focuses on detecting the side-effects of a successful exploit (i.e., the changes to the underlying system), rather than detecting the exploit itself, an approach that some refer to as "state-change-based detection" [46]. While this approach has merits (e.g., it provides very convincing evidence of the maliciousness of a detected page), it also creates an opportunity to attack the detection system. More precisely, an attacker can use the window between the launching of an exploit and the execution of its actual drive-by component (whose effects are detected by a high-interaction honeyclients) to attack and evade the honeyclient.

In this paper, the security model of high-interaction honeyclients is put under the microscope and its weaknesses are evaluated in practice. More precisely, we first review high-interaction honeyclients in general, discussing different possible designs and their security properties. We then introduce a number of possible attacks that leverage weaknesses in the design of high-interaction honeyclients to evade their detection. Finally, we implement these attacks and test them against four popular, well-known implementations of high-interaction honeyclients. Our attacks allow malicious web pages to avoid being detected by a high-interaction honeyclient, while continuing to be effective against regular visitors. Some of these attacks have been previously described; nevertheless, we show concrete implementations that successfully bypass well-known, commonly-used honeyclient tools. In addition, we introduce three novel honeyclient attacks (JavaScript-based honeyclient detection, in-memory execution, whitelist-based attacks) that enable us to detect the presence of a high-interaction honeyclient or to perform a drive-by-download without triggering the honeyclient's detection mechanisms.

We also note that it is relatively easy to retrofit existing drive-by-download toolkits with the evasion techniques that we present here. This makes their impact even more worrisome, and it increases the urgency for implementing adequate defensive mechanisms in high-interaction honeyclients.

2   Related Work

Our work is mainly related to the problems of identifying weaknesses in the defensive systems designed to monitor and detect the execution of malicious programs, and of devising attacks against them. Here, we will review the current state-of-the-art in these areas, focusing in particular on systems that detect web-based and binary malware and on intrusion detection tools.

Web-based malware monitors. Attacks against high-interaction honeyclients have been previously discussed. In particular, Wang et al. discuss three avenues to evade their HoneyMonkey system [46]: *(i)* identifying HoneyMonkey machines (based on detecting their IP addresses, by testing whether the browser is driven by a human, or by identifying the presence of a virtual machine or the HoneyMonkey code itself); *(ii)* running exploits that do not trigger HoneyMonkey's detection (e.g., by using time delays); and *(iii)* randomizing the attack (trading off infection rates for detection rates).

We build on and extend this research in several ways. First, we have implemented the aforementioned attacks and confirmed that they are (still) effective against all current, publicly-available honeyclient systems. Second, we introduce and discuss in detail novel attacks against high-interaction honeyclients, with the goal of providing simple and practical implementations. Finally, we discuss the design trade-offs of these attacks. For example, we show how to detect the presence of a honeyclient from a page's JavaScript and from an exploit's shellcode. JavaScript-based attacks have more limited capability because they are restricted by the JavaScript security model (e.g., they cannot be used to detect hooks in the memory of a process), but they are more difficult to detect by current honeyclients because they do not cause any change on the attacked system (e.g., no new file is created and no exploit is launched).

We also note that Wang's paper concludes its discussion of possible countermeasures by introducing the Vulnerability-Specific Exploit Detector (VSED), a tool that checks the browser with vulnerability-specific predicates to determine when an attack is about to trigger a vulnerability. The attentive reader will notice that VSED represents a significant deviation from the traditional state-change-based approach for the detection of drive-by-download attacks. In fact, while state-change-based approaches focus on detecting the consequences of a successful drive-by-download, VSED attempts to detect the actual exploitation.

Some of the attacks identified in [46] have become standard in several drive-by-download toolkits. In particular, it is common for these kits to launch an attack only once per visiting IP [33], to only attack clients coming from specific geographic regions (determined on the basis of GeoIP location data) [4], and to avoid attacking IPs known to belong to security researchers and security companies [15]. Another attack against detection tools used by some drive-by-download campaigns consists of waiting for some minimal user interaction before launching the exploit. For example, the JavaScript code used by Mebroot triggers only when the user clicks on a page's link or releases the mouse anywhere on the page.

Malware sandboxes. Binary malware is a significant security threat, and, consequently, a large body of work exists to analyze and detect malicious code. Currently, the most popular approach for malware analysis relies on dynamic analysis systems, often called sandboxes [1, 2, 7, 18, 29, 41]. A sandbox is an instrumented execution environment that runs a potentially malicious program, while monitoring its interactions with the operating system and other hosts. Similarly to honeyclients, malware sandboxes execute unknown code and determine its maliciousness based on the analysis of its behavior.

Since system emulators and virtual machines are commonly employed to implement sandboxes, malware authors have developed a number of techniques to identify them (and, thus, avoid the detection of the monitoring system). For example, a number of instructions have been identified that behave differently on a virtualized or emulated environment than on a real machine [9, 22, 30, 36, 38]. This has led researchers to design monitoring systems that are transparent to malware checks (i.e., that cannot be easily distinguished from regular hosts), by either removing artifacts of regular monitoring tools [21] or by introducing mechanisms (such as virtualization and dynamic translation) that by design remain transparent to a wider range of checks [8, 44].

Another class of attacks against a malware sandbox consists of detecting, disabling, or otherwise subverting its monitoring facilities. These threats have prompted researchers to experiment with new designs for monitoring systems, in which the monitoring components are protected by isolating them from the untrusted monitored environment through hardware memory protection and virtualization features ("in-VM" designs) [39] or by removing them from the monitored environment ("out-of-VM" designs) [17].

In this paper we dissect the monitoring and isolation mechanisms employed in high-interaction honeyclient. As we will see, many of the approaches currently used are vulnerable to attacks similar to those devised against malware monitoring systems.

Intrusion detection systems. Our work continues the line of research on attacking tools designed to detect malicious activity, in particular, intrusion detection systems (IDSs). A few notable results include Ptacek and Newsham's attacks against network IDSs [34], Fogla and Lee's evasion attacks against anomaly-based IDSs [11], Vigna et al.'s approach to evade signature-based IDSs [45], and Van Gundy et al.'s "omission" attack against signature generation tools for polymorphic worms [43]. Our research identifies high-interaction honeyclients as a new, important target for offensive techniques, and shows weaknesses in several popular implementations.

3   Honeyclients

High-interaction honeyclients use a full-featured web browser to visit potentially malicious web pages. The environment in which the browser runs is monitored to determine if the visit resulted in the system being compromised. In particular, the honeyclient records all the modifications that occur during the visit of a page, such as files created or deleted, registry keys modified, and processes launched. If any unexpected modification occurs, this is considered as the manifestation of an attack, and the corresponding page is flagged as malicious.

In this section, we first describe the security requirements for honeyclients. Then, we discuss the key design choices in the development of honeyclients, and we conclude examining in detail a specific honeyclient implementation.

3.1   Security Requirements for High-Interaction Honeyclients

An ideal honeyclient system would be capable of detecting all the malicious web pages that it visits. There are three general reasons that may cause a missed detection: 1) the honeyclient is not exploitable, thus the attack performed by the malicious web page is not successful; 2) the honeyclient is incapable of monitoring the changes caused by a successful attack, thus the attack is not detected; and 3) the presence of the honeyclient is detected by the malicious pages, thus the attack is not run.

The first issue (the honeyclient must be vulnerable) can be addressed through careful configuration of the honeyclient system. Old, vulnerable versions of browsers and operating systems are used, and a large number of additional components (plugins and

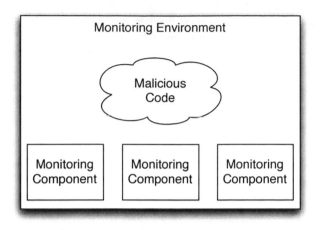

Fig. 1. Malicious code interaction with the Honeyclient system

ActiveX) are installed on the system, to maximize the possibility of successful exploits[1].
Even if this configuration is a complex task, in the rest of this paper, we will assume
that the honeyclient system is vulnerable to at least one of the exploits launched by a
malicious page.

Second, effective monitoring requires that the monitoring facilities used by the honeyclient system cannot be bypassed by an attack. The well-known reference monitor
concept [16] describes a set of requirements that security mechanisms must enforce
to prevent tampering from the attacker and to ensure valid detection of the malicious
activity:

Provide complete mediation: The monitoring mechanism must always be invoked,
when a potentially malicious URL is tested on the system. It is essential in the case
of honeyclients that the mechanism is able to detect all the possible changes that a
successful attack could produce on the targeted system.

Be tamperproof: The monitoring mechanism should not be susceptible to tampering.
For the honeyclient, this means that the malicious code should not be able to affect
it in any way. For example, if the malicious code were able to kill the monitoring
process or to blame another URL for the malicious activity, the reference monitor
would be useless.

Be verifiable: The monitoring mechanism should be easy to verify for completeness
and correctness. Unfortunately, this might not be an easy task, given the complexity
of today's honeyclients, which include large operating systems (e.g., Windows) and
applications (browsers).

---

[1] In [5] we showed that this approach has some inherent limitations, as there is a large number
of vulnerable plugins, some of which may be incompatible with each other. Therefore, it may
be impractical to create an environment that is vulnerable to all known attacks.

A third venue of evasion is related to the **transparency** [13] of a high-interaction honeyclient. The honeyclient system should be indistinguishable from a regular host, to prevent malicious web pages from behaving differently inside a monitoring environment than on a real host.

3.2 Design Choices for High-Interaction Honeyclients

Given the requirements described above, there are a few important design choices that can be made when developing a high-interaction honeyclient.

A first design choice is the placement of the monitoring mechanism inside or outside the guest environment executing the browser process. This "in-VM" vs. "out-of-VM" choice is a well-known and widely-discussed aspect of any malware analysis environment. Developing the monitoring mechanisms within the guest operating system greatly simplifies the architecture of the system, but, at the same time, makes the system vulnerable to detection, as the artifacts that implement the monitoring infrastructure cohabitate with the malicious code. By implementing the monitor at the kernel-level it is possible to better control access to the monitoring artifacts (drivers, processes, etc.) However, this is at the cost of increased complexity. In addition, there exist honeynet vulnerable configurations in which the code that attacks the browser is able to gain access to kernel-level data structures. In this case it might be hard to hide the presence of the monitoring artifact from the malicious code.

We believe that a more appropriate model for honeyclients requires that the monitoring system is completely isolated from the environment. By moving the inspection of the potentially malicious code outside the virtual machine we guarantee that the attacker cannot tamper with the system. In practice, this is not trivial to implement and there are several obstacles to overcome, in order to have a deep insight of the program's execution inside the guest OS without compromising speed. We discuss in more detail the practical implications of running the monitoring system inside a virtual machine in Section 6, and we propose several methods on how to overcome the limitations of this approach.

Another design choice is the type and granularity of monitoring. This is a challenge especially in Windows-based system, because the Windows OS has a very large number of mechanisms for interacting with processes, injecting code, modifying files, etc. and therefore it is not easy to create a monitoring infrastructure that is able to collect the right type of events. This challenge is sometimes simplistically solved by collecting information about the surrounding environment only after the execution of a web page has terminated. By doing so, it is possible to determine if permanent damage has been caused to the guest OS. However, as it will be described later, there are situations in which attacks might not cause side-effects that are detectable.

3.3 Honeyclients in Practice

In this section, we provide a brief discussion of the general architecture and mode of operation of high-interaction honeyclients. As an example, we use Capture-HPC [40], a very popular, open-source honeyclient. To determine whether a URL is suspicious, Capture-HPC visits this URL with a browser (typically, Internet Explorer) that runs in an instrumented virtual machine.

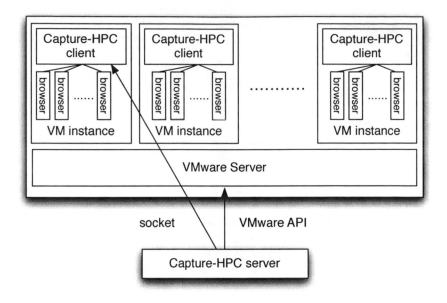

Fig. 2. Capture-HPC Architecture

In Figure 2, a more detailed overview of the architecture of Capture-HPC is shown. The system design follows a client-server model. The server component manages a number of clients and communicates with a VMware Server process to launch new, clean virtual machine instances. Each client component is running inside one of these virtual machines. The client consists of a controller and three kernel modules to monitor file, registry, and process events, respectively. The controller receives a list of URLs from the server and opens a web browser to visit them. When a URL is visited, the kernel modules record all events that are related to the browser (by matching events against the process ID of the browser). The controller then checks the recorded events against a whitelist. This whitelist stores events that are "normal" for the execution of the browser, such as writes to the browser's cache. When events occur that are not filtered by the whitelist, the controller reports these events, together with the URL that triggered them, back to the server. Note that, for performance reasons, Capture-HPC is also capable of spawning multiple browser instances inside the same virtual machine, in order to process URLs in parallel.

In principle, all high-interaction honeyclients share an architecture that is very similar to the one described here. These systems are all based on virtual machine technology to revert to a clean state when a honeyclient instance gets compromised, and they use a client-server model to provide a URL feed and to detect suspicious activity. For example, HoneyClient [24] uses a stand-alone version of Capture-HPC's client as its detection component. Web Exploit Finder (WEF) [27] works in a way similar to Capture-HPC, but instead of using kernel modules for monitoring, the system hooks directly into the System Service Dispatch Table (SSDT) to intercept system calls. Finally, Shelia [37] takes a slightly different monitoring approach. Instead of hooking at the kernel level, it directly hooks interesting Windows API function calls inside the browser process.

As it clear from this discussion, real-world, state-of-the-art honeyclients do not satisfy the security requirements described at the beginning of this section. First of all, they all lack transparency. All the available honeyclients operate within the guest VM, and, therefore, they can easily be detected, by looking at specific artifacts. Second, they are not tamperproof, as in a number of cases these tools can be disabled by the same malicious page that they are analyzing. Third, real-world honeyclients do not provide complete mediation. There are situations in which certain operations performed by the malicious web page can have a negative impact on the security of the browser's environment but are not monitored by the system.

Attacks that explicitly exploit these weaknesses are the subject of the next section.

4   Attacks against Honeyclients

In this section, we describe techniques that an attacker can mount against a honeyclient system. The ultimate goal of the attacker is to avoid the detection of malicious activity while her URL is visited. This can be done by in two ways: *(i)* the attack code can detect the presence of the monitoring system and perform only benign activities, or *(ii)* the attack code is run in such a way that it will avoid detection. That is, the attack does not generate any events that are considered malicious (*e.g.*, no new processes are spawned and no suspicious files or registry keys are accessed). We implemented several attacks and tested their effectiveness against the four popular honeyclients described in the previous section: Capture-HPC, HoneyClient, Shelia, and WEF. For this test, we selected a buffer overflow exploit [6] that is served in a drive-by-download via Metasploit. The victim images (the honeypots) were running Windows XP with Service Pack 2 and a vulnerable version of Internet Explorer 7. We first verified that each of the four honeypots correctly detect the attack. Then, we modified the drive-by exploit to implement each of the evasion attacks that are described below, and we checked whether the technique was successful in preventing (or evading) detection.

4.1   Detection of the Monitoring Environment

A honeyclient system should not be differentiable from a true victim. If the attacker is able to detect the presence of a monitoring system, then the malicious code will compromise true victims but will perform only benign actions inside the honeypot.

Virtual machine detection. Due to the fact that many real-world drive-by attacks install malware that tampers with the operating system, most honeyclients make use of virtual machines. This way, a honeyclient can ensure that any change to the system will be reverted back to a safe state through the use of virtual machine snapshots. Although virtual machines make a honeyclient system immune to the attacks that it monitors, there is a drawback: the attacker has the opportunity to detect the presence of the virtual machine and, when a VM is detected, conclude that the exploit code is running inside a monitored environment.

```
1 var script = document.createElement("script")
2 script.type = "text/javascript";
3 script.src = "res://C:\\Program%20Files\\Capture\\
     CaptureClient.exe";
4 script.onreadystatechange= function () {
5   if(this.readyState == "complete")
6     alert("capture-hpc detected!"); };
7 document.getElementsByTagName("head")[0].appendChild(script);
```

Fig. 3. Detecting Capture-HPC presence in the file system with JavaScript

There are many known methods that can detect if code is running inside a VMware virtual machine [9, 19, 35]. By using one of these techniques, the adversary can perform a check that her code is not inside a virtualized environment. Since all the tested honeyclients make use of VMware, we have chosen the ScoopyNG checks [19] as our method to detect reliably the presence of virtual machines in practice. Although one can argue that there is an increasing tendency to use virtual machines by moving parts of applications to the cloud, we argue that regular end users do not browse the web through a VM. Rather, the normal case is to run the browser in a non-virtualized environment.

Honeyclient detection. Another way to detect the presence of a monitoring system is to check for artifacts of the honeyclient itself. For example, the attacker can detect the presence of Capture-HPC and HoneyClient by looking in the file system for the *CaptureClient.exe* binary, by checking whether specific kernel modules are loaded, or by looking for the active processes that belong to these honey clients. Similarly, Shelia and WEF can be detected by looking for their respective executable files, *shelia.exe* and *BrowserControl.exe*, or for their required DLL files. In all cases, the systems do not take any measures to protect themselves from this kind of detection.

Checking for the presence of particular files can even be done in the JavaScript code that is responsible for launching an attack. This makes the check stealthier, because no actual exploit is launched. In Figure 3, we show how an attacker can perform a simple check to see if there are specific programs installed on the client's machine. This novel attack method tricks the JavaScript engine by asking it to load a source script from the client's local file system. We found out, much to our surprise, that JavaScript does not perform any checks to see if the file requested is actually a JavaScript source file. Instead, it attempts to load the file, and, if it is not of an expected format, a JavaScript runtime error is thrown. This allows us to determine if any local file exists, simply by loading it. In this way, we are also able to detect the presence of *VMware Tools*, which reveals the existence of a virtual machine. Notice that this was tested only with Internet Explorer 7 and might not work with all of its versions.

Detection of hooked functions. Recently, there has been some effort in the research community to detect hooks installed by malware [47]. Along similar lines, we try to detect the hooks set up by the monitoring environment. Certain honeyclients (and Shelia in particular) use function call hooking to monitor and intercept calls to critical functions. In this way, the honeyclient can prevent malicious behavior, in addition to detecting the attack. For example, the honeyclient may avoid calling the real *WinExec* function to prevent malware from executing on the system.

```
 1 checkhooks:
 2    CMP BYTE [DS:EBX], 0xE9     ; 0xE9 == jmp
 3    JE hooked
 4    CMP BYTE [DS:EBX], 0xE8     ; 0xE8 == call
 5    JE hooked
 6    CMP BYTE [DS:EBX], 0x8B     ; 0x8B == mov
 7    JE safe_vprotect
 8 safe_vprotect:
 9    PUSH ESP   ; PDWORD lpflOldProtect
10    PUSH 0x40  ; DWORD flNewProtect,
11               ; PAGE_EXECUTE_READWRITE
12    PUSH 0x7d0 ; SIZE_T dwSize , 2000
13    PUSH EAX   ; LPVOID lpAddress
14    CALL EBX   ; call VirtualProtect
15 hooked:
16    ;function is hooked
17    RET
```

Fig. 4. Function hooks detection: before calling a critical function, we check if it is hooked

To hook functions, honeyclients can make use of the fact that the Windows compiler reserves the first two bytes of library functions for hot-patching. More precisely, the compiler places the instruction *MOV EDI,EDI* at the beginning of each library function prologue, which acts as a two-byte long *NOP* operation. Monitoring systems such as Shelia can then replace this instruction with a jump to a routine of their choice, which, once done, calls the original function properly. In this way, calls to critical functions such as *VirtualProtect, WinExec, etc.* can be intercepted and examined.

In Figure 4, we present the x86 assembly code that can be used to detect the presence of hooks before calling a function. To do this, we verify, before calling a critical function, that the first operation at the memory address where the function is located (*EBX* in our example) contains a *MOV* instruction and not *JMP* or *CALL*. As a result, the exploit code can refuse to run when function hooking is identified, or the attack code could jump over the hook to the first "real" instruction. This technique allows us to successfully detect and evade Shelia. However, this technique does not work against the other tested honeyclients, since they collect information inside the kernel.

HTTP referrer check. As part of a drive-by download attack, the victim issues an HTTP GET request to the attacker's web server to actually download the exploit code. Of course, the attacker is able to check the referrer of this request. If the attacker has any control over (or knowledge about) the site(s) where her malicious URLs are being advertised, then this information can be used to serve malicious content only when the *Referer* header matches one of these expected sites. For example, the exploit might be served only if the referrer is `google.com`. Other *Referer* header values indicate that the requests are from analysis systems such as honeypots (although these systems might be able to set the *Referer* field to an expected value and thwart this check). This attack is effective against all tested honeyclients, since it occurs before the victim's infection and thus is independent of the detection approach.

4.2 Detection Evasion

Although the attacker may be unaware that her malware is running in a monitored system, she can perform some tasks that are not easily detectable by honeyclients. These tasks constitute a barrier that can be used to hide or delay the intended, malicious behavior until the adversary is sure that the attacked system is an actual victim computer.

Delayed exploitation. In a drive-by download, the attacker can decide to wait for some time before performing the exploit, or to trigger the execution of an exploit based on the occurrence of a user-triggered event. For example, the malicious JavaScript code can sleep for some seconds. The idea is that this delay will trigger a time-out on the honeyclient system (after which the analysis of the current page is terminated), but it will enable attacks against a real user who keeps the malicious page open long enough (until the time-out expires). The honeyclients that we examined use a timeout of no more than 30 seconds, and hence, can be evaded when running the exploit is delayed by at least this amount of time.

Unfortunately, setting long timeouts makes the attack unreliable, since real users might leave the malicious site before the attack is invoked. Another way to implement a timebomb consists of waiting for some user interaction before launching the attack. This technique can be implemented by using JavaScript event handlers, such as onMouseOver. In this case, the idea is that a real user will likely move the mouse over the page and, by doing so, will generate the mouseOver event. This will execute the corresponding handler, which, in turn, launches the attack. A honeyclient, on the other hand, will not trigger such events, and, thus, the attack remains undetected.

In-memory execution. Current honeyclient systems focus on monitoring events that are related to file system, registry, and process activity. Thus, an attack remains undetected as long as the malicious code does not interfere with these operating system resources. However, as the adversary, we would still like to execute additional malware code.

To load and execute malicious code in a stealth fashion, we can make use of remote library injection, in particular, a technique called Reflective DLL injection [10]. In this case, a (remote) library is loaded from the shellcode directly into the memory of the running process, without being registered in the process' list of loaded modules, which is stored in the Process Environment Block (PEB). Once the library is loaded, the shellcode calls an initialization function, which, in our case, injects a thread to the browser's process. At this point, the execution is returned back to the browser, which continues to run normally. However, there is now an additional thread running that executes the malicious code.

When injecting the malicious code directly into the process, there are no additional processes spawned, files created, or registry entries manipulated. Thus, the attack evades the tested honeyclients. Of course, the malware code itself cannot write to the file system either (or it would be detect). However, it is possible to open network connections and participate in a botnet that, for example, sends spam, steals browser credentials, or conducts denial of service attacks. A drawback is that the malicious code does not survive reboots (or even closing the browser).

Whitelist manipulation. When visiting any URL, the browser interacts with the operating system and generates a certain number of events. Of course, these events do

```
1  void CrawlDirs(wchar startupdir[]) {
2    WIN32_FIND_DATA ffd;
3    HANDLE hFind;
4    hFind = FindFirstFile(startupdir, &ffd);
5    do {
6      if (ffd.dwFileAttributes & FILE_ATTRIBUTE_DIRECTORY)
7        CrawlDirectories(startupdir+"\\"+ffd.cFileName);
8      else {
9        if(is_js_file(ffd.cFileName))
10         patch_js(ffd, path);
11     }
12   } while (FindNextFile(hFind, &ffd) != 0);
13 }
```

Fig. 5. Browser cache poisoning attack

not indicate malicious behavior, and thus, they need to be removed before analyzing the effects that visiting a page has on the system. To this end, honeyclients use whitelists. However, this also means that the attacker has limited freedom in performing certain, whitelisted (operating system) actions, such as browser cache file writes, registry keys accesses *etc.*, that will not be detected as malicious. The interesting question is whether these actions can be leveraged to compromise the host's security.

The attacks described in this section are not relevant for Shelia, which uses function hooks to identify malicious activity, but apply to the remaining three honeyclients that record and monitor system calls.

To show the weakness of whitelisting, we have implemented a *browser cache poisoning* attack. This attack leverages that fact that write to files in the Internet Explorer cache are typically permitted. The reason is that reads and writes to these files occur as part of the normal browser operation, and hence, have to be permitted (note that Honeyclients could also disable the browser cache, making this attack ineffective).

We have implemented an attack that poisons any JavaScript file found in Internet Explorer's cache. With "poisoning," we mean that we add to every JavaScript file in the browser's cache a small code snippet that redirects the browser to a malicious site. Thus, whenever the browser opens a page that it has visited before, and this page contains a link to a cached script, the browser will load and use the local, *modified* version of the script. As a result, the browser will get redirected and re-infected. The purpose of this attack is that it allows the adversary to make a compromise persistent *without* triggering the detection of a high-interaction honeyclient. That is, an adversary could launch an in-memory attack (as described in the previous section) and poison the cached JavaScript files with a redirect to her exploit site. Even when the victim closes the browser or reboots, it is enough to visit any page that loads a modified, cached script, to re-infect the machine in a way that is not detected by a honeyclient.

In Figure 5, we present a simplified version of our implementation of the cache poisoning attack. The algorithm starts from a predefined directory location (in our implementation, the directory *Temporary Internet Files*) and recursively searches for JavaScript source files. When a JavaScript source file is found, then the file is patched

```
1  void keylogger() {
2    wchar_t buffer[SIZE];
3    while(1) {
4      /* Appends keystrokes to buffer using GetAsyncKeyState */
5      buffer = get_keys();
6      /* Contacts attacker's webserver with buffer appended to
           path requested using WinHttpSendRequest*/
7      httpget(buffer);
8    }
9  }
```

Fig. 6. In-memory keylogger: collects keystrokes and sends them to the attacker with HTTP GET requests

by inserting a redirection to the malicious site, using JavaScript's *window.location* property.

As a proof of concept for an attack that uses both in-memory execution and whitelist manipulation, we developed a keylogger that can survive boots. The keylogger runs entirely in memory, and, instead of writing the pressed keys into a file, it uses GET requests to send collected data directly to a web server.

The outline of our implementation is presented in Figure 6. The code shows the body of the thread that is injected into *Internet Explorer's* process with the use of the Reflective DLL injection technique. The implementation is straightforward: we gather keystrokes by invoking the *GetAsyncKeyState* function offered by the Windows API. When our buffer is full, we send the keystrokes to our webserver by appending the buffer to the path field. Our keylogger is part of *Internet Explorer's* process, and thus, is very hard to detect, as it is normal for this process to perform HTTP GET requests.

To survive reboots, the keylogger also poisons all JavaScript source files in the browser cache. As a consequence, after reboot, the next time the victim visits a URL with cached JavaScript code, she will be re-infected. The honeyclients raise no alert, since all activity appears legitimate to their detection routines.

Honeyclient confusion. For performance reasons, honeyclients are capable of visiting multiple URLs at the same time. This speeds up the analysis process significantly, since the checking of URLs can be done in parallel by multiple browser instances. By using the process IDs of the different browsers, their events can be distinguished from each another.

The adversary can take advantage of this feature and try to confuse the honeyclient. In particular, the malicious code might carry out activities that are properly detected by the honeyclient as malicious, but they are blamed on a (benign) URL that is concurrently examined.

This is done by searching for concurrent, active Internet Explorer processes, as shown in Figure 7. Through the *IWebBrowser2* interface, we can control each browser instance, in the same way as, for example, Capture-HPC does. At this point, we can force any browser instance to visit a URL of our choice. For example, we can force the browser to visit a malicious URL under our control. This malicious URL can serve a drive-by download exploit that, when successful, downloads and executes malware. Of

```
 1 SHDocVw::IShellWindowsPtr spSHWinds;
 2 IDispatchPtr spDisp;
 3 IWebBrowser2 * pWebBrowser = NULL;
 4 HRESULT hr;
 5
 6 // get all active browsers
 7 spSHWinds.CreateInstance(__uuidof(SHDocVw::ShellWindows));
 8
 9 // get one, or iterate va to get each one
10 spDisp = spSHWinds->Item (va);
11
12 // get IWebBrowser2 pointer
13 hr = spDisp.QueryInterface (IID_IWebBrowser2, & pWebBrowser);
14
15 if (SUCCEEDED(hr) && pWebBrowser != NULL) {
16   visitUrl(pWebBrowser); // with the use of IWebBrowser2::
          Navigate2
17 }
```

Fig. 7. Confuse honeyclient: find an Internet Explorer instance and force it to visit a URL of our choice

Table 1. Summary of the attacks: a ✗ indicates that the attack did not evade the honeyclient, a ✓ indicates that the attack was not detected

Attack	Attack successful?			
	Capture-HPC	Shelia	WEF	HoneyClient
Plain drive-by	✗	✗	✗	✗
VM detection	✓	✓	✓	✓
JavaScript FS checks	✓	✓	✓	✓
Hooks detection	✗	✓	✗	✗
HTTP referrer	✓	✓	✓	✓
JS timebomb	✓	✓	✓	✓
In-memory execution	✓	✓	✓	✓
Whitelist manipulation	✓	✗	✓	✓
Confusion attack	✓	✗	✓	✓

course, the honeyclient does not know that the browser has been forced to a different URL (by code in another browser instance), since this could also have been the effect of a benign redirect. Thus, even when the malware performs actions that are detected, they will be blamed on the original, benign URL that Capture-HPC has initially loaded into the misdirected browser.

The purpose of this attack is to invalidate the correctness of the results produced by a honeyclient and thus, we propose to use it only when we have previously identified the presence of a monitoring system. Also, the attack does not work when a honeyclient uses only a single browser instance. However, constraining a honeyclient to test one URL at the time forces the honeyclient system to accept a major performance penalty.

4.3   Summary

We have implemented all the previously-described attacks and tested them against four popular, open-source honeyclients. Table 1 summarizes our results and shows that each honeyclient is vulnerable to most of the proposed attacks. Moreover, different attack vectors are independent and, hence, can be easily combined.

5   Attacks in the Real World

To better understand the extent to which high-interaction honeyclients are attacked in the real-world, we have deployed an installation of Capture-HPC. Then, we have fed this popular, high-interaction honeyclient with 33,557 URLs that were collected from various sources, such as spam URLs, web crawls, and submissions to Wepawet [5].

Then, we compared the detection results of Wepawet and Capture-HPC for the collected URLs. Wepawet is a tool, developed by our group, that uses anomaly-based detection to identify malicious web pages by looking directly for malicious JavaScript, without checking for the byproducts of a successful attack. Notice that a page marked by Wepawet as malicious contains some type of an attack that could compromise a system, but not every system will get compromised by executing the code. We have found that Wepawet has very low false positive and negative rates, and hence, its output serves as ground truth for the purpose of this evaluation [5]. Looking at Table 2, we can see that Wepawet found significantly more malicious sites in the wild. Of particular interest are 8,835 cases in which Wepawet detected malicious or suspicious activity, while Capture-HPC marked the URLs as benign, because there is a significant chance that these attacks try to avoid detection by systems such as Capture-HPC.

As a first step, we searched the pages that correspond to the malicious URLs for VM detection methods that are commonly employed by shellcode. Since the shellcode is typically encoded and, in addition, often obfuscated, we performed this search on the decoded JavaScript output provided by Wepawet. Moreover, we attempted to "break" the possible obfuscation of shellcode by xor'ing all shellcode strings with all possible (256) one-byte values and checking for a regular expression that indicates a (malware download) URL. Unfortunately, despite these efforts, we could not identify any shellcode that used known VM detection code.

In the next step, we checked for common JavaScript evasion techniques (as described in Section 4). In this case, our search turned out to be more fruitful, and we found a number of instances in which JavaScript code makes use of timeouts and event handlers (as shown in Table 3). Notice that the dominating technique is the HTTP *Referer* check.

We also found an interesting case in which, after the victim got infected, the malware rebooted the virtual machine. Although the attacker probably did not have the intention

Table 2. Capture-HPC and Wepawet analysis results

Detection system	Total URLs	Malicious	Benign
Capture-HPC	33,557	644	32,913
Wepawet	33,557	9,230	24,327

Table 3. Possible JavaScript evasion techniques against Capture-HPC found in the wild

Malicious/Suspicious URLs undetected by Capture-HPC

JS Method	Occurrences
oetTimeOut	347
onMouseOver	419
onmouseout	403
onClick	137
Referrer	1,894

to avoid detection from Capture-HPC, she actually did. In fact, since the machine is rebooting, all running processes are killed. This means that Capture-HPC's client is also killed. This happens immediately after infection. Because Capture-HPC's client waits for all browser instances to finish loading their URLs, this event precedes reporting back to Capture-HPC's server. As a result, the server loses the connection with the client. When this happens, the server simply believes that the client has crashed, so it restores the virtual machine to a safe snapshot and restarts the client. This means that all the information gathered by the previous instance of the client is lost. Thus, although the virtual machine is rebooting, an obvious malicious act, Capture-HPC is unable to detect the malicious URL that caused it.

Another (possibly involuntary) evasion technique that we observed has to do with the fact that Capture-HPC is built as a Windows Console Application. After the infection, we noticed that a new command (DOS) window was spawned by the exploit code. After a few seconds, this command prompt was killed. But, by doing so, the Capture-HPC process was killed as well. The reason is that Capture-HPC is also invoked from the Windows command prompt (*cmd.exe*). Thus, when the exploit code kills all command prompts as part of its operations, the Capture-HPC process is killed as well. From this point on, the detection fails for the same reasons described in the previous paragraph.

6   Countermeasures

In this paper, we have shown a number of attacks that an adversary can use to prevent the detection of her malicious web pages by a honeyclient system. In this section, we focus on the countermeasures that existing honeyclient systems may implement to detect attacks more robustly.

6.1   Transparency

We have seen that it is often easy for a malicious page to detect that it is running in a high-interaction honeyclient (as opposed to a regular host). This issue should be addressed at several levels.

File system level. The attacker should not be able to discover the files related to the monitoring infrastructure on the honeyclient's file system. For example, in the default setup of Capture-HPC, a simple search into the *Program Files* directory reveals the use of VMware Tools and Capture-HPC. These files should be hidden in the file system so that the attacker must put significant effort in finding them, and the honeyclient should be able to detect the attacker's attempt to locate these files.

Kernel level. The attacker should not be able to detect the presence of kernel drivers that honeyclients use for monitoring system level changes. We are not aware of any method offered by the Windows API that can be used to hide the presence of a driver from a process. Therefore, honeyclients could rely on rootkit techniques, such as Direct Kernel Object Manipulation (DKOM) [42], to hide the presence of these modules. Notice that, by using the same techniques, a honeyclient could hide processes and files that it uses for its monitoring.

Network level. If the monitored system is deployed on a static location on the Internet, its IP address or subnet may be identified by attackers [20]. It is, therefore, necessary to deploy the monitored system in several locations, using multiple ISPs in order eliminate the possibility of getting blacklisted by the attacker at the network level.

Hypervisor level. Implementing the monitoring system at the hypervisor level offers complete isolation between the analysis environment and the malware. Although this approach seems ideal, inspecting the operating system from "outside the box" is not trivial, and it requires a significant effort to reverse engineer the necessary operating system data structures to bridge the semantic gap.

Thwarting virtual machine detection. The virtual machines currently used for malicious behavior analysis are not designed to be transparent [13]. As we have seen in Section 2, there has been significant effort to create stealthier virtual machines, such as MAVMM [28], and transparent monitoring systems, such as Ether [8]. These techniques could be used in future honeyclient systems.

6.2   Protecting the Monitoring System

Protecting the browser. A successful exploit against a browser vulnerability typically gives the attacker the ability to execute arbitrary code in the context of the exploited browser process. The attacker can then subvert other browser processes, compromising the integrity of the detection, as we have seen in the case of the confusion attack. High-interaction honeyclients that run multiple browser instances should take steps to isolate each instance from the others, for example by executing them under different principals. Alternatively, the honeyclient process could monitor browser processes to detect attempts to manipulate their execution. For example, the honeyclient system could monitor the *Handles* that belong to each browser's process, using the *GetProcessHandleCount* function provided by the Windows API. In this fashion, one can monitor for cases when the attacker attempts to manipulate a browser and protect the results produced by revisiting one by one the URLs associated with the manipulated browser's instances.

Protecting the honeyclient processes. Any honeyclient process that runs inside the virtual machine needs to be protected from tampering (e.g., from getting terminated) by the attacker. One way to achieve this is by running the honeyclient processes with elevated privileges compared to the browser's processes. It is also possible to check for and intercept attempts to terminate the honeyclient processes.

7   Conclusions

In this paper, we examined the security model that high-interaction honeyclients use, and we evaluated their weaknesses in practice. We introduced and discussed a number of possible attacks, and we test them against several popular, well-known high-interaction honeyclients. In particular, we have introduced three novel attack techniques (JavaScript-based honeyclient detection, in-memory execution, and whitelist-based attacks) and put under the microscope already-known attacks. Our attacks evade the detection of the tested honeyclients, while successfully compromising regular visitors. Furthermore, we suggest several countermeasures aiming to improve honeyclients. By employing these countermeasures, a honeyclient will be better protected from evasion attempts and will provide more accurate results.

References

1. Anubis: Analyzing Unknown Binaries, http://anubis.seclab.tuwien.ac.at
2. Bayer, U., Kruegel, C., Kirda, E.: TTAnalyze: A Tool for Analyzing Malware. In: Proceedings of the European Institute for Computer Antivirus Research Annual Conference, EICAR (2006)
3. Boscovich, R. et al.: Microsoft Security Intelligence Report. Technical Report, vol. 7, Microsoft, Inc. (2009)
4. Broersma, M.: Web attacks slip under the radar (2007), http://news.techworld.com/security/10620/web-attacks-slip-under-the-radar/
5. Cova, M., Kruegel, C., Vigna, G.: Detection and Analysis of Drive-by-Download Attacks and Malicious JavaScript Code. In: Proceedings of the International World Wide Web Conference, WWW (2010)
6. CVE. Windows ANI LoadAniIcon() Chunk Size Stack Overflow (HTTP), http://cve.mitre.org/cgi-bin/cvename.cgi?name=2007-0038.
7. CWSandbox (2009), http://www.cwsandbox.org/
8. Dinaburg, A., Royal, P., Sharif, M., Lee, W.: Ether: Malware analysis via hardware virtualization extensions. In: Proceedings of the ACM Conference on Computer and Communications Security, CCS (2008)
9. Ferrie, P.: Attacks on Virtual Machines. In: Proceedings of the Association of Anti-Virus Asia Researchers Conference (2007)
10. Fewer, S.: Reflective DLL injection, http://www.harmonysecurity.com/files/HS-P005_ReflectiveDllInjection.pdf
11. Fogla, P., Lee, W.: Evading Network Anomaly Detection Systems: Formal Reasoning and Practical Techniques. In: Proceedings of the ACM Conference on Computer and Communications Security CCS (2006)
12. Frei, S., Dübendorfer, T., Ollman, G., May, M.: Understanding the Web browser threat: Examination of vulnerable online Web browser populations and the insecurity iceberg. In: Proceedings of DefCon, vol. 16 (2008)
13. Garfinkel, T., Adams, K., Warfield, A., Franklin, J.: Compatibility is Not Transparency: VMM Detection Myths and Realities. In: Proceedings of the USENIX Workshop on Hot Topics in Operating Systems (2007)
14. Google. Safe Browsing API, http://code.google.com/apis/safebrowsing/
15. Holz, T.: AV Tracker (2009), http://honeyblog.org/archives/37-AV-Tracker.html

16. Jaeger, T.: Reference Monitor Concept. Encyclopedia of Cryptography and Security (2010)
17. Jiang, X., Wang, X., Xu, D.: Stealthy Malware Detection and Monitoring through VMM-Based Out-of-the-Box Semantic View Reconstruction. ACM Transactions on Information and System Security (TISSEC) 13(2) (February 2010)
18. Joebox: A Secure Sandbox Application for Windows (2009), http://www.joebox.org/
19. Klein, T.: ScoopyNG - The VMware detection tool, http://www.trapkit.de/research/vmm/scoopyng/index.html
20. Krebs, B.: Former anti-virus researcher turns tables on industry (October 27, 2009), http://voices.washingtonpost.com/securityfix/2009/10/former_anti-virus_researcher_t.html
21. Liston, T., Skoudis, E.: On the Cutting Edge: Thwarting Virtual Machine Detection (2006), http://handlers.sans.org/tliston/ThwartingVMDetection_Liston_Skoudis.pdf
22. Martignoni, L., Paleari, R., Roglia, G.F., Bruschi, D.: Testing CPU Emulators. In: Proceedings of the International Symposium on Software Testing and Analysis, ISSTA (2009)
23. Microsoft. What is SmartScreen Filter?, http://www.microsoft.com/security/filters/smartscreen.aspx
24. MITRE. HoneyClient, http://www.honeyclient.org/
25. Moshchuk, A., Bragin, T., Deville, D., Gribble, S., Levy, H.: SpyProxy: Execution-based Detection of Malicious Web Content. In: Proceedings of the USENIX Security Symposium (2007)
26. Moshchuk, A., Bragin, T., Gribble, S., Levy, H.: A Crawler-based Study of Spyware in the Web. In: Proceedings of the Symposium on Network and Distributed System Security, NDSS (2006)
27. Müller, T., Mack, B., Arziman, M.: Web Exploit Finder, http://www.xnos.org/security/web-exploit-finder.html
28. Nguyen, A., Schear, N., Jung, H., Godiyal, A., King, S., Nguyen, H.: MAVMM: Lightweight and Purpose Built VMM for Malware Analysis. In: Proceedings of the Annual Computer Security Applications Conference, ACSAC (2009)
29. Norman Sandbox (2009), http://www.norman.com/about_norman/technology/norman_sandbox/
30. Paleari, R., Martignoni, L., Roglia, G.F., Bruschi, D.: A Fistful of Red-Pills: How to Automatically Generate Procedures to Detect CPU Emulators. In: Proceedings of the USENIX Workshop on Offensive Technologies, WOOT (2009)
31. Polychronakis, M., Mavrommatis, P., Provos, N.: Ghost Turns Zombie: Exploring the Life Cycle of Web-based Malware. In: Proceedings of the USENIX Workshop on Large-Scale Exploits and Emergent Threats, LEET (2008)
32. Provos, N., Mavrommatis, P., Rajab, M., Monrose, F.: All Your iFRAMEs Point to Us. In: Proceedings of the USENIX Security Symposium (2008)
33. Provos, N., McNamee, D., Mavrommatis, P., Wang, K., Modadugu, N.: The Ghost in the Browser: Analysis of Web-based Malware. In: Proceedings of the USENIX Workshop on Hot Topics in Understanding Botnet (2007)
34. Ptacek, T., Newsham, T.: Insertion, Evasion, and Denial of Service: Eluding Network Intrusion Detection. Technical report, Secure Networks, Inc. (1998)
35. Quist, D., Smith, V., Computing, O.: Detecting the Presence of Virtual Machines Using the Local Data Table, http://www.offensivecomputing.net/files/active/0/vm.pdf
36. Raffetseder, T., Kruegel, C., Kirda, E.: Detecting System Emulators. In: Proceedings of the Information Security Conference (2007)

37. Rocaspana, J.: SHELIA: A Client HoneyPot For Client-Side Attack Detection (2009), http://www.cs.vu.nl/~herbertb/misc/shelia/
38. Rutkowska, J.: Red Pill. or how to detect VMM using (almost) one CPU instruction (2004), http://www.invisiblethings.org/papers/redpill.html
39. Sharif, M., Lee, W., Cui, W., Lanzi, A.: Secure In-VM Monitoring Using Hardware Virtualization. In: Proceedings of the ACM Conference on Computer and Communications Security, CCS (2009)
40. The Honcynet Project. Capture-HPC, https://projects.honeynet.org/capture-hpc
41. ThreatExpert (2009), http://www.threatexpert.com/
42. Tsaur, W., Chen, Y., Tsai, B.: A New Windows Driver-Hidden Rootkit Based on Direct Kernel Object Manipulation. In: Proceedings of the Algorithms and Architectures for Parallel Processing Conference (2009)
43. Van Gundy, M., Chen, H., Su, Z., Vigna, G.: Feature Omission Vulnerabilities: Thwarting Signature Generation for Polymorphic Worms. In: Proceedings of the Annual Computer Security Applications Conference, ACSAC (2007)
44. Vasudevan, A., Yerraballi, R.: Cobra: Fine-grained Malware Analysis using Stealth Localized Executions. In: Proceedings of the IEEE Symposium on Security and Privacy (2006)
45. Vigna, G., Robertson, W., Balzarotti, D.: Testing Network-based Intrusion Detection Signatures Using Mutant Exploits. In: Proceedings of the ACM Conference on Computer and Communications Security CCS (2004)
46. Wang, Y.-M., Beck, D., Jiang, X., Roussev, R., Verbowski, C., Chen, S., King, S.: Automated Web Patrol with Strider HoneyMonkeys: Finding Web Sites That Exploit Browser Vulnerabilities. In: Proceedings of the Symposium on Network and Distributed System Security, NDSS (2006)
47. Yin, H., Poosankam, P., Hanna, S., Song, D.: HookScout: Proactive Binary-Centric Hook Detection. In: Proceedings of the Conference on Detection of Intrusions and Malware & Vulnerability Assessment, DIMVA (2010)

An Assessment of Overt Malicious Activity Manifest in Residential Networks

Gregor Maier[1,2], Anja Feldmann[2], Vern Paxson[1,3],
Robin Sommer[1,4], and Matthias Vallentin[3]

[1] International Computer Science Institute, Berkeley, CA, USA
[2] TU Berlin / Deutsche Telekom Laboratories, Berlin, Germany
[3] University of California at Berkeley, CA, USA
[4] Lawrence Berkeley National Laboratory, Berkeley, CA, USA

Abstract. While conventional wisdom holds that residential users experience a high degree of compromise and infection, this presumption has seen little validation in the way of an in-depth study. In this paper we present a first step towards an assessment based on monitoring network activity (anonymized for user privacy) of 20,000 residential DSL customers in a European urban area, roughly 1,000 users of a community network in rural India, and several thousand dormitory users at a large US university. Our study focuses on security issues that *overtly manifest* in such data sets, such as scanning, spamming, payload signatures, and contact to botnet rendezvous points. We analyze the relationship between overt manifestations of such activity versus the "security hygiene" of the user populations (anti-virus and OS software updates) and potential risky behavior (accessing blacklisted URLs). We find that hygiene has little correlation with observed behavior, but risky behavior—which is quite prevalent—more than doubles the likelihood that a system will manifest security issues.

1   Introduction

Conventional wisdom holds that residential users experience a high degree of compromise and infection, due to a dearth of effective system administration and a plethora of users untrained or unwilling to observe sound security practices. To date, however, this presumption has seen little in the way of systematic study. Such analysis can prove difficult to conduct due to major challenges both in obtaining access to monitoring residential activity, and in determining in a comprehensive fashion whether a given system has been subverted given only observations of externally visible behavior.

In this paper we develop first steps towards such an investigation. We examine the network activity of 20,000 residential DSL customers within a European urban area, roughly 1,000 users of a community network in rural India, and several thousand dormitory users at a large US university. As a baseline, we include in our assessment the same analyses for Internet traffic seen at a large research laboratory that has a track record of effectively protecting its roughly 12,000 systems without employing a default-deny firewall policy.

We in addition investigate the relationship between problems flagged by our analyses and the level of apparent "security hygiene" in our populations. One may expect that

T. Holz and H. Bos. (Eds.): DMIVA 2011, LNCS 6739, pp. 144–163, 2011.

users who perform regular OS updates and deploy anti-virus software are less likely to have their systems compromised. Likewise, one might presume that users who partake in risky behavior have more security problems. To check these assumptions, we examine the end-user systems in our data sets for signs of regular operating system updates, anti-virus deployments, and contacts to URLs blacklisted by Google's Safe Browsing API [8].

We emphasize that given our data we can only assess malicious activity that *overtly manifests* in network traffic. Clearly, this reflects only a (perhaps quite small) subset of actual security problems among the users. Thus, what we provide constitutes only a first step towards understanding the nature and prevalence of such problems. Given that caution, we frame some of our more interesting findings as:

- In all of our environments, only a small fraction of hosts manifest malicious activity.
- We do not find significant differences between the environment in rural India and the other residential environments, though the former poses a number of analysis difficulties, so this finding is only suggestive.
- While OS software updates and anti-virus technology are widely deployed, we do not find that their use correlates with a lower degree of overt malicious activity.
- We observe frequent risky behavior, and users exhibiting such risky behavior are roughly twice as likely to manifest malicious activity.

We structure the remainder of this paper as follows. After introducing our data sets and methodology in §2, we study security hygiene in §3 and then investigate malicious activity in §4. We present related work in §5. Finally, we discuss our results and present avenues for future work in §6.

2   Methodology

We start our discussion by summarizing the specifics of the data sets we captured in the four network environments we examine in this study. We then discuss how, using these traces, we identify the operating systems used by individual hosts. Finally, we present the metrics we deploy for detecting overt malicious activity.

2.1   Data Sets

We started our work by recording network traces in all environments. However, due to high traffic volume it did not prove feasible to record the full network data stream for an extended period of time in most environments. We therefore leveraged Maier et al.'s "Time Machine" system [13] to reduce the stored amount of data. The Time Machine records only the first N bytes of each connection, discarding the remainder. For example, in the ISP environment, using N=50 KB allowed us to record $\approx 90\%$ of all connections in their entirety while only retaining 10% of total volume.[1]

We used the Bro system [14] with Dynamic Protocol Detection [6] to detect and extract application layer headers. Our capturing processes made sure to anonymize the

---

[1] We note that due to operational constraints we used different cutoff values in each environment, as detailed in the corresponding sections.

Table 1. Data sets for European ISP, Univ, and LBNL. We collected all these using the *Time Machine*.

Location	Start	Duration	Total volume	After cutoff applied	Loss
ISP	Mar 13, 2010	14 days	> 90 TB	> 9 TB	0 %
Univ	Sep 10, 2010	7 days	> 35 TB	> 2 TB	0.005 %
LBNL	Apr 29, 2010	4 days	> 25 TB	> 350 GB	0.2 %

Table 2. Data sets for AirJaldi

Name	Start	Duration	#IPs	Size	Loss
AirJaldi1	Mar 10, 2010	40 h	263	65 GB	0.35 %
AirJaldi2	Mar 13, 2010	34 h	188	31 GB	1.07 %
AirJaldi3	Apr 22, 2010	34 h	261	51 GB	0.44 %

data in accordance with the network operators' policies, and all data classification and header extraction executed directly on the secured measurement infrastructures. Table 1 and Table 2 summarize our data sets.

Lawrence Berkeley National Laboratory. The *Lawrence Berkeley National Laboratory* (LBNL) is a large research institute with more than 12,000 hosts connected to the Internet via a 10 Gbps uplink, and we use it a baseline for our study. Since LBNL offers an open research environment, LBNL's security policy defaults to fairly unrestricted access, with only limited firewalling at the border. LBNL's security team actively monitors its network for malicious activity, deploying a toolbox of strategies including detectors for scanning and spamming. Systems detected as compromised are quickly taken off the network. Thus, we expect to find little malicious activity in this environment.

We analyze one 4-day packet-level trace. The trace covers two weekdays and a weekend, with a total of 7,000 hosts active during that period. Large individual flows are common at this site, so the Time Machine proved especially effective at reducing volume of collected data. We ran it with a cutoff value of 25 KB. During our recording interval, the capture mechanism reported 0.2 % of all packets as dropped.

In terms of application protocol mix, we find that HTTP contributes about 42 % of bytes at LBNL and SSH 21 %. About 23 % of the traffic remains unclassified.

European ISP. Our largest data set represents a 14-day anonymized packet-level trace of more than 20,000 residential DSL lines, collected at an aggregation point within a large European ISP. The ISP does not employ any traffic shaping or blocking (such as filtering outbound SMTP connections), providing us with an unobstructed view of potential malicious activity.

We used the Time Machine with a cutoff value of 50 KB. Since we employed Endace monitoring cards and discarded the bulk of the data, we did not experience any packet loss. In addition, we also have access to several further day-long traces for comparison purposes.

This ISP data set includes meta-data associating the anonymized IP addresses in the trace with the corresponding (likewise anonymized) DSL line IDs, which enables us to distinguish customers even in the presence of the frequent address reassignment employed by this ISP [11]. For our study, we thus use these line IDs as our basic analysis unit.

Furthermore, the NAT detection approach developed in [12] works well in this environment and allows us to reliably identify the presence of NATs on any of the DSL lines. In addition, the NAT detection approach enables us to estimate the number of hosts connected at a DSL line. We find that 90% of the DSL lines use NAT and that 46% connect more than one device to the Internet.

The application protocol mix in the monitored ISP network is dominated by HTTP (> 50% of the total volume), while the prevalence of peer-to-peer applications is rather small (15%). NNTP accounts for roughly 5%, and less than 15% of the traffic remains unclassified but is likely P2P.

Indian community network.. The AirJaldi [1] wireless network is a non-profit community network in the Himalayas of India. Using approximately 400 wireless routers, it covers a radius of 80 km in and around the city of Dharamsala. AirJaldi connects thousands of users and machines with two leased lines from broadband ISPs, which provide a total uplink capacity of 10 Mbps. The majority of the rural population accesses the Internet via publicly shared machines in cybercafes or libraries. In addition, some residential users connect to the network with individually administered machines.

In the AirJaldi network, a single IP address is assigned to each "customer site", such as a specific building, library, or village. Customer sites can in turn provide connectivity to anywhere from one to several hundred systems, and the larger ones typically employ a multi-tiered NAT architecture on their inside, with NAT gateways connecting further NAT gateways.

Due to this architecture, we cannot directly distinguish individual systems at our monitoring point which is located at the central uplink router. Likewise, the NAT detection approach we use for the European ISP cannot reliably determine the number of hosts behind the larger gateways. We therefore report only aggregate findings for malicious activity and risky behavior for the AirJaldi environment.

However, to get an idea of the size of the user population, we can still estimate the number of *active* individual users by extracting (anonymous) user ID cookies found in HTTP traffic: the IDs sent to google.com, Doubleclick, and Google Analytics consistently indicate that we are seeing at least 400–600 users in each trace.

In our traces, HTTP dominates AirJaldi's application protocols mix, accounting for 56–72% of the total traffic volume, similar to the European ISP. However, in contrast to the ISP, interactive communication protocols (instant messaging, VoIP, Skype, etc.) account 2.5–10% at AirJaldi, while NNTP and P2P are not prevalent.

University Dormitories. We also examine network traffic recorded at dormitories of a major US University, where our monitoring point allows us to observe all their external traffic. While the dormitory network generally employs a default-open firewall, it deploys a custom "light-weight" Snort setup configured to detect a small set of recent malware. Users flagged by Snort are automatically moved over to a containment network from where they can then only access resources for disinfecting their systems.

Note that this containment prevents such victims from further triggering our malicious activity metrics once the dorm setup has restricted their access.

The IP address space for the dorm users is large enough to assign public IP addresses to each local system, with no need for a central gateway NAT. In our data set, we observe about 10,000 active IP addresses. Analyzing user IDs (as we discussed with the AirJaldi network), we find roughly 14,000 distinct ones, suggesting that a single public IP is only used by few machines. We also find that user-to-IP mappings remain mostly stable, and thus we can use IP addresses as our main analysis unit here. Similar to the ISP, however, we cannot further distinguish between different hosts/devices connected potentially through a user-deployed NAT gateway.

We note that the NAT detection approach developed in [12] does not work well in this environment. As it leverages IP TTLs, it relies on a well-known hop distance between the monitoring point and the user system, which is not the case in the dorm environment.

We analyze one 7-day packet-trace from the Univ environment, recorded using the Time Machine with a 15 KB cutoff (i.e., smaller than for the European ISP). The application protocol mix in the dorm network is dominated by HTTP, which accounts for over 70 % of all bytes, with 20–25 % of traffic unclassified.

2.2 Operating Systems

Malware often targets particular operating systems, and some OSes are perceived as more secure due to architectural advantages or smaller market shares that render them less attractive targets. To assess these effects, we annotate our traces with the operating system(s) observed in use with each DSL line (for the European ISP) or IP address (for the other environments). We determine operating systems by analyzing HTTP user-agent strings reflecting the most popular browsers (Firefox, Internet Explorer, Safari, and Opera).

Doing so, we can identify one or more operating systems on more than 90 % of all DSL lines of the European ISP. Analyzing the operating system mix, we find that 59 % of the lines use only a single version of Windows, while 23 % use different Windows versions. Mac OS is present on 7.6 % of the lines, and used exclusively on 2.7 %. We find Linux on 3.7 % of the lines. However, we also observe that Linux is generally used in combination with other operating systems, and the fraction of lines with only Linux is too small to assess malicious activity separately.

At LBNL, we can identify at least one operating system for 60 % of all active IPs. We find that 70 % of these IPs use only a single version of Windows. We see Macs in use with 19 % of those IPs, and Linux with 8.6 %.

In the Univ environment, we are able to determine operating systems for 73 % of all active IPs. Mac OS is the dominating operating system here, present on 56 % of them. 34 % of IPs use a single version of Windows exclusively, and Linux is present on just over 4 % of IPs.

At AirJaldi, we observe a large number of operation systems per IP due to its extensive NAT deployment and thus cannot further estimate the distribution.

2.3   Manifestations of Compromised Systems

To identify end systems that overtly manifest malicious activity or signs of likely compromise, we search for three behavioral indicators—*address scanning, port scanning,* and *spamming*—and also monitor for network-level signatures aimed at detecting three malware families, Zlob, Conficker, and Zeus.

To take advantage of the long duration of our traces, we analyze and report manifestations of malicious activity first separately for each day of our multi-day traces (European ISP, Univ, and LBNL). We then further aggregate the results by accumulating all activity over increasing trace durations into cumulative data sets. For example, consider a local system (DSL line or IP address) that started to be a scanner on day 4. In the daily data set this system is marked as a scanner on day 4. In the cumulative data set, it is marked as scanner on day 4 as well as for *all following days*, regardless of whether the system is again acting as a scanner on any of the subsequent days or not. In particular, the cumulative data for the last day of a trace reflects the aggregate behavior over the full observation period.

Scanning. Extensive *address scanning* often reflects the precursor of an attack that targets services that answer the scan. Most network intrusion detection systems (NIDS) therefore detect and report such scanners but their detectors typically target *external* hosts probing a monitored network. For our study, however, we instead wish to find *outbound* scanners. This can prove harder to do, as the potential probes are embedded within the host's benign activity.

We found that for our environments, a simple threshold-based scan detector often erroneously flags benign user activity such as web browsers. Detectors that count *failed* connection attempts work better, but still can misfire for P2P-style traffic patterns. We therefore use an approach loosely modeled on that of TRW [10]: we compute the *ratio* of successful vs. unsuccessful TCP connections initiated by a local host. We define a connection as unsuccessful if a client sends a SYN but either receives a RST back or no answer at all.

We find that our data exhibits a sharply bi-modal distribution of success ratios: Connections between a specific pair of local and remote hosts tend to either always succeed or always fail. However, when investigating the fraction of remote destinations *per* local host that tend to fail, we do not find such a clear distribution. Presumably, P2P clients can have similarly large numbers of mostly unsuccessful destinations, thus rendering this approach impractical. We can overcome this ambiguity, however, by limiting our scan analysis to 14 ports that frequently appear in inbound scanning, as identified by the security monitoring in our baseline environment, LBNL. These ports include, e.g., the Windows services 135–139, 445, and 1433. For activity targeting these ports, we indeed find that local systems either have a small (< 20) or large (> 100, often $> 1,000$) number of unsuccessful remote contacts; see Figure 1. We thus deem activity as overtly manifesting a compromised local system if a host unsuccessfully attempts to contact > 100 destinations.

Another dimension of scanning regards *port scanning*: probing many ports on a single remote host. Since few benign applications need to contact numerous distinct ports on a single system, we use a simple threshold-based approach: we consider a local

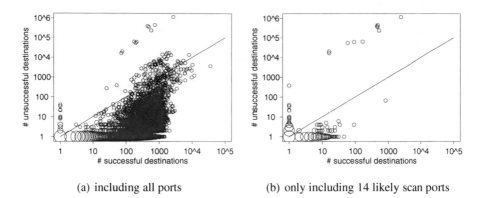

(a) including all ports   (b) only including 14 likely scan ports

Fig. 1. Scatter plot showing number of successful vs. unsuccessful connections with remote IPs per DSL line, computed for a single day of the ISP trace. The size of the circles is proportional to the number of lines having the corresponding ratio.

system to manifest malicious activity if it *unsuccessfully* contacts at least two remote hosts on more than 50 ports within a single day.

Spamming. Another manifestation of malicious activity concerns local hosts sending spam. To find an appropriate indicator for classifying a host as a spammer, we examined SMTP activity of local systems in terms of how many remote SMTP servers they contact. The number of distinct SMTP servers can be an indicator since we do not expect many users to run their own SMTP servers, but instead to rely on a (small) number of e-mail providers to deliver their mails. Particularly in the ISP environment, e-mail providers are necessary since the IP range of the monitored DSL lines is dynamically assigned and many SMTP servers generally reject mails from any dynamic addresses unless specifically authenticated. We find that DSL lines consistently contact either less than 25 SMTP servers or more than 100. Indeed, most lines contact less than 10. We ultimately classify a system as a *spammer* if it contacts > 100 distinct SMTP servers in one day.

Known malware families. We can also observe manifestations of host compromise by flagging activity related to known malware families. To do so, we focused on Zlob, Conficker, and Zeus.

The Zlob malware family [24] changes the DNS resolver settings of infected hosts (and even broadband routers), altering them to a well-known set of malicious remote systems. We thus classify a system as reflecting a Zlob infection if it uses one of those known DNS resolvers. We note that Zlob targets both Windows and Mac systems, subverting systems using social engineering in the guise of a fake codec download.

Another malware family that has attracted much attention is Conficker [15]. For April 2010, the Conficker Working Group [4] reported 5–6 M distinct Conficker A+B infected IPs and 100–200 K distinct Conficker C infected IPs. Note however that the number of IPs does not necessarily provide a good estimation of the population size due to aliasing. The group estimates the true population size to be between 25–75 % of the IP addresses seen per day.

To find rendezvous points, Conficker A and B generate a list of 250 different domain names each day (Conficker C uses 50,000 domains) and then try to resolve them. Since the algorithm for generating the domain names is known [22], we can compute the relevant domain names for our observation periods and check which local hosts try to resolve any of these. To account for potential clock skew on the client machines, we also include the domain names for the days before and after our observation period.

Conficker C sometimes generates legitimately registered domains, due to its frequent use of very short names. To rule out false positives, we therefore only flag a system as manifesting a Conficker infection if it issued ≥ 50 lookups for known Conficker domains. We note that Conficker also uses address-scanning to find other vulnerable machines and spread itself. Thus, we expect to find a correlation between address scanning and Conficker lookups.

We use the Zeus Domainblocklist [25] to identify local systems infected with Zeus. Since the list does not only contain seemingly random domain names but also some indicating scare-ware (e. g., updateinfo22.com) or typo squatting (e. g., google-analytiics.cn), we require ≥ 4 lookups per system and day to classify a system as infected. We found that fewer lookups often reflect embedded ads or other artifacts not due to compromise. Since we initially lacked a continuous feed of the Zeus domain list, we used a one-day snapshot from Mar 23, 2010 for the ISP trace and Air-Jaldi1/AirJaldi2. We used another snapshot from May 6, 2010 for LBNL and AirJaldi3. For Univ, we were able to continuously update the list during the measurement period.

Alternative Manifestations of Compromised Systems. We also examined further alternative approaches to detect compromised systems, which however did not turn out to generate sufficiently reliable results.

One obvious approach is to leverage a NIDS' output directly. Consequently, we attempted using a standard signature set: the Emerging Threats rules [7] loaded into Snort [18]. We excluded all rules that are labeled as aiming at finding "inappropriate" activity (e. g., gaming traffic or P2P) as such is not in scope for our study. Still, analyzing a single day of ISP traffic, we get more than 1 million hits, flagging more than 90 % of the monitored local systems. Clearly, such results have to include many false positives.

We can reduce the number of hits by restricting the analysis to examine only outbound activity, and whitelisting rules that are likely to flag benign activity. However, Snort still reports too many alarms to be a reliable indicator for us. The main problems with the Emerging Threats rules are their sheer size (more than 3,500 rules in total), and a general lack of documentation (many rules are not documented at all). In particular, the rules do not include any indication on how tight they are (i. e., what their likelihood of false positives is), nor how severe one should consider the activity they target (e. g., is this rule triggered by a C&C channel or by adware).

Another approach we tried as an indicator of likely system compromise is checking whether a local system's IP address appears on an anti-spam blacklist, such as Spamhaus. However, we find that doing so proves difficult in our settings: address assignments are dynamic and can often reflect numerous different hosts over short time intervals. Thus a single blacklist entry can tar the reputation of many distinct local systems. In addition, some anti-spam providers proactively blacklist *all* dynamically assigned IP address ranges.

3   Security Hygiene and Risky Behavior

To analyze whether residential users are aware of potential hazards and take recommended countermeasures, we analyze *(i)* whether local systems use anti-virus scanners; *(ii)* if they regularly update their OS software (e. g., Windows Update); and *(iii)* whether they download Google's Safe Browsing blacklist.

Most anti-virus and OS software updates are done using HTTP, and they use specific user-agents and/or HTTP servers. Searching for those allows us to classify a local system as a software updater and/or anti-virus user. Likewise, the HTTP servers serving Google's blacklist are well-known, and we can thus identify local systems which use the blacklist. Moreover, we also check if local systems downloading the blacklist still request any blacklisted URLs. Such behavior clearly has to be considered risky. For finding such "bad" requests, we determine whether a requested URL was blacklisted at the time of the request by keeping a local change history of the blacklist over the course of our measurement interval.

We note that me might over-estimate the number of actual OS or anti-virus updates. OS updaters often only check whether an update is available and then ask the user to install it, however the user might decline to do so. Likewise, anti-virus products might download (or check for) new signatures but not use them unless the user has a current license for the anti-virus software. Our analysis flags these cases as anti-virus user and OS updater respectively. However, we cross-checked our results by only considering a local system as anti-virus user if the anti-virus software transferred at least 1 MB and 100 KB of HTTP body data.

3.1   European ISP

Figure 2 shows the fraction of active DSL lines vs. lines performing anti-virus or OS updates. On any given day 57–65 % of DSL lines perform OS software updates, and 51–58 % update their anti-virus signatures (or engines). From the cumulative data we see that over the 14 day observation period up to 90 % of lines check for updates to their OS and 81 % use anti-virus software. This highlights that the user-base in principle exhibits elementary "security hygiene" and performs recommended precautions.

When focusing on DSL lines exhibiting exclusively MacOS activity, we find that up to 2 % do anti-virus updates and up to 78 % perform software updates.

But what about risky behavior such as requesting potentially dangerous URLs? Overall, we find that only about 0.03 % of all HTTP requests appear on Google's Safe Browsing blacklist. However, investigating the per-DSL line behavior, we find that on any given day up to 4.4 % of the DSL lines request at least one blacklisted URL (see Figure 3). Across the whole 14-day period we see that a striking 19 % of lines request at least one blacklisted URL.

To check if the browser may have warned the user about doing these requests, we next examine if the user-agent placing them actually downloaded the blacklist from

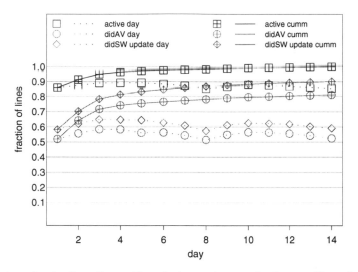

Fig. 2. Fraction of active lines, lines with anti-virus updates, and software updates for daily and cumulative data sets from the ISP

Google earlier. For doing so, we distinguish three cases when a user accesses a black-listed URL:

- notDownloaded: The browser did not download the blacklist at all, thus the user could not have been warned.
- beforeBlacklisted: The browser downloaded the blacklist, however the URL was requested *before* it appeared on the blacklist, thus the user could likewise not have been warned.[2]
- whileBlacklisted: The browser downloaded the blacklist and requested the URL while it was blacklisted. That is, the user placing the request (presumably by click-ing on a link) *should have been warned* by the browser that the URL is considered malicious.

In Table 3 we list for each combination of cases the fraction of DSL lines exhibiting this combination. We find that for the majority of lines requesting blacklisted URLs the browser either did not download the blacklist (notDownloaded), or the request occurred before the URL was blacklisted and thus the browser could not have warned the user about the URLs potential malignity. However, we find a significant number, 33.6 %, of DSL lines that request blacklisted URLs even though the users should have been warned by their browsers (any combination in which whileBlacklisted is present). When we investigate how often DSL lines request URLs that are on Google's blacklist, we

---

[2] We allow for a 1 hr grace period, relative to the time when a URL has appeared on our local copy of the list. Google suggests that browser developers implement a 25–30 minute update interval for the blacklist. Furthermore, Google states that a warning can only be displayed to the user if the blacklist is less than 45 minutes old, thus forcing browsers to regularly update the list.

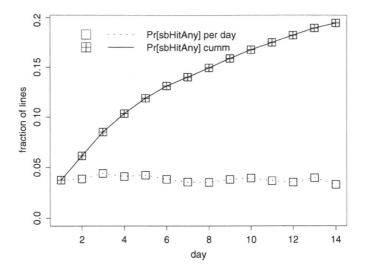

Fig. 3. Fraction of lines requesting URLs blacklisted by Google

Table 3. Possible cases when DSL lines access blacklisted URLs for ISP dataset. 100 % represents all lines requesting at least one blacklisted URL.

Fraction	Cases
43.8 %	notDownloaded
19.5 %	beforeBlacklisted
16.9 %	whileBlacklisted
11.0 %	whileBlacklisted, beforeBlacklisted
3.0 %	notDownloaded, whileBlacklisted
2.7 %	notDownloaded, whileBlacklisted, beforeBlacklisted
3.1 %	notDownloaded, beforeBlacklisted

find that 53 % of such lines do so on only a single day. This indicates that although many lines request blacklisted URLs, they do not request such URLs every day.

3.2 University

Analyzing security hygiene at the Univ environment, we find that 78 % of all local IP addresses perform OS software updates over the 7-day trace duration, and that 60 % perform anti-virus updates. While these numbers are lower than the numbers for the European ISP, we note that we observe significantly more IP addresses on which only MacOS systems (and no Windows systems) are active than at the European ISP. For IP addresses on which we only observe Macs, we find that 45 % perform anti-virus and 73 % perform software updates.

When we turn to risky behavior we find that after the 7-day observation period roughly 20 % of local IP addresses have requested URLs blacklisted by Google. This is higher than at the European ISP, where we reach 19 % after 14 days (after the first 7 days the European ISP environment reaches 14 %). Similar to the ISP we find that

36.4 % of the IPs requesting blacklisted URLs do so although the browser should have warned the user.

3.3 AirJaldi

Comparing security hygiene at the European ISP with the AirJaldi network in India, we find them quite similar. In terms of HTTP requests, we find that at AirJaldi approximately 0.02 % are blacklisted by Google (European ISP: 0.03 %), and 0.5–1.12 % are related to anti-virus software (European ISP: 1 %). For OS software updates, the numbers differ more: up to 2.8 % of all HTTP requests at AirJaldi, vs. only 0.3 % at the European ISP. Assessing security hygiene on a per host basis is difficult in this environment, however, given the layered NAT structure. We find that 29.6 %–40.7 % of the observed sites at AirJaldi perform anti-virus and OS software updates, and 3.8–5.4 % request blacklisted URLs. Recall, however, that each site can connect anywhere between a handful and several hundred users.

3.4 LBNL

We next turn to security hygiene at LBNL. We find relatively few hosts there updating anti-virus software (24 %) or operating systems (31 %). This can be explained however by the fact that LBNL uses centralized, internal update servers. The operating system distribution also differs notably from the ISP environment, with significantly more Linux and Mac hosts in use at LBNL. Turning to risky behavior, we find that only 0.01 % of all HTTP requests are blacklisted. In terms of the fraction of hosts requesting blacklisted URLs, we also find a smaller number than at the European ISP: up to 0.92 % of hosts per day and less 1.25 % overall. However, we find that users at LBNL still request blacklisted URLs even though they should have been warned by their browser; 23.4 % of IPs requesting blacklisted URLs do so.

4   Malicious Activity

After finding that even though users appear to be security aware and take appropriate precautions they still engage in risky behavior, we now use our indicators for identifying malicious behavior. Moreover, we also study the influence of security awareness, risky behavior, NAT deployment, and operating systems on infection probability. We emphasize that the overall estimate of malicious activity that we derive can only be a lower bound of the total present in these environments.

We start by studying the characteristics of the DSL customers of the European ISP since that is our richest data set. We then compare the results from the European ISP with those from the university dorms (Univ), the AirJaldi community network, and the LBNL setting, as applicable.

4.1   European ISP

Figure 4 shows the likelihood that a DSL line triggers any of the malicious activity indicators for the European ISP. We find that both on a per-day basis as well as overall

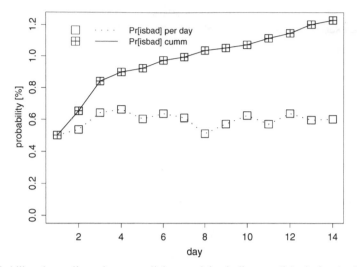

Fig. 4. Probability that a line triggers malicious activity indicators (isbad) for the ISP, shown separately for the daily and cumulative data sets

only a small fraction of local systems manifest overtly malicious activity; $< 0.7\,\%$ and $< 1.3\,\%$, respectively. Moreover, these percentages do not vary much across days.

However, even though the cumulative probabilities remain small, they are increasing over our 14-day period. This indicates that over time we are able to identify more lines that manifest malicious activity, and it may imply that longer observation periods would reveal even more lines manifesting such activity.

We find that *overall* the malware families and spammers contribute most to the observed manifestations of compromised systems, while scanners are less prominent; see Table 4. On a *per-day* basis, only the malware-based indicators are prominent.

More than 44% of the spammers are only active on a single day, i. e., they trigger the indicator only on a single day. In contrast, only 11% of the scanning activity is limited to a single day. On average (mean and median) scanners are seen for 4 days.

For most indicators, we observe a difference between the mean number of days that the indicator is triggered and the median number of days. This indicates that there is no consistent behavior by the local systems manifesting malicious activity. Indeed, an in-depth analysis reveals that some spammers and scanners start their malicious behavior as soon as the DSL line becomes active, while others stop temporarily or are only active for a short period. The fact that the malware families typically trigger on 5–8 days (mean) confirms that the bots engage in activity on a regular basis. However, malicious activity such as port scanning or spamming seems to be limited to sub-periods.

We find only a small overlap among the lines that trigger any of the indicators. Most lines that manifest malicious activity trigger only a single indicator (92%); about 7% trigger two. There is some correlation (0.227) between lines that manifest Conficker and scanning activity, as we would expect due to Conficker's regular network scans in search of further vulnerable hosts. We also observe a correlation of 0.109 between DSL lines triggering the Spam and Zeus metrics.

Table 4. Probability that a DSL line triggers a malicious activity indicator. The daily numbers summarize the range of the probability values per day. To estimate the persistence of the activity, we include the mean/median number of days that each indicator triggered and the percentage of lines for which the indicator triggered only on a single day.

Indicator	Probability			Activity prevalence	
	daily prob.	cumm. prob.		mean / median	only single day activity
Spam	0.03–0.10 %	0.25 %		3.6 / 2 days	44 %
Scan	0.01–0.06 %	0.09 %		4.3 / 4 days	11 %
Port Scan	0.01–0.03 %	0.06 %		3.5 / 2 days	39 %
Zlob	0.13–0.19 %	0.24 %		8.4 / 10 days	10 %
Conficker	0.17–0.26 %	0.23 %		6.5 / 6 days	27 %
Zeus	0.07–0.15 %	0.28 %		4.9 / 2 days	38 %
Total	0.50–0.66 %	1.23 %		5.9 / 4 days	28 %

Next we check whether the likelihood that a local system manifests malicious activity is influenced by other parameters.

Security Hygiene. We start our investigation by examining the impact of anti-virus deployment and OS software updates. Surprisingly, we do not see any strong effects in this regard. Anti-virus software does not noticeably reduce the likelihood of a DSL line manifesting malicious activity (1.10 % with anti-virus vs. 1.23 % without, considering all indicators). We cross-check these numbers for a potential over-estimation by only considering DSL lines that transferred at least 100 KB (1 MB) of anti-virus HTTP payload, we find that still 1.06 % (0.82 % for 1 MB) of lines trigger our metrics. While the latter is a drop of roughly 30 %, anti-virus software still seems less effective than one might presume. Likewise, we do not observe any particular impact of performing OS updates. We verified that these findings are not biased by NATed DSL lines with multiple hosts. That is, even for lines that do not show multiple hosts, the likelihood of infections is not significantly changed by using anti-virus or doing updates.

Google Blacklist. Given the large fraction of DSL lines requesting blacklisted URLs, we next study whether such behavior increases the chance of manifesting malicious activity (see Figure 5). Indeed, we find that the probability of a line triggering any of our indicators rises by a factor of 2.5, up to 3.19 % (from 1.23 %) if we also observe the same line requesting at least one URL found on Google's blacklist. While in absolute terms the elevated level still remains low, our indicators only track *overt* manifestations of security issues, so the more salient takeaway concerns the more-than-doubled rate of host compromise for systems with poor "security hygiene".

NAT. Next, we evaluate whether NAT influences the probability of triggering our malicious activity indicators. We find that DSL lines that connect multiple hosts are 1.5 times more likely to trigger one (1.81 %). Lines on which no NAT gateway is present are as likely to trigger an indicator as all DSL lines.

Malicious activity on Macs. Next, we turn to DSL lines on which all traffic is from Macs (2.7 % of all lines) and evaluate their likelihood of manifesting malicious activity. When analyzing the full 14-day observation period, we find that Mac lines trigger one of our indicators at less than half the rate of all systems (0.54 % vs 1.23 %), and they

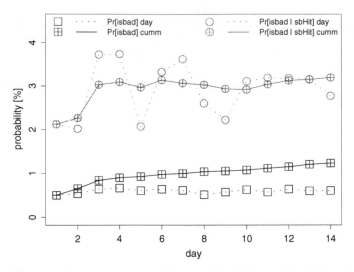

Fig. 5. Probability that a line triggers any malicious activity indicator (isbad) given it requested a blacklisted URL (BlkLst) for ISP

do so via a single indicator, infection with Zlob. In this regard, however, Macs are more than *twice* as likely to manifest an infection as all systems (0.24 %).

These findings are somewhat difficult to interpret. They appear to suggest that in general, Mac systems fare better than Windows systems in terms of resisting infection— but possibly only because most infection targets only the latter, and when infection also targets Macs, they may in fact be more vulnerable, perhaps due to less security vigilance.

4.2   University

We next turn to manifestations of malicious activity in the Univ dorm environment. As the dorm network provides central DNS resolvers to all local systems, we are not able to observe DNS requests from local systems unless they specifically configure a different, external DNS resolver. This implies that we cannot use our DNS-based indicators (Conficker and Zeus) for directly identifying infected local systems. We are however able to observe DNS requests from the central resolvers, allowing us to recognize whether any local systems are infected. Analyzing the DNS requests in Univ's traffic, we find no Conficker lookups at all, indicating that no hosts infected with Conficker were active (outside the containment network) during our measurement interval. We do however observe lookups for Zeus domains.

When using the other indicators, we observe that only a few local systems (0.23 %) manifest overtly malicious activity during our 7-day observation period. At the European ISP, 1 % of DSL lines manifest such activity over 7 days (1.23 % over 14 days), and 0.8 % excluding Zeus. In contrast to the European ISP, we find that port scanners at Univ contribute most to the overall number of local systems manifesting malicious activity. Scanners trigger on 0.13 % of local systems and all other indicators combined trigger on 0.1 % of local systems.

We do not observe any local systems that trigger more than one of our malicious activity indicators. This is however not surprising given that we cannot observe Conficker and Zeus activity. Recall that at the European ISP, these two tend to correlate most with other indicators.

Similar to the European ISP, we find that risky behavior (requesting blacklisted URLs) nearly doubles the rate of manifesting malicious activity, with the 0.23 % overall figure rising to 0.4 % in that case. Again, we find that neither OS software nor anti-virus update activities affect the rate at which security problems manifest.

4.3 AirJaldi

Within the Indian AirJaldi network, we observe very limited malicious activity. However, given that AirJaldi uses a multi-tiered NAT hierarchy, we can only explore malicious activity by customer site rather than per end-system. Within each trace we observe between 188 to 263 active customers sites. Each customer site can connect multiple, possibly hundreds, of hosts. However, exploring the number of destinations for scanners and spammers for each flagged site, we find that they are well within the range of what we observe at the European ISP. Therefore, we conclude that each of the reported scanning and spamming sites is likely due to a small number of infected hosts. Indeed, most likely it is due to a single one.

Across all three traces only a total of 12 customer sites triggered any of our indicators. Figure 6 summarize the results, listing all 12 customer sites that triggered any of our indicators. An "X" indicates that a site was not observed in a particular trace. We also further annotate each site with labels based on whether any of its systems requested blacklisted URLs (*BLK*), or updated anti-virus (*AV*) or OS software (*SW*).

	AirJaldi 1				AirJaldi 2				AirJaldi 3			
Site 1	ZeuS		AV	SW	ZeuS		AV	SW	ZeuS		AV	SW
Site 2	Conficker(799)			SW	Conficker(275)			SW	Spam	BLK	AV	SW
Site 3		BLK	AV	SW			AV	SW	Scan	BLK	AV	SW
Site 4	X				X				Spam		AV	SW
Site 5	X				X				Spam	BLK		SW
Site 6	X				X				Spam	BLK	AV	
Site 7	X				X				Spam	BLK	AV	
Site 8		BLK	AV	SW	Scan	BLK	AV	SW		BLK	AV	SW
Site 9		BLK		SW	Spam	BLK	AV	SW		BLK	AV	SW
Site 10	Conficker(291)		AV	SW			AV	SW			AV	SW
Site 11	Spam? Scan				X				X			
Site 12	Scan	BLK	AV	SW				AV				AV

AV = anti-virus   SW = software update   BLK = Blacklist hit
Shaded background =   malicious activity

Fig. 6. Summary of malicious activity and security hygiene for all AirJaldi traces

A detailed look at the spammers shows that *site 11* contacted 56 remote SMTP servers, less than our cutoff of 100. However, since no other site contacts more than 10 SMTP servers, we flag this site as a likely spammer (Spam?) rather than a certain spammer (Spam).

Only two sites trigger our malicious activity indicators in more than one trace. We never observe more than 7 sites manifesting malicious activity in any single trace, and in only one case do we find multiple forms of malicious activity at a single customer site. We note that *sites 4–7* are in the same /24 network and could potentially be a single customer site using multiple IP addresses over the trace duration.

Even though we cannot reliably determine the number of infected hosts at each customer site, we can attempt to estimate it. For Conficker this is possible since each infected host will in general generate 250 DNS lookups per day. Thus we estimate the number of infected hosts by dividing the total number of Conficker lookups by 250. We list the number of Conficker lookups per site in parentheses (Conficker(n)) in Figure 6.

Given the inability to identify end hosts, we cannot soundly correlate activity levels, anti-virus, OS software updates, or Google blacklist hits with malicious activity.

4.4   LBNL

At LBNL, our indicators trigger only for a small number of benign hosts. Not surprisingly, local mail servers are reported as "spammers"; and hosts deployed by the Lab's security group for penetration testing purposes are flagged as "scanners". While confirming that our detectors are working as expected, such false alarms are unlikely to occur in the residential environments. Other than these, we do not find any further malicious activity reported at LBNL.

5   Related Work

In our study, we examine several manifestations for malicious activity including scanning and spamming which are established indicators of compromised systems. Most network intrusion detection systems (NIDS), such as the open-source systems Snort [18] and Bro [14], use simple threshold schemes to find scanners. Bro also provides a more sensitive detector, *Threshold Random Walk* [10], that identifies scanners by tracking a system's series of successful and failed connection attempts. However, existing detectors do not work well for finding *outbound* scans, as needed for our study.

Spamming is often countered by blocking known offenders via DNS-based blacklists, such as SORBS [19] or Spamhaus [21]. However, due to the high IP address churn we experience (for example, due to DSL lines frequently changing their IP address [11]), such blacklists do not provide us with a reliable metric. Furthermore, many blacklists include the *full* dynamic IP space. Ramachandran et al. [17] identify spammers by observing the destinations they try to connect to. This eliminates the need for content inspection. The Snare system [9] extends this approach by building a reputation-based engine relying on additional non-payload features. These approaches, however, deploy clustering algorithms, and thus rely on suitable training sets, which are not available for our data set.

We also check our data sets for indicators of specific malware, all of which are analyzed and tracked in detail by other efforts: *Conficker* [15, 4]; Zlob [24]; and Zeus [25]. For example, Bailey et al. [2] survey botnet technology and Dagon et al. [5] examine malware that changes a client's DNS resolver, including the Zlob trojan.

Carlinet et al. [3] ran Snort on DSL traffic from about 3,000 customers of a French ISP to study what contributes to a user's risk of being infected with malware. For their study, Carlinet et al. simply removed the 20 Snort signatures triggering the most alarms. However, they do not further analyze how the remaining signatures contribute to the overall results, what their false-positive rate is, or whether there is relevant overlap between them.

We also leverage Google's Safe Browsing blacklist [8]; the approach used for collecting the blacklist is originally described by Provos et al. in [16].

Stone-Gross et al. [20] try to identify malicious (or negligent) Autonomous Systems (AS). They analyze data from their honeyfarm to identify IP addresses of botnet C&C servers and use four data feeds to find IP addresses of drive-by-download hosting servers and phishing servers. They correlate the information from these sources and the longevity of these malicious servers to compute a "malicious score" for the ASes hosting such malicious servers. ASes with high scores can then be blacklisted or de-peered by other ISPs or network operators. Thus their focus is on the hosting infrastructure rather than individual infected machines.

There has been some work on the prevalence of individual malware. The Conficker Working Group states that 3 million infected hosts is a "conservative minimum estimate", and it cites the study of an anti-virus vendor that finds that 6% of the monitored systems are infected. Weaver [23] estimates the hourly Conficker C population size in March/April of 2009 to average around 400-700 K infections.

6   Conclusion

In this work we have aimed to develop first steps towards understanding the extent of security problems experienced by residential users. Such studies face major difficulties in obtaining in-depth monitoring access for these users. To this end, we have made partial progress by acquiring network-level observations for tens of thousands of users. However, we lack direct end-system monitoring, and as such in this study we must limit our analysis to security issues that *overtly manifest* in network traffic. On the other hand, we were able to obtain such observations from a number of sites that differ in size, geographic location, and nature of the residential users. This diversity then gives us some initial sense of what facets of the residential security experience appear to hold regardless of the specific environment, and what relationships we find behind different facets of each environment and the differing behavior of individual users.

In this regard, our analysis develops a number of findings:

- A typical residential system is unlikely to engage in scanning or spamming, nor to contact known botnet command-and-control servers.
- Residential users generally exhibit good "security hygiene": many of them update their systems regularly and deploy anti-virus software.

- However, such hygiene does not appear to have much impact on the likelihood of becoming infected with malware.
- A significant subset of users exhibit risky behavior: they contact malicious sites even though, as best as we can deduce, their browsers have warned them in advance.
- Such risky behavior roughly doubles the likelihood of becoming infected with malware.

Our range of data sets allows us to also infer *relative* comparisons between different residential environments. Our main finding in this regard is that seemingly quite different sites—a European ISP, a US university dorm complex, and a rural Indian network—all exhibit similar levels of both security hygiene and risky behavior. Fairly assessing levels of overt malicious activity across these environments is challenging, in part due to ambiguity and limited information for the rural Indian network and limited observability (no DNS based metrics) at the Univ dorm environment. However, for both the European ISP and the Univ environment often only a single indicator manifests per local system. In contrast, for our baseline system at LBNL, we do not observe any overt malicious activity, and significantly less risky behavior.

Finally, our work establishes that much more detailed data will be required to build up a fully comprehensive picture of security issues in residential environments. We have shown that *overt* malicious activity is in fact fairly tame for these networks. The next, very challenging, step is to determine how to construct a sound understanding of *covert* malicious activity.

Acknowledgments. We would like to thank Yahel Ben-David of AirJaldi for helping us with the AirJaldi network and the anonymous reviewers for their valuable comments. We would also like to thank our data providers: the European ISP, the US University, the AirJaldi network, and the Lawrence Berkeley National Laboratory.

This work was supported in part by NSF Awards CNS-0905631 and NSF-0433702; the U.S. Army Research Laboratory and the U.S. Army Research Office under MURI grant No. W911NF-09-1-0553; a grant from Deutsche Telekom Laboratories Berlin; and a fellowship within the postdoctoral program of the German Academic Exchange Service (DAAD). Opinions, findings, and conclusions or recommendations are those of the authors and do not necessarily reflect the views of the National Science Foundation, the U.S. Army Research Laboratory, the U.S. Army Research Office, or DAAD.

References

1. AirJaldi Network, http://www.airjaldi.org
2. Bailey, M., Cooke, E., Jahanian, F., Xu, Y., Karir, M.: A survey of botnet technology and defenses. In: Proc. Cybersecurity Applications & Technology Conference for Homeland Security (2009)
3. Carlinet, Y., Me, L., Debar, H., Gourhant, Y.: Analysis of computer infection risk factors based on customer network usage. In: Proc. SECUWARE Conference (2008)
4. Conficker Working Group, http://www.confickerworkinggroup.org
5. Dagon, D., Provos, N., Lee, C.P., Lee, W.: Corrupted DNS resolution paths: The rise of a malicious resolution authority. In: Proc. Network and Distributed System Security Symposium, NDSS (2009)

6. Dreger, H., Feldmann, A., Mai, M., Paxson, V., Sommer, R.: Dynamic application-layer protocol analysis for network intrusion detection. In: Proc. USENIX Security Symposium (2006)
7. Emerging Threats, http://www.emergingthreats.net/
8. Google, Google safe browsing API, http://code.google.com/apis/safebrowsing/
9. Hao, S., Feamster, N., Gray, A., Syed, N., Krasser, S.: Detecting spammers with SNARE: spatio temporal network-level automated reputation engine. In: Proc. USENIX Security Symposium (2009)
10. Jung, J., Paxson, V., Berger, A., Balakrishnan, H.: Fast portscan detection using sequential hypothesis testing. In: Proc. IEEE Symp. on Security and Privacy (2004)
11. Maier, G., Feldmann, A., Paxson, V., Allman, M.: On dominant characteristics of residential broadband internet traffic. In: Proc. Internet Measurement Conference, IMC (2009)
12. Maier, G., Schneider, F., Feldmann, A.: NAT usage in residential broadband networks. In: Spring, N., Riley, G.F. (eds.) PAM 2011. LNCS, vol. 6579, pp. 32–41. Springer, Heidelberg (2011)
13. Maier, G., Sommer, R., Dreger, H., Feldmann, A., Paxson, V., Schneider, F.: Enriching network security analysis with time travel. In: Proc. ACM SIGCOMM Conference (2008)
14. Paxson, V.: Bro: A system for detecting network intruders in real-time. Computer Networks Journal 31, 23–24 (1999) Bro homepage, http://www.bro-ids.org
15. Porras, P., Saidi, H., Yegneswaran, V.: An analysis of Conficker's logic and rendezvous points. Tech. rep., SRI International (2009)
16. Provos, N., Mavrommatis, P., Rajab, M.A., Monrose, F.: All your iFRAMEs point to us. In: Proc. USENIX Security Symposium (2008)
17. Ramachandran, A., Feamster, N., Vempala, S.: Filtering spam with behavioral blacklisting. In: Proc. ACM Conf. on Computer and Communications Security, CCS (2007)
18. Roesch, M.: Snort: Lightweight intrusion detection for networks. In: Proc. Systems Administration Conference, LISA (1999)
19. SORBS, http://www.au.sorbs.net
20. Stone-Gross, B., Kruegel, C., Almeroth, K., Moser, A., Kirda, E.: FIRE: FInding Rogue nEtworks. In: Proc. Computer Security Applications Conference, ACSAC (2009)
21. The Spamhaus Project, http://www.spamhaus.org
22. Universität Bonn,
    http://net.cs.uni-bonn.de/wg/cs/applications/containing-conficker/
23. Weaver, R.: A probabilistic population study of the conficker-C botnet. In: Krishnamurthy, A., Plattner, B. (eds.) PAM 2010. LNCS, vol. 6032, pp. 181–190. Springer, Heidelberg (2010)
24. Wikipedia. Zlob trojan, http://en.wikipedia.org/wiki/Zlob_trojan
25. ZeuS Tracker, https://zeustracker.abuse.ch

What's Clicking What?
Techniques and Innovations of Today's Clickbots*

Brad Miller[1], Paul Pearce[1], Chris Grier[1,2], Christian Kreibich[2], and Vern Paxson[1,2]

[1] Computer Science Division
University of California Berkeley
{bmiller1,pearce,grier}@cs.berkeley.edu
[2] International Computer Science Institute
{christian,vern}@icir.org

Abstract. With the widespread adoption of Internet advertising, fraud has become a systemic problem. While the existence of *clickbots*—malware specialized for conducting *click-fraud*—has been known for a number of years, the actual functioning of these programs has seen little study. We examine the operation and underlying economic models of two families of modern clickbots, "Fiesta" and "7cy." By operating the malware specimens in a controlled environment we reverse-engineered the protocols used to direct the clickbots in their activities. We then devised a *milker* program that mimics clickbots requesting instructions, enabling us to extract over 360,000 click-fraud directives from the clickbots' control servers. We report on the functioning of the clickbots, the steps they employ to evade detection, variations in how their masters operate them depending on their geographic locality, and the differing economic models underlying their activity.

1 Introduction

Online advertising forms a vital part of the modern Internet economy. Millions of websites profit from an ecosystem of advertising networks and syndication chains. This widespread adoption of internet advertising has given rise to systematic fraud. The percentage of fraudulent ad clicks, called *click-fraud*, has steadily increased over recent years. Recent estimates suggest the fraud-rate is as high as 22% [8].

In the predominant form of click-fraud, a malicious party sets up a website filled with ads and deceives an advertising network into registering ad clicks, earning revenue for each click[1]. *Clickbots*, malware which automatically click on ads, can produce this fraudulent traffic. A challenge for clickbot operators is producing traffic in such a way that advertising agencies do not detect it as non-human or fraudulent.

In this study, we present an analysis of clickbot techniques and the associated infrastructure that supports click-fraud. We obtained samples of two clickbot families, which we named "Fiesta" and "7cy," in order to study the operation of clickbots. We executed the binaries in a controlled environment to prevent harmful side effects, such as actually participating in click-fraud. By monitoring the controlled execution of the bots, we

---

* Student co-leads listed alphabetically.
[1] In a second form of click-fraud, a malicious party deliberately focuses clicks on a competitors advertisements in an attempt to exhaust that party's advertising budget [18].

T. Holz and H. Bos. (Eds.): DMIVA 2011, LNCS 6739, pp. 164–183, 2011.

reverse-engineered their command and control (C&C) protocols to determine how the bots respond to the commands they receive. This analysis enabled us to develop C&C servers and websites for the bots to interact with, allowing greater exploration of bot behaviors. We then devised a *milker* program that mimics a clickbot requesting instructions, enabling us to extract 366,945 click-fraud directives from the clickbots' control servers.

Throughout our analysis, we compare both families of clickbots to Clickbot.A [9] in order to illuminate how clickbots have evolved in recent years. We find two major innovations. The first regards the underlying economic model used by the Fiesta family. In this model a middleman has emerged, acting as a layer of abstraction between ad syndicates and the clickbots that generate traffic. This middleman provides an intermediary between the traffic originator (bots and users) and the ad syndicates. Fiesta clickbots generate traffic that flows towards this middleman and is then laundered through a series of ad syndicates in an effort to hinder fraud detection.

The second innovation concerns complex behavior that attempts to emulate how humans browse the web. 7cy mimics a human browsing the web by both randomizing the click targets as well as introducing human-scale jitter to the time between clicks. Through the use of our milker we also discover that 7cy control servers distribute fraud directives that vary by the geographic region of the bot. Thus, while Fiesta generally uses indirection to accomplish click-fraud, 7cy uses random clicks, timing, and location-specific behavior to ostensibly present more realistic browsing behavior.

In § 2 we survey the related work in the field. § 3 describes our methodology for executing bots in a safe environment. § 4 discusses the Fiesta clickbot in depth, and § 5 looks at 7cy. We discuss potential defenses and then conclude in § 6.

2   Related Work

While there is a well-developed body of literature describing both botnets and click-fraud, there has been little work directly studying clickbots themselves. We discuss existing work dealing with clickbots, as well as tangential work describing the various aspects of click-fraud and botnets.

Clickbots: The only academic work analyzing the functionality of a botnet performing click-fraud focused on a bot named Clickbot.A [9]. Clickbot.A conducted low-noise click-fraud through the use of syndicated search engines. Daswani et al. employed a combination of execution, reverse-engineering, and server source code analysis to determine how Clickbot.A performed fraud. The clickbot used compromised web servers for HTTP-based C&C, and restricted the number of clicks performed for each bot, presumably to limit exposure to the ad agency. In addition to describing the botnet behavior, the investigators estimate the total fraud against Google using economic aspects of syndicate search and click pricing. Our work analyzes multiple clickbot specimens to understand the changes in both the economic model and bot operation in two modern clickbots. We expect that criminals are constantly improving bot technology in order to remain competitive against ad agencies that improve their fraud detection. Throughout this paper we use Clickbot.A as a reference for comparison.

Detecting Automated Search: Researchers have dedicated considerable effort to methods for differentiating search queries from automated and human sources. Yu et al. observe details of bot behavior in aggregate, using the characteristics of the queries to identify bots [23]. Buehrer et al. focus on bot-generated traffic and click-through designed to influence page-rank [3]. Kang et al. propose a learning approach to identify automated searches [15]. These efforts do not examine bot binaries or C&C structure, focusing instead on techniques for the search engine to identify automated traffic.

Defending Against Click-Fraud: Both academia and industry have explored click-fraud defenses. Tuzhilin studied Google's click-fraud countermeasures in response to a lawsuit filed against Google over potentially fraudulent clicks, and concluded that the countermeasures are reasonable [20]. Separately, academia has proposed purely technical solutions. Not-A-Bot (NAB) [11] combats bot activity through detection mechanisms at the client. In the NAB system the client machine has a trusted component that monitors keyboard and mouse input to attest to the legitimacy of individual requests to remote parties. In addition to NAB, Juels et al. likewise propose dealing with click-fraud by certifying some clicks as "premium" or "legitimate" using an attester instead of attempting to filter fraudulent clicks [14]. Kintana et al. created a system designed to penetrate click-fraud filters in order to discover detection vulnerabilities [16]. Our work complements click-fraud defenses by exploring the techniques clickbots use and has the potential to improve click-fraud detection.

Botnets: There is extensive work examining botnets and reverse-engineering bots and their C&C protocols [1, 5–7, 12, 13, 19]. Dispatcher is a technique that automatically reverse-engineers botnet C&C messages and was used to uncover details in the MegaD spamming botnet C&C protocol [5]. In a later work, Cho et al. used Dispatcher to conduct an extensive infiltration of the MegaD botnet, developing milkers to determine the C&C structure and mine data about the botnet's internal operations [7]. We employ a similar milking technique to explore the C&C structure of the clickbots under study.

3   Methodology

In this section we outline our environment and procedures for executing clickbots without risk of malicious side effects. We studied two "families" of clickbots, Fiesta and 7cy, within our experimental framework[2]. Since we obtained samples that did not have useful or consistent anti-virus labels we took the names Fiesta and 7cy from domain names the bots visited while performing click-fraud.

We obtained the Fiesta and 7cy samples by infiltrating several malware Pay-Per-Install (PPI) services as part of a larger study on malware distribution [4]. PPI services use varied means to compromise machines and then distribute malware to the compromised hosts in exchange for payment on the underground market [21]. We used behavioral characteristics to group multiple harvested binaries representing different

---

[2] The MD5 hashes of the Fiesta specimens are c9ad0880ad1db1eead7b9b08923471d6 and 5bae55ed0eb72a01d0f3a31901ff3b24. The hashes of the 7cy specimens are 7a1846f88c3fba1a 2b2a8794f2fac047, b25d0683a10a5fb684398ef09ad5553d, 36ca7b37bb6423acc446d0bf0722 4696, and 782538deca0acd550aac8bc97ee28a79.

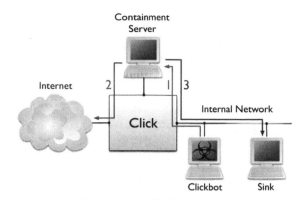

Fig. 1. Our basic containment architecture, showing how a containment server can interact with an infected VM and a "sink" server. The clickbot's communication is routed through the containment server (1), which can allow the traffic (perhaps modified) out to the Internet (2), or redirect it back into the farm to the sink (3).

versions of a given family of malware. We selected Fiesta and 7cy for further analysis because their connection behavior and content was the most interesting. A third potential clickbot family remains unanalyzed.

We executed the clickbots in virtual machines hosted on VMware ESX servers. A central gateway, implemented using Click [17], moderates network access for the VMs. The gateway routes each outbound connection to a "containment server" that decides on a per-flow basis whether traffic is forwarded, dropped, rewritten, or reflected back into the contained network. The containment server makes these decisions based on packet header information as well as packet content. Figure 1 shows a simplified view of this approach.

Given this architecture, we implemented containment policies that allowed us to execute the clickbot specimens safely. These policies required understanding the basic behavioral patterns of the bots and the other parties involved. This was an iterative process in which we repeatedly examined the bot behavior connection by connection, starting from a default-deny policy. Each step in this iterative process involved manually examining connections and packet payloads by hand to verify the nature of the communication. In some cases, this meant examining data logs, and in other cases it involved manually visiting websites. We white-listed connections deemed safe, and then restarted the bot in order to identify the next communication.

We needed the capability to replay pre-recorded communication and interact with the bot entirely within the farm in order to explore each clickbot's behavior and C&C protocol. Therefore, we built a special HTTP "sink" server that impersonated the destinations of outbound clickbot flows. This server allowed us to respond to network communication using a server under our control rather than releasing the traffic from the farm or dropping the flow. The sink server accepted all incoming connections and returned predefined responses as a function of the HTTP header data. Since the bot used HTTP for C&C as well as web browsing, we used the same HTTP server to simulate both C&C and web traffic. Initially, we replayed previously seen C&C responses. Then, we manually explored and perturbed the plain-text C&C protocol and fed these modified responses back into the bots within the farm. Using this technique we reverse-engineered much of the protocol used for both bot families. As we understood more of the C&C protocols, we modified the responses to change the behavior of the bot. Using our capability to replay previously observed communications and explore new communication variants, we accelerated our analysis and developed a broader understanding of the clickbots' behavior.

4   The Fiesta Clickbot

We selected the Fiesta clickbot as the first specimen for in-depth analysis. The primary innovation we discovered during this evaluation is the monetization opportunity created by separating traffic generation (bots) from ad network revenue. In this model intermediate pay-per-click (PPC) services "launder" clicks generated by bots and then deliver them to ad networks. The intermediate PPC service abstracts the botmaster from advertising networks and is a new development since the investigation into Clickbot.A. We have not found any record of the security community studying the Fiesta clickbot[3]. In this section we describe Fiesta's behavior and structure, then discuss an economic model for click-fraud based on our observations. We conclude with a discussion of the bot's prevalence.

4.1   C&C Structure

There are two key players in the operation of Fiesta: a botmaster running a C&C server, and the self-described "Fiesta Pay-Per-Click (PPC) Profitable Traffic Solution." Fiesta PPC operates a store-front complete with signup and forum services. Although we named this clickbot Fiesta after the Fiesta PPC service, we believe the PPC service and the botmaster to be separate entities with different economic incentives. This relationship is discussed further in § 4.2.

Immediately upon infection the Fiesta bot establishes an HTTP connection with the bot's C&C server. The server's IP address is statically coded into the binary and remains constant for the lifetime of the bot. Using this server, the bot performs a one-time connection that informs the C&C server that a new infection has occurred. After this initial connection the bot settles into a constant cycle of click-fraud. Figure 2 gives a high-level overview of Fiesta's behavior for a single click. One click constitutes one act of click-fraud and involves multiple queries to the C&C server and multiple interactions with web pages. We observed our Fiesta bot performing about three such clicks per minute.

A fraudulent click begins with Fiesta requesting a list of search query terms from its C&C server, shown as step 1 in Figure 2. In response the bot receives several hundred varied terms; Table 1 shows some samples. We observed these terms changing frequently, appearing arbitrary in nature, and containing typographical errors. Once the bot receives this query list, it randomly selects one term that it will use for the remainder of this click.

---

[3] One variant observed was classified by an Anti-Virus vendor as the parasitic Murofet trojan [2]. We believe this to be a case of mistaken identity resulting from a standard Fiesta binary becoming infected and playing host to an instance of Murofet.

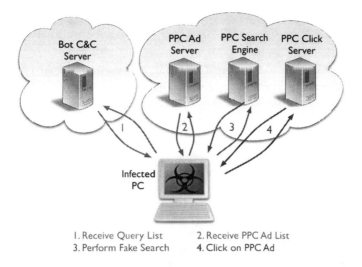

1. Receive Query List   2. Receive PPC Ad List
3. Perform Fake Search   4. Click on PPC Ad

Fig. 2. The basic behavioral architecture of the Fiesta clickbot. Communication occurs in the order specified by the numeric labels. This pattern repeats indefinitely.

Table 1. A sample of search query terms returned to the bot by the Bot C&C Server during a single exchange

nerdy shirts	cruise special	fifa world cup qualifiers
potato canon	among the hidden solution	kitchen aid dishwashers
ftv plus	scooby doo online games	yahoo real estate
online video	card cheap credit machine	oakland newspaper
cheap insurance life uk	camera disposable pentax	tapes on self help
celtic names	debt and consolidation	bozeman schools. mt
justin om	dallas nursing institute	anniversary gifts by year
vxb bearings	discount hotel booking	station nightclub fire video

After the bot selects a search query, the bot begins communicating with the Fiesta PPC service, labeled step 2 in Figure 2. Initially the bot performs a request to receive ads that correspond to the selected search query. In response, the PPC Ad Server returns approximately 25 ads in XML format. Figure 3 shows an example of the PPC Ad Server XML response. Information contained in each record includes an ad URL, title, keywords, and "bid." The PPC Ad Server returns ads that vary greatly. Some ads directly relate to the search, while others appear random. The bot selects one of the ads at random from the PPC Ad Server response, biasing its selection towards high bid values. After selecting an ad, the bot performs a search for the original search query at a search engine operated by the PPC service. The bot then informs the search engine which ad it is about to click via a separate HTTP request (step 3 in Figure 2). Lastly, the bot will contact the PPC Click Server and actually perform the ad click (step 4 in Figure 2).

The PPC Ad Server returns ad URLs that point to the PPC Click Server. Each ad URL contains a unique 190-character identifier that is used when the bot issues an HTTP request to the PPC Click Server to signal a click. The PPC Click Server responds

```
 1  <?xml version="1.0" encoding="UTF-8"?>
 2  <records>
 3   <query>u2 tour</query>
 4   ...
 5   <record>
 6    <title>Looking for u2 tour?</title>
 7    <description>Find u2 tour here!</description>
 8    <url>http://u2-tour.com</url>
 9    <clickurl>http://CLICK_SERVER/click.php?c=UNIQUE_ID</clickurl>
10    <bid>0.0004</bid>
11    <fi>52</fi>
12   </record>
13    ...
14   <record>
15    <title>Style Fashion Show Review</title>
16    <description>Chanel</description>
17    <url>http://www.style.com</url>
18    <clickurl>http://CLICK_SERVER/click.php?c=UNIQUE_ID</clickurl>
19    <bid>0.0023</bid>
20    <fi>39</fi>
21   </record>
22   ...
23  </records>
```

Fig. 3. Sample Fiesta ad C&C returned in response for a fake search for "u2 tour." The C&C syntax is abbreviated as necessary for space.

to all clicks with HTTP 302 redirect responses, beginning the fraudulent click. Figure 4 shows the process that occurs once the bot issues a request to the PPC Click Server, with arrows representing HTTP redirects. A single click will cause the bot to receive redirects to three or four different locations, eventually settling on a legitimate website such as style.com or accuweather.com. The resolution of this redirection chain completes a single act of click-fraud.

We believe the sites directly linked to the PPC Click Server along the redirection chains in Figure 4 are advertising sub-syndicates (i.e., entities that show ads generated by other ad networks in exchange for some portion of generated revenue) that have entered into syndication agreements with legitimate advertising services. The legitimate advertising services include *BidSystems* and *AdOn Network*. We believe some of the ad sub-syndicates are illegitimate based on other services hosted on the same IP addresses, as well as the frequency with which the sub-syndicate's IP addresses appear in malware reports.

Interestingly, the Fiesta bot issues requests to the Fiesta Ad Server with HTTP referrers from Fiesta search engines, yet performs searches *after* issuing ad requests. This implies that the PPC service could detect clicks occurring by this bot given the improper request ordering.

4.2   Fiesta Economic Model

Based on our observations of the Fiesta clickbot and our investigation of the Fiesta PPC service, we believe that we have identified the economic model of both the Fiesta PPC service and the Fiesta clickbot. This model introduces the notion of a click-fraud middleman whose job is to abstract ad revenue from the generation of fraudulent traffic.

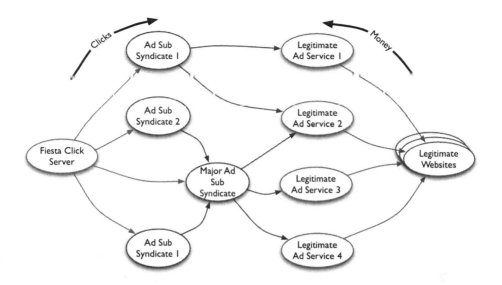

Fig. 4. The expanded Fiesta click redirection chain. This graph represents the possible redirection paths beginning with a click on the Fiesta click-server and ending at a legitimate website. One click will take one path through the graph. Redirections flow from left to right, and money flows from right to left.

This is a significant change in the economic structure of the click-fraud ecosystem that was not present for Clickbot.A.

We suspect that Fiesta PPC has entered into revenue sharing agreements with several advertising sub-syndicates. As part of this agreement, Fiesta PPC operates a search engine that displays the ad sub-syndicate's ads. Each of these ads is routed through the Fiesta Click Server. When an ad click occurs, the revenue is divided between the parties. The Fiesta PPC service then distributes the search engine traffic amongst their ad sub-syndicates through the use of the Fiesta PPC Click Server.

Investigation of the Fiesta PPC website supports these theories. The site contains links to traffic bid information based on region, web forums (which are currently not working), and an affiliate application form.

Inserting a middleman into the click-fraud path is an innovative structural development. A PPC service allows botmasters to generate revenue without regard to the specifics or defenses of advertising networks, while simultaneously allowing the middleman service to focus on ad revenue without engaging in traffic generation.

Concurrent with our own work, a separate study discovered a business relationship between the Fiesta PPC service and the operators of the Koobface botnet [22]. This study detailed the economics of Koobface, revealing that the botnet generated some of its revenue by interacting with various affiliate services in exchange for payment. Koobface utilized Fiesta PPC as an affiliate in addition to other PPC services. We believe the Fiesta bot operator has established a similar business relationship with the Fiesta PPC service.

4.3 Prevalence

We observed two different PPI services distributing Fiesta bots across a three month timespan. In one instance, a PPI service served the Fiesta bot binary for over 12 hours. Through creative use of the Google search engine combined with our own samples, we were able to locate four different C&C server IP addresses across three different domain names. Since the C&C server used by our bot was hard-coded into the binary and varied between dropper services, we suspect that Fiesta bots released via different mechanisms use different C&C servers. Using the same Google techniques, we have also identified 22 domain names that act as search engines for the Fiesta service, spread across three IP addresses.

5   The 7cy Clickbot

Clickbot.A, 7cy and Fiesta differ significantly in their behavior. While Fiesta and Click-bot.A use levels of indirection between organizations to launder clicks, 7cy attempts to evade detection by simulating human web-browsing behavior. The 7cy C&C language controls the bot's click behavior by specifying an initial site to "surf," a series of page content patterns for identifying desirable links to click on, and an inter-click delay time. The bot then leverages timing by introducing a random amount of jitter into the delay between clicks. Separately, the C&C directs the bot to generate more browsing traffic during popular times such as the evening and the workday. Compared to Fiesta, 7cy requires a substantially different C&C language and surrounding botmaster infrastructure, which we detail next.

5.1   C&C Structure

A 7cy bot locates the C&C server by resolving the domain name in.7cy.net, and then communicates with that server using HTTP. We show a sample C&C request in Figure 5. Line 1 includes the bot's network MAC address, presumably as a unique identifier. Line 3 presents a user-agent specific to the bot family, as well as a version number.

After receiving a request, the C&C server will respond with one of three messages: (*i*) an instruction to wait for a specified time period, (*ii*) an HTTP 302 response redirecting the bot to another C&C server, or (*iii*) specific click-fraud instructions. We refer to the latter as an instruction "batch." Each batch is comprised of "jobs," and each job is comprised of "clicks." Within a given batch, each job specifies a different site to target for click-fraud, and each click corresponds to an HTML link to visit. Jobs specify

```
1  GET /p6.asp?MAC=00-0C-29-24-29-12&Publicer=bigbuy HTTP/1.1
2  Host: in.7cy.net
3  User-Agent: ClickAdsByIE 0.7.4.3
4  Accept-Language: zh-cn,zh;q=0.5
5  Referer: http://in.7cy.net/p6.asp
6  Content-Type: application/x-www-form-urlencoded
7  Connection: Close
```

Fig. 5. Initial 7cy C&C request. The MAC-based bot ID and user-agent are shown in bold.

```
 1  http://housetitleinsurance.com
 2  http://www.google.com/url?sa=t&source=web&ct=res&cd=8&url=http://housetitleins...
 3  90
 4  15
 5  CLICK
 6  /'search/{|||}api={|||}yt={|||}qs
 7  RND
 8  5
 9  NOSCRIPT
```

Fig. 6. Excerpt of response from C&C server. Note that whitespace between lines is removed.

web-surfing sessions: their clicks are applied to sites as they result from previous clicks, rather than to the initial site. On average there are 18 jobs per batch and 9 clicks per job.

Figure 6 shows an excerpt of one batch. Lines 1 through 4 constitute a header for a single job. Line 1 specifies the website at which the bot should begin the browsing session. Line 2 specifies the referrer to use in the initial request to the target site, although an actual request to the referring site is never made. Line 3 specifies a time limit after which new instructions will be requested if the clicks have not been completed yet. Line 4 specifies the number of clicks in the job. The structure seen in lines 5 through 9 describes a particular click. This structure (with possibly different values) repeats the number of times denoted on line 4 to complete the job. Line 5 specifies the action to perform. Several values other than CLICK have been observed, but seem to be ignored by our specimens. Given the rarity of these other commands (less than 0.01% of total commands), we suspect they are erroneous, or a new feature still in testing. Line 6 specifies token patterns to search for on the current page when selecting the next click. Tokens are delimited by the five characters "{ | | | }". Line 8 specifies a time delay for the bot to wait before performing the next click. Once all clicks in the job are specified, a new job header occurs or the C&C transmission ends.

After receiving a batch of instructions from the C&C server, a bot will begin traversing web pages as described in the instructions. Many of the sites targeted by the bot are hosted at parked domains. Examples include housetitleinsurance.com, quickacting.com, and soprts.com. We call these websites *publishers*. These sites mainly consist of links and ads within the page body, and keywords in the HTML meta tag which relate to the theme suggested by the domain name. They may also provide a link to contact the owner and purchase the domain name.

Although the domains and advertising networks vary across jobs, the traffic patterns follow progressions that we can aggregate into a graph, shown in Figure 7. Edges correspond to HTTP requests made by the bot. The origin of an edge corresponds to the domain of the referrer used in the request, and destination of an edge corresponds to the host to which the request is made. The first HTTP request a bot makes in a job is always for the URL of the publisher's website, using a referrer header mimicking a previous Google search (not actually performed) which could plausibly lead the user to the publisher's website (step 1). Next, the bot loads the publisher's website as a browser would, fetching all supporting objects (pictures, scripts, etc.) as dictated by the initial request (steps 2, 3). Once the bot has downloaded the publisher's webpage, it selects an in-page ad matching the search pattern specified via C&C for clicking. If multiple

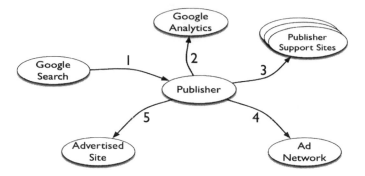

Fig. 7. General progression of a 7cy "job." Arrows represent HTTP requests and go from the domain of the refer to the domain of the host. Note that the publisher is often a parking page.

links on the page match the pattern, the bot makes a random selection. Each link on the webpage points to a "trampoline" page at the publisher's site, resulting in HTTP 302 redirects to the ad network and on to the actual advertised site. This behavior allows the publisher and the ad network to detect when the bot clicks on an ad. The bot follows this redirection chain (step 4) and loads the advertised site (step 5). A job often includes several clicks designed to simulate link-clicking behavior on the advertised site.

5.2   Specific Fraud Example

In order to demonstrate several details of the traffic produced by a 7cy bot, we now present excerpts of traffic from an actual job. In this job, the publisher is housetitleinsurance.com, the ad network is msn.com, and the advertised site is insureme.com. Figure 8 shows the bot's initial request to the publisher's website and the corresponding response. Note that as the bot is now issuing requests to published websites, the User-Agent presented in line 3 of the request has been changed to Mozilla/4.0 rather than ClickAdsByIE.

In this instance, after the bot had loaded the publisher's site the bot clicked on a link to the publisher's own domain. This caused the bot to send another series of requests to the publisher as the corresponding site was loaded. Throughout this exchange, we observed that the publisher changed a portion of the cookie originally set on the bot in Figure 8 and began including a value similar to the cookie in links included on the page. This is seen in Figures 8-10 as the bold portion of the cookie changes.

The use of cookies and referrers represents an increase in complexity over the techniques used by Clickbot.A [9]. Clickbot.A strips the referrer from requests in order to obscure the site at which the traffic originated. While there are plausible reasons for removing the referrer in normal use cases, removing the referrer does introduce a notable characteristic into the traffic. Likewise, cookies help the traffic produced by 7cy to appear more natural and could potentially be used to construct the illusion of a user or browsing session for an ad network.

The bot will ultimately browse away from the publisher's website when a request is issued to the ad network in order to obtain a redirect to the actual website being advertised. This request is shown in Figure 9. Note that this request uses a Referer

```
1 GET / HTTP/1.0
2 Referer: http://www.google.com/url?sa=t&source=web&ct=res&cd=8&url?sa=t&source...
3 User-Agent: Mozilla/4.0 (compatible; MSIE 6.0; Windows NT 5.1; SV1)
4 Host: housetitleinsurance.com
```

```
1 HTTP/1.1 200 OK
2 Cache-Control: no-cache
3 Pragma: no-cache
4 Content-Length: 13776
5 X-AspNet-Version: 4.0.30319
6 Set-Cookie: SessionID=6492595d-c592-419a-bf16-0cad97eef767; path=/
7 Set-Cookie: VisitorID=5f68a43f-6cf3-4a2f-831c-127ce007b646&Exp=11/29/2013 8:38...
8 Set-Cookie: yahooToken=qs=06oENya4ZG1YS6...HO8xG7uLE1uBAe5qKwGUov0xhAWIvfCJZ1E...
```

Fig. 8. Selected headers from request (top) and response (bottom) of a publisher's webpage

```
1 GET /?ld=4vnjCbJ-GAvwzaNZFHBC2hWDhbZSs2HbnQAVmreNgXqjJdTOCGnrnZiVXS01aPdMH1DdL...
2 Referer: http://housetitleinsurance.com/online/find/home/owner/find/home/owner...
3          ...yt=qs%3d06oENya4ZG1YS6...HO8xG7uLGV-ZMa5qKwGUov0xhAWIvfCJZ1EtVWLO1...
4 User-Agent: Mozilla/4.0 (compatible; MSIE 6.0; Windows NT 5.1; SV1)
5 Host: 948677.r.msn.com
```

```
1 HTTP/1.1 302 Object Moved
2 Cache-Control: no-cache, must-revalidate
3 Pragma: no-cache
4 Location: http://www.insureme.com/landing.aspx?Refby=614204&Type=home
5 Set-Cookie: MSConv=4vfcf6a1f935caa89943fce63a4bbf1574fc5c1f28c000945ebcd99d208...
6 Set-Cookie: MSAnalytics=4v76de0ef30bff74b972b5855ec3be14bc0c26342d22158a9ceaa6...
7 Content-Length: 202
```

Fig. 9. Selected request (top) and response (bottom) headers for an advertised site's URL

which includes a value similar to the `yahooToken` value previously set as a cookie on the bot by the publisher. The changed portion is shown in bold.

Lastly, a request is made to load the actual site being advertised. In this particular case the parking page has been moved within the same domain so a `301` redirect is issued. This is unrelated to the click-fraud infrastructure. As shown in Figure 10 this request also includes a referrer header which includes the `yahooToken` value used in other requests.

```
1 GET /landing.aspx?Refby=614204&Type=home HTTP/1.0
2 Referer: http://housetitleinsurance.com/online/find/home/owner/find/home/owner...
3          ...yt=qs%3d06oENya4ZG1YS6...HO8xG7uLGV-ZMa5qKwGUov0xhAWIvfCJZ1EtVWLO1...
4 User-Agent: Mozilla/4.0 (compatible; MSIE 6.0; Windows NT 5.1; SV1)
5 Host: www.insureme.com
```

```
1 HTTP/1.1 301 Moved Permanently
2 Cache-Control: no-cache, no-store
3 Pragma: no-cache
4 Content-Length: 44447
5 Location: http://www.insureme.com/home-insurance-quotes.html
6 Set-Cookie: ASP.NET_SessionId=4u4vxv45vupmetvi2f4ghoqu; path=/; HttpOnly
```

Fig. 10. Selected request (top) and response (bottom) headers for a request for an advertised site

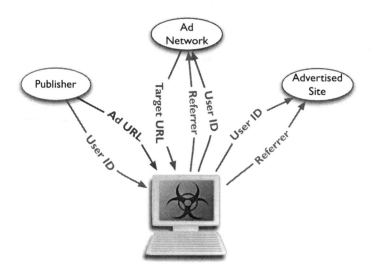

Fig. 11. Flow of critical information in 7cy click-fraud

We summarize the pattern of traffic described above in Figure 11. Each line corresponds to a piece of information and each bubble corresponds to a distinct server. The publisher's domain name is included in the referrer to both the ad network and the advertised site. The ad URL is supplied by the publisher and contains the domain of the ad network. The target URL is supplied by the ad network and contains the advertised site domain name. Lastly, the `yahooToken` likely containing a user ID is set by the publisher and given to the ad network and the advertised site.

5.3 7cy Economic Model

While the economic structure of 7cy is relatively clear, the parties involved and their roles are not. The pattern of traffic suggests that the advertised site (e.g., `insureme.com`) is paying the ad network (e.g., `msn.com`), which is paying the publisher (e.g., `housetitleinsurance.com`). Additionally, the domain names appear to be registered to multiple distinct parties. Unfortunately, it is unclear whether the publisher is paying the botmaster, or the publisher itself is the botmaster. If the publisher is paying the botmaster then it is unclear exactly how many distinct parties are acting as publishers.

5.4 Timing and Location Specific Behaviors

Timing Variance: In order to appear more human, the bot introduces jitter into the delays specified by the C&C language. The results labeled "Experiment" in Figure 12 show the differences we observed between the time delay specified in the C&C and the bot's actions in our contained environment. We conducted these measurements by feeding the bot artificial C&C with specific wait times while reflecting all HTTP traffic internally to a sink server within our farm. We then measured the inter-arrival time of requests at that sink. In order to confirm that the jitter observed was the result of the

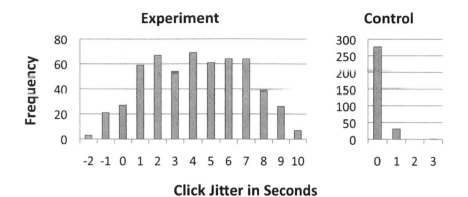

Fig. 12. Measurement of the amount of jitter introduced into inter-click delay by the clickbot binary and surrounding infrastructure compared to jitter introduced by infrastructure alone

bot's own behavior and not our honeyfarm environment, we also performed a control experiment in which we made HTTP requests at a constant rate from within an inmate VM, and then measured the variance in the same way as with the actual bot. The results labeled "Control" in Figure 12 indicate that the jitter introduced by the honeyfarm is infrequent, small, and always positive. Combined, these results show that the 7cy click-bot is introducing both positive and negative variance, on the order of seconds, into the inter-click delay.

Instructions Over Time: In order to gather data about the characteristics of the C&C over time and the influence of bot location on the behavior of control servers, we also conducted a C&C milking study of the 7cy infrastructure. As part of our study we build a milker which connected to 7cy C&C servers via Tor [10] exit nodes in 9 countries throughout North America, Europe and Asia. These countries were Canada (CA), Spain (ES), France (FR), Hong Kong (HK), Japan (JP), South Korea (KR), Russia (RU), Singapore (SG), and the United States (US).

Our milker mimics the behavior of a 7cy bot by contacting the 7cy C&C server and requesting work. We record all network traffic in the exchange, but do not carry out any of the fraud specified by the C&C server. Our milker is implemented entirely in Python and is approximately 370 lines of code. Our study milked the C&C server continuously for five days starting Thursday, January 13 2011, at 5am GMT.

All initial C&C requests, regardless of the Tor exit node, were sent to in.7cy. net. This mimicked the behavior we observed in our actual specimens. Recall from Section 5.1 that the C&C server's responses can be classified as "Wait" (delay for a fixed time period), "Moved" (a 302 redirect to another server), or "Batch" (instructions for click-fraud). On occasion the C&C server returned a 400-level error code, empty response, or no response, all of which we classify as "Other." When connecting from Japan, the C&C server occasionally returned a web page which seemed to be under development. We likewise classify this as "Other."

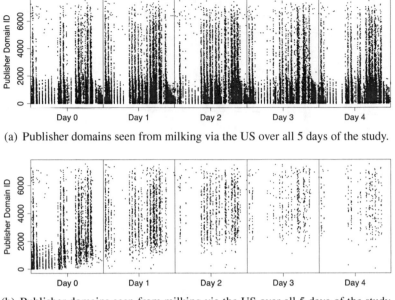

(a) Publisher domains seen from milking via the US over all 5 days of the study.

(b) Publisher domains seen from milking via the US over all 5 days of the study, with domains plotted only the first time they occur.

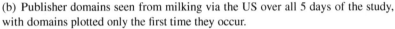

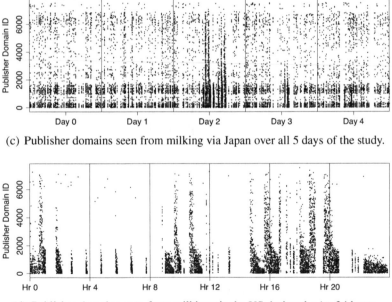

(c) Publisher domains seen from milking via Japan over all 5 days of the study.

(d) Publisher domains seen from milking via the US during the 1st 24 hours.

Fig. 13. The plots above show the domains the milker was directed to for click-fraud as a function of time. The vertical axis represents all domains observed, ordered from most frequently seen (bottom) to least frequently seen (top). Frequency was defined with respect to the entire study. Note that Day 0 begins at 5am GMT.

We observe that the C&C servers target some sites for click-fraud more often than others. The C&C samples obtained by our milker contained 366,945 jobs directing traffic towards 7,547 unique domains. An analysis of the traffic reveals that although 7,547 unique domains were seen across all countries, 75% of jobs targeted only 1,614 of the domains.

Figure 13 shows the domains targeted by the 7cy bots with respect to both country and time. The horizontal axis represents the time in seconds since the start of the milking study. The vertical axis is the sorted target domain ID, where domain 0 is the most targeted domain, and domain 7,546 is targeted least. Figure 13(a) plots the domains sent to our US Tor exit node milker over the 5 day period. The distinctive gaps in the data are the result of successive wait commands given to us by the C&C server. Figure 13(d) is an expanded view of the first day of Figure 13(a). We see that the server seems to work on an hourly cycle, dispensing a minimum amount of click-fraud instructions to the most trafficked sites each hour. The US exit node received more click-fraud instructions during peak US Internet use times, such as the work day and evening. In non-peak hours, the US exit node received more wait instructions to generate a lower volume of traffic. Interestingly, all exit nodes except Japan and Korea showed timing patterns in sync with the US despite time zone differences.

Japan and Korea, however, display a pattern similar to each other and distinct from other countries examined. Figure 13(c) shows domains served to the Japanese Tor exit nodes with respect to time, over the entire 5-day milking period. This figure shows the same distinctive bands, however the distances between bands and widths vary. While these countries do appear to have a strong, periodic schedule and do visit some sites considerably more than others, traffic appears to be distributed relatively uniformly throughout the day.

Figure 13(b) shows the same data as Figure 13(a) except all duplicate domains have been removed. This means once a specific domain has been observed at time t, it is no longer plotted for time greater than t. This figure illustrates that although there is a clear periodic pattern to the traffic, the domain names involved vary throughout the observed time. The other countries surveyed have similar behavior.

Beyond differences in timing, the distinct behavior seen in Japan and Korea is also characterized by differences in the C&C instructions received. Table 2 depicts the requests and responses made by the milker. Japan and Korea are redirected to 3.95622. com relatively frequently, although no other countries are directed there. Similarly, Russia, Spain, Germany, Hong Kong, Canada and the United States are redirected to 1. 95622.com, although Japan and Korea are rarely directed to that domain. Only Singapore received no redirects.

In addition to differences in traffic handling and timing, milked C&C revealed a correlation in which domains were served to which countries. In order to determine the degree of correlation between two countries, we calculate for each country the percentage of overlap of its domains to the two countries' combined set of domains. In order to develop a standard of correlation, Table 3 shows the result of correlating a randomly selected half of a country's traffic with the remaining half. This provides a standard for determining that two countries are similar. Pairwise analysis of countries revealed that all countries other than Japan and Korea are strongly correlated. These results are

Table 2. Types of C&C responses received at geographically diverse locations

Country	Host	Total Req.	Wait	Batch	Moved to 1.95622.com	Moved to 3.95622.com	Other
CA	1.95622.com	193	24	167	0	0	2
	in.7cy.net	2,947	338	2,360	193	0	56
ES	1.95622.com	217	35	178	0	0	4
	in.7cy.net	2,935	327	2,333	216	0	59
FR	1.95622.com	215	18	192	0	0	5
	in.7cy.net	2,883	336	2,252	215	0	80
HK	1.95622.com	323	26	290	0	0	7
	in.7cy.net	2,253	438	1,465	323	0	27
JP	1.95622.com	10	0	10	0	0	0
	3.95622.com	777	378	396	0	0	3
	in.7cy.net	1,656	176	292	10	778	400
KR	1.95622.com	1	1	0	0	0	0
	3.95622.com	1,191	598	590	0	0	3
	in.7cy.net	1,286	22	37	1	1,193	33
RU	1.95622.com	139	14	121	0	0	4
	in.7cy.net	3,520	259	3,048	139	0	74
SG	in.7cy.net	4,238	160	4,000	0	0	78
US	1.95622.com	225	29	194	0	0	2
	in.7cy.net	3,022	322	2,425	225	0	50

presented in more detail in Table 4, where we see that Japan and Korea are somewhat correlated with each other and relatively uncorrelated with the rest of the world.

Although there is a strong correlation between domains served and country, the cause for this correlation is not clear as the domains served to Japan and Korea appear similar to domains served to all other countries. The domains which are more common in Japan and Korea do not appear to host content in either Japanese or Korean nor contain ads specific to Japan or Korea. The correlation between Japanese and Korean IP addresses and domains served may be related to the ad network being targeted by the bot, rather than the target audience for the content on the domain. We speculate that perhaps some ad networks are more tolerant of or prefer traffic from one country as opposed to others, and so it is more profitable to direct traffic from those countries to those ad networks. As the format of the ad URL is determined by the ad network, this viewpoint is supported by the fact that a similar correlation was seen in tokens to search for in URLs to click on.

The location and time-specific behaviors displayed by 7cy represent a notable departure from the methods of Clickbot.A [9]. 7cy displays time-sensitive behavior both in the randomness introduced to inter-click timings as well as the variations of traffic load

Table 3. Correlation within each country if visits are partitioned randomly in half. Correlation is measured as the percent of domains seen in both halves which were seen in either half.

	CA	ES	FR	HK	JP	KR	RU	SG	US
Internal Correlation	63.7	61.7	59.8	55.6	43.7	65.2	68.0	74.4	63.0

Table 4. Correlation of domain names served to various countries. Note that all countries except Japan and Korea are strongly correlated to each other as evidenced by their correlation to the US.

	CA	ES	FR	HK	JP	KR	RU	SG	US
US	79.5	79.6	78.0	72.5	32.0	12.1	81.0	83.3	100.0
JP	32.2	32.2	31.8	32.7	100.0	42.6	31.5	31.4	32.0
KR	12.4	12.3	12.1	12.3	42.6	100.0	12.0	12.1	12.1

with respect to time-of-day. The evidence of location-specific behavior also represents an added degree of complexity over Clickbot.A. These behaviors make bot-generated traffic appear more realistic and represent an advance in emulating human behavior.

6   Discussion and Conclusion

We have presented an in-depth analysis of two distinct families of clickbots: Fiesta and 7cy. From our analysis we have derived extensive behavioral information about these families. This allowed us to establish a profile of the capabilities of the bots as well as the economic motives and incentives of the parties involved. Utilizing these insights into bot behavior and the structure of click-fraud systems, we are now able to discuss potential techniques for defenses and safeguards against bot-generated traffic.

Through our study of the Fiesta clickbot we have described a click-fraud model in which a service provider acts as a middleman for fraudulent traffic. The middleman pays money for generated traffic, and generates his own revenue through agreements with ad sub-syndicates. This previously undescribed approach could allow advances in traffic generation to be abstracted away from advances in hiding fraudulent clicks, potentially driving click-fraud innovation.

Studying the 7cy clickbot allowed us to observe the specific mechanisms employed by a clickbot attempting to mimic the behavior of a human. The C&C protocol allows the botmaster to dictate or sell traffic at a fine granularity. We observed the attempt to simulate human-like behaviors, including random browsing of the advertised site and randomized inter-click delays. By milking 366,945 click-fraud instructions from the C&C servers via IP addresses in 9 countries we were able to study this botnet's click-fraud in detail and discover region-specific behavior.

Having described the behavior of both the Fiesta and 7cy clickbots, we would like to offer a brief discussion of potential techniques for detecting bot-generated traffic. One approach sites could employ is to develop a set of features characteristic of legitimate traffic and flag browsing sessions which appear abnormal according to these features. Features which would address the bots seen in this paper include the user's mouse movements on the page and the depth of browsing through the site, as these bots differ significantly in these regards from a typical human. Advertised sites may further this technique by correlating atypical features with the domain name of the referrer, and in doing so build a list of publisher domains in use by botmasters. Another conceivable detector is the invisible embedding of HTML links into a site's pages. Any visitor clicking such "honeylinks" is likely to be a bot. In addition to the above suggestions for potential detection techniques, we have pursued collaboration with industry to enhance bot detection.

Building upon this work, we plan to further develop evasion techniques, our understanding of clickbot size and population diversity, and build a more complete taxonomy of modern clickbots.

Acknowledgements

We would like to thank Chia Yuan Cho for his assistance with our efforts to locate bot C&C via Google searches, Eric Brewer for his direction in project development, and the anonymous reviewers of this paper for their helpful guidance.

This work was supported by the Office of Naval Research (ONR) under MURI Grant No. N000140911081, the National Science Foundation (NSF) under Grant No. 0433702 and 0905631, and the Team for Research in Ubiquitous Secure Technology (TRUST). TRUST receives support from NSF Grant No. 0424422. Any opinions, findings, and conclusions or recommendations expressed in this material are those of the authors and do not necessarily reflect the views of ONR, NSF, or TRUST.

References

1. Abu Rajab, M., Zarfoss, J., Monrose, F., Terzis, A.: A Multifaceted Approach to Understanding the Botnet Phenomenon. In: Proc. of SIGCOMM (2006)
2. Bodmer, S., Vandegrift, M.: Looking Back at Murofet, a ZeuSbot Variants Active History (November 2010) http://blog.damballa.com/?p=1008
3. Buehrer, G., Stokes, J.W., Chellapilla, K.: A Large-scale Study of Automated Web Search Traffic. In: Proc. of Workshop on Adversarial Information Retrieval on the Web (2008)
4. Caballero, J., Grier, C., Kreibich, C., Paxson, V.: Measuring Pay-per-Install: The Commoditization of Malware Distribution. In: Proc. of the USENIX Security (2011)
5. Caballero, J., Poosankam, P., Kreibich, C., Song, D.: Dispatcher: Enabling Active Botnet Infiltration using Automatic Protocol Reverse-Engineering. In: Proc. of ACM CCS (2009)
6. Chiang, K., Lloyd, L.: A Case Study of the Rustock Rootkit and Spam Bot. In: Proc. of the 1st Workshop on Hot Topics in Understanding Botnets, USENIX Association (2007)
7. Cho, C.Y., Caballero, J., Grier, C., Paxson, V., Song, D.: Insights from the Inside: A View of Botnet Management from Infiltration. In: Proc. of LEET (2010)
8. Click Fraud Rate Rises to 22.3 Percent in Q3 2010 (October 2010), http://www.clickforensics.com/newsroom/press-releases/170-click-fraud-rate-rises-to-223-percent-in-q3-2010.html
9. Daswani, N., Stoppelman, M.: The Anatomy of Clickbot.A. In: Proc. of the Workshop on Hot Topics in Understanding Botnets (2007)
10. Dingledine, R., Mathewson, N., Syverson, P.: Tor: The Second-Generation Onion Router. In: Proc. of USENIX Security (2004)
11. Gummadi, R., Balakrishnan, H., Maniatis, P., Ratnasamy, S.: Not-a-Bot: Improving Service Availability in the Face of Botnet Attacks. In: Proc. of the 6th USENIX Symposium on Networked Systems Design and Implementation, pp. 307–320 (2009)
12. Holz, T., Steiner, M., Dahl, F., Biersack, E., Freiling, F.: Measurements and Mitigation of Peer-to-Peer-based Botnets: A Case Study on Storm Worm. In: Proc. of the LEET (2008)
13. John, J.P., Moshchuk, A., Gribble, S.D., Krishnamurthy, A.: Studying Spamming Botnets Using Botlab. In: Proc. of the USENIX NSDI (2009)
14. Juels, A., Stamm, S., Jakobsson, M.: Combating Click Fraud Via Premium Clicks. In: Proc. of the USENIX Security (2007)

15. Kang, H., Wang, K., Soukal, D., Behr, F., Zheng, Z.: Large-scale Bot Detection for Search Engines. In: Proc. of WWW (2010)
16. Kintana, C., Turner, D., Pan, J.Y., Metwally, A., Daswani, N., Chin, E., Bortz, A.: The Goals and Challenges of Click Fraud Penetration Testing Systems. In: Proc. of the Intl. Symposium on Software Reliability Engineering (2009)
17. Kohler, E., Morris, R., Chen, B., Jannotti, J., Kaashoek, M.F.: The Click Modular Router. ACM Transactions Computer Systems 18, 263–297 (2000), http://doi.acm.org/10.1145/354871.354874
18. Kshetri, N.: The Economics of Click Fraud. IEEE Security Privacy 8, 45–53 (2010)
19. Polychronakis, M., Mavrommatis, P., Provos, N.: Ghost turns Zombie: Exploring the Life Cycle of Web-based Malware. In: Proc. of LEET (2008)
20. Tuzhilin, A.: The Lane's Gift vs. Google Report (2006) ,http://googleblog.blogspot.com/pdf/Tuzhilin_Report.pdf
21. The Underground Economy of the Pay-Per-Install (PPI) Business (September 2009), http://www.secureworks.com/research/threats/ppi
22. Villeneuve, N.: Koobface: Inside a Crimeware Network (November 2010), http://www.infowar-monitor.net/reports/iwm-koobface.pdf
23. Yu, F., Xie, Y., Ke, Q.: SBotMiner: Large Scale Search Bot Detection. In: Proc. of the Intl. Conference on Web Search and Data Mining (2010)

MISHIMA: Multilateration of Internet Hosts Hidden Using Malicious Fast-Flux Agents (Short Paper)

Greg Banks, Aristide Fattori, Richard Kemmerer,
Christopher Kruegel, and Giovanni Vigna

University of California, Santa Barbara
{nomed,joystick,kemm,chris,vigna}@cs.ucsb.edu

Abstract. Fast-flux botnets are a growing security concern on the Internet. At their core, these botnets are a large collection of geographically-dispersed, compromised machines that act as proxies to hide the location of the host, commonly referred to as the "mothership," to/from which they are proxying traffic. Fast-flux botnets pose a serious problem to botnet take-down efforts. The reason is that, while it is typically easy to identify and consequently shut down single bots, locating the mothership behind a cloud of dynamically changing proxies is a difficult task.

This paper presents techniques that utilize characteristics inherent in fast-flux service networks to thwart the very purpose for which they are used. Namely, we leverage the geographically-dispersed set of proxy hosts to locate (multilaterate) the position of the mothership in an abstract n-dimensional space. In this space, the distance between a pair of network coordinates is the round-trip time between the hosts they represent in the network. To map network coordinates to actual IP addresses, we built an IP graph that models the Internet. In this IP graph, nodes are Class C subnets and edges are routes between these subnets. By combining information obtained by calculating network coordinates and the IP graph, we are able to establish a group of subnets to which a mothership likely belongs.

1 Introduction

In recent years, there has been a dramatic change in the goals and modes of operation of malicious hackers. As hackers have realized the potential monetary gains associated with Internet fraud, there has been a shift from "hacking for fun" [1] to "hacking for profit" [2]. As part of this shift, cybercriminals realized that it was necessary to create large-scale infrastructures to provide services (e.g., spam delivery) and protect important parts of their operations from identification and countermeasures. To this end, botnets and fast-flux networks were introduced.

Botnets are sets of compromised hosts (usually thousands) that are under the control of an attacker, who can then use them to provide services and perform distributed attacks. Hosts in a botnet can also be used as reverse web proxies to serve the content of malicious web sites. In this case, the proxying bots are usually organized as a fast-flux service network [3].

T. Holz and H. Bos. (Eds.): DMIVA 2011, LNCS 6739, pp. 184–193, 2011.

In a fast-flux service network, the hosts associated with a domain name are constantly changed to make it harder to block the delivery of the malicious web pages and effectively hide the address of the actual web server, often referred to as the "mothership." A number of countermeasures against botnets have been proposed, but none of these is able to address the problem of identifying the location of mothership hosts with good approximation.

In this paper, we present a novel approach that utilizes characteristics inherent in fast-flux service networks to thwart the very purpose for which they are used. Namely, we leverage the geographically-dispersed set of proxy hosts in order to multilaterate (more commonly, and mistakenly, referred to as "triangulate") the position of the mothership host in an abstract n-dimensional space. In this space, the distance between a pair of coordinates is the round-trip time between the hosts they represent in the network. Unfortunately, calculating the network coordinates of a host does not give any information about its IP address. To overcome this limitation, we built an IP graph that models the Internet. In this graph, nodes represent Class C subnets and edges represent routes between these subnets. This IP graph is then used to map network coordinates to a set of likely IP addresses. This leads to a significant reduction of the effort needed to shutdown a fast-flux botnet's mothership.

This paper makes the following two main contributions: (I) we introduce a novel approach to compute the location of a mothership host that is hidden behind a fast-flux service network; (II) we create an IP graph representing a model of the Internet topology, which allows us to map network coordinates to actual Class C subnets.

2   Background and Related Work

Given the continuous rise in malicious botnet activity, there has been a significant amount of recent work both in botnet analysis and botnet mitigation. Analysis efforts [2,4,5] have attempted to quantify the number and sizes of botnets. As for mitigation, researchers examined the life cycle of bots [6] and, in particular, the command and control (C&C) channels that are used to exchange information between a botmaster and the infected machines.

2.1   Fast-Flux Service Networks

A particularly troubling development related to botnets is the advent of fast-flux service networks. In a nutshell, fast-flux service networks utilize existing botnets to hide a particular resource or server. This server is generally a host to phishing scams or malicious web content that attempts to infect the end user. Two types of fast-flux networks have been observed in the wild: single-flux and double-flux. In single-flux networks, the DNS A records for a domain are constantly updated with the addresses of bots that act as reverse proxies for the content associated with the domain. Double-flux networks add a second layer of redirection to this scheme. In these networks, the NS records associated with the authoritative name servers for a malicious domain are also short-lived and rotated.

Much of the work involving fast-flux networks has been related to detection and understanding. Holz *et al.* identify the issue and suggest metrics for detection [7]. The authors characterize fast-flux service networks and introduce a function to calculate the "flux-score" for a domain. Similarly, Passerini *et al.* developed a tool, called FluXOR, to detect and monitor fast-flux service networks [8]. Nazario *et al.* use a globally distributed set of honeypots to collect suspect domains, which are then analyzed according to a set of heuristics and identified as being hosted by a fast-flux service network or not [9].

Even though the approaches mentioned above represent a fundamental step toward understanding and detecting fast-flux networks, none of them is able to determine or characterize the location of a mothership. Thus, they assume that the fast-flux service network provides an impenetrable cloaking mechanism to the mothership host.

2.2   Network Coordinates

While fast-flux networks are able to hide much about the mothership, they still expose round-trip times and provide a large number of beacons (e.g., bots acting as reverse proxies) through which to communicate. Similar prerequisites (i.e., beacons and a distance metric) are necessary for systems dealing with location estimation, such as GPS, triangulation, and multilateration, all of which have an Internet counterpart: network coordinate systems.

Techniques dealing with network coordinate systems were first developed to predict Internet latencies. One of the early approaches to predict latency between hosts was a service called IDMaps [10]. The problem with this method is that it requires an additional underlying infrastructure for which the end user is just a client. Ng and Zhang proposed a different method, called global network positioning (GNP), by which Internet hosts interested in latency prediction would interactively participate to create a model of the network as a 3-dimensional Euclidean space [11]. Given this model, each host in the network is assigned a set of coordinates. Latency estimation then becomes a simple calculation of Euclidean distance given the coordinates of two hosts. In 2004, Dabek *et al.* developed a network coordinate system called Vivaldi, which is based on GNP [12]. Vivaldi describes the network as a series of nodes connected by springs and tries to minimize the energy in this network. In this way, each node in the network has a push or pull effect on neighboring nodes and the system settles or converges on a set of coordinates that accurately predicts latencies. Costa *et al.* developed the PIC algorithm around the same time as Vivaldi [13]. PIC also builds on GNP using the same idea of a multi-dimensional space to model network latencies.

A concurrent work by Castelluccia *et al.* was developed simultaneously to MISHIMA [14]. The technique presented in this work aims at geolocalizing proxied services, with a particular focus on fast-flux hidden servers. Their approach is somewhat similar to ours, as they also use multilateration of Internet hosts, but we believe their technique to be both less precise and less complete. The reason is that they can only give an idea of the geographical location of a fast-flux server with an approximation of 100 km^2 or more. This makes it difficult to actually identify the network location (IP address) of a host and the network carrier responsible for take-down.

3   Approach

We developed a system, called MISHIMA (Multilateration of Internet hostS Hidden usIng Malicious fast-flux Agents), to actively calculate the coordinates of motherships associated with various domains that have been identified as being hosted by fast-flux service networks. Our main goal in doing this is to determine the location of a mothership, where by "location," we mean a Class C subnet (or a set of them) to which the mothership likely belongs.

Our approach to fast-flux mothership multilateration works in three steps: In the first step, we make use of existing network coordinate calculation techniques to determine the coordinates of the various proxies, or bots, that are part of a proxy network for a particular fast-flux domain. The coordinates of a proxy (or, in general, any host) represent a point in an n-dimensional Euclidean space where the measure of *distance* between hosts is their round-trip time (RTT). In the second step, we utilize three characteristics of fast-flux service networks in order to multilaterate the position of the mothership that is used to host the actual content for a domain. In the third step, we use network coordinates and attempt to map them to IP addresses, using a network model of the Internet.

3.1   Calculation of Proxy Network Coordinates

We calculate the network coordinates for the proxies of a fast-flux service network using the algorithm by Costa *et al.* [13], while incorporating ideas by Gummadi *et al.* [15] and Ledlie *et al.* [16]. Costa *et al.* provide a general algorithm to calculate the network coordinates for hosts in an n-dimensional space given the measurement of actual round-trip times between hosts. The goal of the coordinate system is to be able to estimate the latency between two hosts whose coordinates are known, by calculating the Euclidean distance between the coordinates. This means that two nodes who lie close to each other in the coordinate space are likely in the same network, while those that lie far away from each other are likely in different networks.

Network coordinate systems require a large number of geographically-dispersed beacons to perform well [11]. A *legitimate* resource available to the research community that fits these characteristics is PlanetLab. Therefore, we make use of approximately 150-200 PlanetLab nodes distributed throughout North America, Europe, and Asia at any given time.

For our system, we need to know the coordinates of these beacons as well as their distance from a target (which we get using various probing techniques). We have created a centralized database containing a large number of coordinates. This allows us to do a simple linear scan over the appropriate nodes to find the closest ones. In the case that we have no coordinates for a particular target, we have to estimate them *before* we can actually find their closest nodes. To this end, we first use random nodes (beacons) to estimate the coordinates of the target, and then scan the database of known coordinates to find beacons that are close to it.

In addition to having a large number of geographically-dispersed beacons, we also need a supply of malicious domains to work with. To this end, we utilize two sources: the Arbor Networks Atlas repository [17] and a locally-collected repository of domains harvested from the .COM zone file. The DNS resource records for each domain are checked against a simple set of heuristics throughout the process to determine whether they are still hosted by fast-flux networks. The heuristics used are as follows:

- There must be at least nine distinct A records associated with the domain.
- The TTL associated with each record must be less than 1,000 seconds.
- The percentage of A records from the same /16 must be less than 70.
- The NS records for a query must not belong to a small blacklist of those used to "park" domains.

Unlike most network coordinates studies, we have very specific constraints on our ability to probe the machines whose coordinates we want to calculate. Traditionally, latency measurements are performed using ICMP echo probes or some application-level probe (usually UDP-based), in the case that ICMP probes are filtered. For our purposes, we use directed TCP-based application-level probes in the case of both fast-flux agents and mothership network coordinate calculations, and ICMP-based echo probes for our PlanetLab (beacon) nodes. In fact, we have to use TCP-based probes in the case of the proxy agents for two reasons: first, since most of the fast-flux agents reside in residential and DHCP assigned networks, ICMP ping probes are filtered; second, we need a way to measure the round-trip-time from the proxy node to the mothership. To calculate the RTT to the mothership, we measure the RTT to the proxy as the time difference from the outgoing TCP packet containing the GET request to its respective ACK. The RTT from the proxy to the mothership is the time difference between the outgoing GET request and the incoming HTTP response minus the RTT to the proxy node.

To calculate the network coordinates for a target given the RTTs extracted from our probes, we use the Nelder-Mead simplex method using the sum of the squared relative errors between the actual distance and the predicted distance as the objective function to be minimized.

3.2   Mothership Network Coordinate Calculation

We calculate the network coordinates for a mothership by leveraging a side-effect of the first step. More precisely, in calculating the network coordinates for a fast-flux proxy node we are also able to estimate the RTT to the mothership from the proxy. Since we can estimate the RTT from a proxy to the mothership and we are able to calculate the coordinates of hundreds, or even thousands, of proxies associated with a particular mothership, we satisfy the two prerequisites for multilateration: (1) a significant number of geographically-dispersed beacon nodes, and (2) distance measurements from those beacons to the node whose coordinates are unknown. By doing this, we can use the algorithm by Costa et al. [13] using these proxies and their RTTs as input.

We need to calculate the coordinates for at *least* sixteen proxies before we attempt to calculate the coordinates of a mothership. In our implementation, we consider a domain ready for mothership multilateration when we have calculated the coordinates for at least 100 proxies. This gives us enough beacons to calculate at least eight coordinates for the mothership using the hybrid approach in [13], the flexibility to choose a varied set of beacons, and the opportunity to discard outliers.

3.3   IP Graph

Even if it is possible to determine the network coordinates of a mothership, this information does not allow one to directly determine the corresponding IP address. Therefore, we need a way to map the network coordinates of a host to its IP address (or a set of likely IP addresses). To do this, we first build an IP graph. In this graph, nodes are Class C subnets and edges represent routes between these subnets.

To build the IP graph, we made use of the CAIDA topology datasets [18]. This data is generated through the use of geographically-distributed machines that continuously calculate routes toward a large set of hosts, and it is made available daily, thus granting very up-to-date data. To create our graph, we parse all CAIDA data but we take into consideration only Class C subnets, as routing information within the same subnet is too fine-grained for our purposes.

Once the IP graph has been built, we pre-compute the network coordinates for a large number of IP addresses on the Internet. Then, given the network coordinates of a particular machine of interest, we can find all nodes in the IP graph that have close (pre-computed) network coordinates. After that, we use the IP graph (and its edges) to look for other nodes that are close. These nodes represent likely Class C networks where the machine of interest is located.

More precisely, the algorithm works as follows: We first calculate the set K of the n nearest networks to the target t, of which we only know the network coordinates NC. To determine which networks are in this set, we calculate the Euclidean distance between every node in the IP graph G and NC, and we pick the n closest nodes. Then, for each $k \in K$, we compute the set of nodes that are reachable from k via a maximum number d of hops in G, and we call these sets of close nodes *candidate sets* C_k. Finally, we create the set K' that contains only the nodes that appear in a certain percentage p of the candidate sets C_k generated during the previous step. Of course, K' will contain some nodes that are far away from t. We prune these nodes by eliminating all nodes that are farther away from t than a given threshold.

In Figure 1, we show a simple example of this technique applied to a small partition of the graph. Assume t is our target, $d = 2$, $p = 1$ (100%), and the set of closest nodes, based only on the Euclidean distance computed from network coordinates, is $K := \{a, b, c\}$. As we explained before, we take every element of K, and, for each element, we find all the nodes in G that are a maximum number of hops d away. This results in the new sets C_a, C_b, and C_c, marked in the example with a dotted, a full, and a dashed line, respectively. We then compute the intersection of these three sets. In these example, the result is the set $K' := \{a, t\}$. In real-world cases, the sets C_k can become quite large. For this reason, as we will show in Section 4, a choice of $p < 1$ leads to better results.

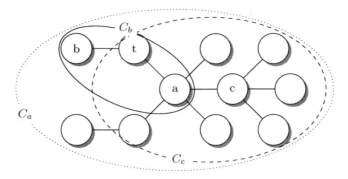

Fig. 1. From Network Coordinates to Subnet(s)

4   Experimental Results

In a first test, we picked a set of known hosts (targets). We then computed their network coordinates and evaluated the effectiveness of our approach to map these network coordinates back to IP addresses. More precisely, we applied our technique to eight distinct hosts, using different settings for p (the fraction of candidate sets in which a Class C network must appear before it is reported in the results). A larger value of p results in fewer networks that are reported (that is, the result set is tighter). On the other hand, it is also more likely that the true location of a host is missed. All experiments have been performed with $n = 10$, $d = 2$, and $threshold = 10$.

In Table 1, we report the results of our experiments. For each target host, we show the percentage of candidate sets to which a node (network) must belong to

Table 1. Real-World Experiments

Target	p	Intersection	Found	Target	p	Intersection	Found
128.111.4.0	100%	2	✓	159.149.153.0	100%	0	
128.111.4.0	50%	75	✓	159.149.153.0	50%	2	
128.111.4.0	30%	75	✓	159.149.153.0	30%	31	✓
128.111.4.0	10%	75	✓	159.149.153.0	10%	31	✓
114.108.44.0	100%	0		99.54.140.0	100%	0	
114.108.44.0	50%	6		99.54.140.0	50%	0	
114.108.44.0	30%	54	✓	99.54.140.0	30%	0	
114.108.44.0	10%	77	✓	99.54.140.0	10%	1	
85.17.143.0	100%	1		114.108.82.0	100%	0	
85.17.143.0	50%	48	✓	114.108.82.0	50%	6	
85.17.143.0	30%	48	✓	114.108.82.0	30%	71	✓
85.17.143.0	10%	82	✓	114.108.82.0	10%	71	✓
59.136.176.0	100%	0		93.160.107.1	100%	0	
59.136.176.0	50%	149	✓	93.160.107.1	50%	2	
59.136.176.0	30%	196	✓	93.160.107.1	30%	10	
59.136.176.0	10%	222	✓	93.160.107.1	10%	115	✓

be reported in the detection results (column p) as well as the number of Class C networks that appear in the result set (column *intersection*). We also report whether the true target was part of the result set.

From Table 1, we can see that a value of $p = 30$ seems to offer a good trade-off between detection and precision. That is, in 6 out of 8 cases, the true location of the network was detected, and the number of potential Class C networks is typically less than a hundred. It is interesting to note that we are not able to find any non-empty intersection (except for $p = 10\%$) when looking for the target subnet 99.54.140.0/24. We investigated the reason for this, and we discovered that we have very little knowledge of the network coordinates of nodes close to this subnet. Because of this, the elements belonging to the set of closest nodes are at a medium distance of 30 from the target, while in the other successful cases we have a medium distance between 0.5 and 8. Therefore, knowing the network coordinates of hosts in the neighborhood of the target is a prerequisite to be able to determine a set of nodes to which the target likely belongs.

We also performed our tests with different parameter settings for the number of initial nodes n, the distance d, and the threshold t. For space reasons, we can discuss these results only briefly. When using $d = 3$ instead of $d = 2$, the results remain similar, but the precision starts to decrease and the result sets grow. Also, changing the initial number of near nodes n does not improve the results significantly. The most interesting parameter was the *threshold* value. Indeed, by using a *threshold* smaller than 10, we can reduce the size of the intersection considerably. For example, with a *threshold* = 2, we can prune the intersection to two nodes, or even to one, and still find our target. However, we decided to use a more conservative approach (*threshold* = 10) since, in the case of real-world motherships, we have to take into account noise.

We also investigated how many different Autonomous Systems (AS) cover the subnets in the resulting intersection. Our findings are encouraging. In fact, in most of our experiments, all of the subnets contained in the intersection belong to the same AS. This can help in obtaining a more precise identification of the mothership, as, once we discover the AS to which the mothership belongs, it could be possible to start a collaboration with the corresponding ISP or institution to analyze network traffic or to perform scanning in the AS network in order to detect the mothership with greater precision.

To demonstrate the effectiveness of our approach on a real-world botnet, we decided to analyze the then-active Waledac botnet. To do this, we fed four fast-flux domains associated with this botnet to MISHIMA and we identified 335 hosts that are acting as proxies for its mothership. Next, we calculated their network coordinates and ran the IP detection algorithm. This yielded 48 Class C subnets where the mothership was likely located. To confirm our result, we set up a honeypot Windows XP machine and infected it with the latest sample of the malware associated with Waledac. To get the most up to date sample, we retrieved it directly from botnet hosts that are serving it. By doing this, we were able to infiltrate the botnet and discover the mothership IP address. We were able to successfully confirm that the actual mothership was in one of the 48 networks that we found. We want to point out that the knowledge of the IP address of the mothership has been used **only** to validate our results and not, in any way, to determine the set where the mothership might have been located.

5   Attacks & Shortcomings

There are several ways in which a knowledgeable attacker might try to prevent the correct identification of the mothership's location.

First, fast-flux proxies could artificially delay the HTTP responses that we require for our probes, thus invalidating our coordinate calculations. If this delay were a static value, our coordinates would simply represent a point far away in the coordinate space from the actual coordinates. If the delay was random, we would only be able to calculate the general area where the mothership would likely lie. Over the course of our measurements, we did not see anything that indicated this behavior was taking place.

Second, since we are heavily reliant on a relatively large number of probes to each beacon, we cannot deal with proxies that recognize this behavior and cease to proxy connections. We saw this behavior with some domains (e.g., a request to a domain from the same IP address within a few-minutes period would only return the malicious web page for the first several requests). The most likely method to mitigate this attack would be to throttle our probes to an appropriate speed.

Third, there are several network topologies that would confuse our measurements and invalidate the coordinates we calculate. If the proxies are set up to load-balance requests among a number of motherships, we will most likely calculate incorrect, or at least inconsistent, coordinates. Currently, we assume that there is exactly one mothership. If this is not the case, the RTTs associated with our probes will conflict, and our results will likely resemble those in the case of random artificial delay being inserted into our probes. Even though it may be possible to identify and cluster RTTs in an effort to identify those that were destined for a different mothership, we did not see results that indicated that load-balancing was being performed.

6   Conclusions

We have presented *MISHIMA*, a system that helps to automatically identify and cluster fast-flux hosted domains by their respective motherships. By integrating our knowledge of network coordinates and of the Internet topology, we are able to determine a set of subnets to which the mothership likely belongs. Last but not least, *MISHIMA* goes beyond previous heuristic-based approaches to mothership clustering and makes use of more robust characteristics at the network and application level, allowing it to identify motherships in spite of the presence of different fast-flux service networks and disparate web content. In conclusion, we believe that *MISHIMA* will constitute a useful contribution to the efforts undertaken to counteract the threat of fast-flux botnets.

References

1. Bailey, M., Cooke, E., Jahanian, F., Watson, D., Nazario, J.: The Blaster Worm: Then and Now. In: IEEE Security & Privace, pp. 26–31 (2005)
2. Cooke, E., Jahanian, F., McPherson, D.: The Zombie Roundup: Understanding, Detecting, and Disrupting Botnets. In: Proceedings of the USENIX SRUTI Workshop, pp. 39–44 (2005)
3. The Honeynet Project: Know Your Enemy: Fast-Flux Service Networks (2007), www.honeynet.org/book/export/html/130
4. Freiling, F., Holz, T., Wicherski, G.: Botnet Tracking: Exploring a Root-Cause Methodology to Prevent Distributed Denial-of-Service Attacks. In: 10th European Symposium On Research In Computer Security (2005)
5. Rajab, M.A., Zarfoss, J., Monrose, F., Terzis, A.: A Multifaceted Approach to Understanding the Botnet Phenomenon. In: 6th ACM SIGCOMM Internet Measurement Conference, IMC (2006)
6. Gu, G., Porras, P., Yegneswaran, V., Fong, M., Lee, W.: BotHunter: Detecting Malware Infection Through IDS-Driven Dialog Correlation. In: Proceedings of the 16th USENIX Security Symposium (2007)
7. Holz, T., Gorecki, C., Rieck, K., Freiling, F.C.: Measuring and detecting fast-flux service networks. In: Network & Distributed System Security Symposium (2008)
8. Passerini, E., Paleari, R., Martignoni, L., Bruschi, D.: FluXOR: Detecting and Monitoring Fast-Flux Service Networks. LNCS (2008)
9. Nazario, J., Holz, T.: As the Net Churns: Fast-Flux Botnet Observations. In: Conference on Malicious and Unwanted Software, Malware 2008 (2008)
10. Francis, P., Jamin, S., Jin, C., Jin, Y., Raz, D., Shavitt, Y., Zhang, L.: IDMaps: A Global Internet Host Distance Estimation Service. IEEE/ACM Transactions on Networking 9(5), 525 (2001)
11. Ng, T., Zhang, H.: Towards global network positioning. In: Proceedings of the 1st ACM SIGCOMM Workshop on Internet Measurement, pp. 25–29. ACM, New York (2001)
12. Dabek, F., Cox, R., Kaashoek, F., Morris, R.: Vivaldi: a decentralized network coordinate system. ACM SIGCOMM Computer Communication Review 34(4), 15–26 (2004)
13. Costa, M., Castro, M., Rowstron, R., Key, P.: PIC: Practical Internet Coordinates for Distance Estimation. In: Proceedings of the International Conference on Distributed Computing Systems, pp. 178–187 (2004)
14. Castelluccia, C., Kaafar, D., Perito Pente, D.: Geolocalization of Proxied Services and its Application to Fast-Flux Hidden Servers. In: 9th ACM SIGCOMM Internet Measurement Conference, IMC (2009)
15. Gummadi, K., Saroiu, S., Gfibble, S.: King: Estimating Latency between Arbitrary Internet End Hosts. In: Proceedings of SIGCOMM Workshop on Internet Measurment, pp. 5–18 (2002)
16. Ledlie, J., Gardner, P., Seltzer, M.: Network Coordinates in the Wild. In: Proceedings of USENIX NSDI (April 2007)
17. Arbor Networks: Arbor Atlas, http://atlas.arbor.net
18. Hyun, Y., Huffaker, B., Andersen, D., Aben, E., Shannon, C., Luckie, M., claffy, K.C: The CAIDA IPv4 Routed /24 Topology Dataset. http://www.caida.org/data/active/ipv4_routed_24_topology_dataset.xml (07/2009-09/2009)

Code Pointer Masking: Hardening Applications against Code Injection Attacks

Pieter Philippaerts[1], Yves Younan[1], Stijn Muylle[1], Frank Piessens[1],
Sven Lachmund[2], and Thomas Walter[2]

[1] DistriNet Research Group
[2] DOCOMO Euro-Labs

Abstract. In this paper we present an efficient countermeasure against
code injection attacks. Our countermeasure does not rely on secret values such as stack canaries and protects against attacks that are not addressed by state-of-the-art countermeasures of similar performance. By
enforcing the correct semantics of code pointers, we thwart attacks that
modify code pointers to divert the application's control flow. We have
implemented a prototype of our solution in a C-compiler for Linux. The
evaluation shows that the overhead of using our countermeasure is small
and the security benefits are substantial.

1 Introduction

A major goal of an attacker is to gain control of the computer that is being
attacked. This can be accomplished by performing a so-called *code injection
attack*. In this attack, the attacker abuses a bug in an application in such a
way that he can divert the control flow of the application to run binary code
— known as *shellcode* — that the attacker injected in the application's memory
space. The most basic code injection attack is a stack-based buffer overflow that
overwrites the return address, but several other — more advanced — attack
techniques have been developed, including heap based buffer overflows, indirect
pointer overwrites, and others. All these attacks eventually overwrite a *code
pointer*, i.e. a memory location that contains an address that the processor will
jump to during program execution.

According to the NIST's National Vulnerability Database [1], 9.86% of the
reported vulnerabilities are buffer overflows, second to only SQL injection attacks
(16.54%) and XSS (14.37%). Although buffer overflows represent less than 10%
of all attacks, they make up 17% of the vulnerabilities with a high severity rating.

Code injection attacks are often high-profile, as a number of large software
companies can attest to. Apple has been fighting off hackers of the iPhone since it
has first been exploited with a code injection vulnerability in one of the iPhone's
libraries[1]. Google saw the security of its sandboxed browser *Chrome* breached[2]

---

[1] CVE-2006-3459.
[2] CVE-2008-6994.

T. Holz and H. Bos. (Eds.): DMIVA 2011, LNCS 6739, pp. 194–213, 2011.

because of a code injection attack. And an attack exploiting a code injection vulnerability in Microsoft's Internet Explorer[3] led to an international row between Google and the Chinese government. This clearly indicates that even with the current widely deployed countermeasures, code injection attacks are still a very important threat.

In this paper we present a new approach, called *Code Pointer Masking (CPM)*, for protecting against code injection attacks. CPM is very efficient and provides protection that is partly overlapping with but also complementary to the protection provided by existing efficient countermeasures.

By efficiently masking code pointers, CPM constrains the range of addresses that code pointers can point to. By setting these constraints in such a way that an attacker can never make the code pointer point to injected code, CPM prevents the attacker from taking over the computer.

In summary, the contributions of this paper are:

- It describes the design of a novel countermeasure against code injection attacks on C code.
- It reports on a prototype implementation for the ARM architecture that implements the full countermeasure. A second prototype for the Intel x86 architecture exists, but is not reported on in this paper because of page limit constraints and because it is still incomplete. It does, however, show that the concepts can be ported to different processor architectures.
- It shows by means of the SPEC CPU benchmarks that the countermeasure imposes an overhead of only a few percentage points and that it is compatible with existing large applications that exercise almost all corners of the C standard.
- It provides an evaluation of the security guarantees offered by the countermeasure, showing that the protection provided is complementary to existing countermeasures.

The paper is structured as follows: Section 2 briefly describes the technical details of a typical code injection attack. Section 3 discusses the design of our countermeasure, and Section 4 details the implementation aspects. Section 5 evaluates our countermeasure in terms of performance and security. Section 6 further discusses our countermeasure and explores the ongoing work. Section 7 discusses related work, and finally Section 8 presents our conclusions.

2   Background: Code Injection Countermeasures

Code injection attacks have been around for decades, and a lot of countermeasures have been developed to thwart them. Only a handful of these countermeasures have been deployed widely, because they succeed in raising the bar for the attacker at only a small (or no) performance cost. This section gives an overview of these countermeasures.

---

[3] CVE-2010-0249.

Stack Canaries try to defeat stack-based buffer overflows by introducing a se-cret random value, called a *canary*, on the stack, right before the return address. When an attacker overwrites a return address with a stack-based buffer over-flow, he will also have to overwrite the canary that is placed between the buffer and the return address. When a function exits, it checks whether the canary has been changed, and kills the application if it has.

ProPolice [2] is the most popular variation of the stack canaries countermea-sure. It reorders the local variables of a function on the stack, in order to make sure that buffers are placed as close to the canary as possible. However, even ProPolice is still vulnerable to information leakage [3], format string vulnerabil-ities [4], or any attack that does not target the stack (for example, heap-based buffer overflows). It will also not emit the canary for every function, which can lead to vulnerabilities[4].

Address Space Layout Randomization (ASLR, [5]) randomizes the base ad-dress of important structures such as the stack, heap, and libraries, making it more difficult for attackers to find their injected shellcode in memory. Even if they suc-ceed in overwriting a code pointer, they will not know where to point it to.

ASLR raises the security bar at no performance cost. However, there are dif-ferent ways to get around the protection it provides. ASLR is susceptible to information leakage, in particular buffer-overreads [3] and format string vul-nerabilities [4]. On 32-bit architectures, the amount of randomization is not prohibitively large [6], enabling an attacker to correctly guess addresses. New attacks also use a technique called heap-spraying [7]. Attackers pollute the heap by filling it with numerous copies of their shellcode, and then jump to somewhere on the heap. Because most of the memory is filled with their shellcode, there is a good chance that the jump will land on an address that is part of their shellcode.

Non-executable memory is supported on most modern CPUs, and allows applications to mark memory pages as non-executable. Even if the attacker can inject shellcode into the application and jump to it, the processor would refuse to execute it. There is no performance overhead when using this countermeasure, and it raises the security bar quite a bit. However, some processors still do not have this feature, and even if it is present in hardware, operating systems do not always turn it on by default. Linux supports non-executable memory, but many distributions do not use it, or only use it for some memory regions. A reason for not using it, is that it breaks applications that expect the stack or heap to be executable.

But even applications that use non-executable memory are vulnerable to at-tack. Instead of injecting code directly, attackers can inject a specially crafted fake stack. If the application starts unwinding the stack, it will unwind the fake stack instead of the original calling stack. This allows an attacker to direct the processor to arbitrary functions in libraries or program code, and choose which parameters are passed to these functions. This type of attack is referred to as a *return-into-libc* attack [8]. A related attack is called *return-oriented programming* [9], where

---

[4] CVE-2007-0038.

a similar effect is achieved by filling the stack with return addresses to specifically chosen locations in code memory that execute some instructions and then perform a return. Other attacks exist that bypass non-executable memory by first marking the memory where they injected their code as executable, and then jumping to it [10].

Control Flow Integrity (CFI, [11]) is not a widely deployed countermeasure, but is discussed here because it is the countermeasure with the closest relation to CPM. CFI determines a program's control flow graph beforehand and ensures that the program adheres to it. It does this by assigning a unique ID to each possible control flow destination of a control flow transfer. Before transferring control flow to such a destination, the ID of the destination is compared to the expected ID, and if they are equal, the program proceeds as normal. CFI has been formally proven correct. Hence, under the assumptions made by the authors, an attacker will never be able to divert the control flow of an application that is protected with CFI.

CFI is related to CPM in that both countermeasures constrain the control flow of an application, but the mechanisms that are used to enforce this are different. The evaluation in Section 5 shows that CFI gives stronger guarantees, but the model assumes a weaker attacker and its implementation is substantially slower.

3   Code Pointer Masking

Existing countermeasures that protect code pointers can be roughly divided into two classes. The first class of countermeasures makes it hard for an attacker to change specific code pointers. An example of this class of countermeasures is Multistack [12]. In the other class, the countermeasures allow an attacker to modify code pointers, but try to detect these changes before any harm can happen. Examples of such countermeasures are stack canaries [13], pointer encryption [14] and CFI [11]. These countermeasures will be further explained in Section 7.

This section introduces the *Code Pointer Masking (CPM)* countermeasure, located somewhere between those two categories of countermeasures. CPM does not prevent overwriting code pointers, and does not detect memory corruptions, but it makes it hard or even impossible for an attacker to do something useful with a code pointer.

3.1   General Overview

CPM revolves around two core concepts: *code pointers* and *pointer masking*. A code pointer is a value that is stored in memory and that at some point in the application's lifetime is copied into the program counter register. If an attacker can change a code pointer, he will also be able to influence the control flow of the application.

CPM introduces masking instructions to mitigate the effects of a changed code pointer. After loading a (potentially changed) code pointer from memory into a register, but before actually using the loaded value, the value will be sanitized by combining it with a specially crafted and pointer-specific bit pattern. This process is called *pointer masking*.

By applying a mask, CPM will be able to selectively set or unset specific bits in the code pointer. Hence, it is an efficient mechanism to limit the range of addresses that are possible. Any bitwise operator (e.g. AND, OR, BIC (bit clear — AND NOT), ...) can be used to apply the mask on the code pointer. Which operator should be selected depends on how the layout of the program memory is defined. On Linux, using an AND or a BIC operator is sufficient. Even though an application may still have buffer overflow vulnerabilities, it becomes much harder for the attacker to exploit them in a way that might be useful.

The computation of the mask is done at link time, and depends on the type of code pointer. For instance, generating a mask to protect the return value of a function differs from generating a mask to protect function pointers. An overview of the different computation strategies is given in the following sections. The masks are not secret and no randomization whatsoever is used. An attacker can find out the values of the different masks in a target application by simply compiling the same source code with a CPM compiler. Knowing the masks will not aid the attacker in circumventing the masking process. It can, however, give the attacker an idea of which memory locations can still be returned to. But due to the narrowness of the masks (see Section 5.1), it is unlikely that these locations will be interesting for the attacker.

3.2 Assumptions

The design of CPM provides protection even against powerful attackers. It is, however, essential that two assumptions hold:

1. *Program code is non-writable.* If the attacker can arbitrarily modify program code, it is possible to remove the masking instructions that CPM adds. This defeats the entire masking process, and hence the security of CPM. Non-writable program code is the standard nowadays, so this assumption is more than reasonable.
2. *Code injection attacks overwrite a code pointer eventually.* CPM protects code pointers, so attacks that do not overwrite code pointers are not stopped. However, all known attacks that allow an attacker to execute arbitrary code overwrite at least one code pointer.

3.3 Masking the Return Address

The return address of a function is one of the most popular code pointers that is used in attacks to divert the control flow. Listing 1.1 shows the sequence of events in a normal function epilogue. First, the return address is retrieved from the stack and copied into a register. Then, the processor is instructed to jump to the address in the register. Using for instance a stack based buffer overflow, the attacker can overwrite the return address on the stack. Then, when the function executes its epilogue, the program will retrieve the modified address from the stack, store it into a register, and will jump to an attacker-controlled location in memory.

Listing 1.1. A normal function epilogue

```
[get return address from stack]
[jump to this address]
```

CPM mitigates this attack by Inserting a masking instruction inbetween, as shown in Listing 1.2. Before the application jumps to the code pointer, the pointer is first modified in such a way that it cannot point to a memory location that falls outside of the code section.

Listing 1.2. A CPM function epilogue

```
[get return address from stack]
[apply bitmask on address]
[jump to this masked address]
```

The mask is function-specific and is calculated by combining the addresses of the different return sites of the function using an OR operation. In general, the quality of a return address mask is proportional to the number of return sites that the mask must allow. Hence, fewer return sites results on average in a better mask. As the evaluation in Section 5.2 shows, it turns out that most functions in an application have only a few callers.

However, the quality is also related to how many bits are set in the actual addresses of the return sites, and how many bits of the different return addresses overlap. Additional logic is added to the compiler to move methods around, in order to optimize these parameters.

Example. Assume that we have two methods M1 and M2, and that these methods are the only methods that call a third method M3. Method M3 can return to a location somewhere in M1 or M2. If we know during the compilation of the application that these return addresses are located at memory location 0x0B3E (0000101100111110) for method M1 and memory location 0x0A98 (0000101010011000) for method M2, we can compute the mask of method M3 by ORing the return sites together. The final mask that will be used is mask 0x0BBE (0000101110111110).

By ANDing this generated mask and the return address, the result of this operation is limited to the return locations in M1 and M2, and to a limited number of other locations. However, most of the program memory will not be accessible anymore, and all other memory outside the program code section (for example, the stack, the heap, library memory, ...) will be completely unreachable.

3.4   Masking Function Pointers

It is very difficult to statically analyze a C program to know beforehand which potential addresses can be called from some specific function pointer call. CPM solves this by overestimating the mask it uses. During the compilation of the program, CPM scans through the source code of the application and detects for which functions the address is taken, and also detects where function pointer calls are located. It changes the masks of the functions that are called to ensure that they can also return to any return site of a function pointer call. In addition, the masks that are used to mask the function pointers are selected in such a way that they allow a jump to all the different functions whose addresses have been taken somewhere in the program. As Section 5.1 shows, this has no important impact on the quality of the masks of the programs in the benchmark.

The computation of the function pointer mask is similar to the computation of the return address masks. The compiler generates a list of functions whose addresses are taken in the program code. These addresses are combined using an OR operation into the final mask that will be used to protect all the function pointer calls.

A potential issue is that calls of function pointers are typically implemented as a *JUMP* <*register*> instruction. There is a very small chance that if the attacker is able to overwrite the return address of a function and somehow influence the contents of this register, that he can put the address of his shellcode in the register and modify the return address to point to this *JUMP* <*register*> instruction. Even if this jump is preceded by a masking operation, the attacker can skip this operation by returning to the JUMP instruction directly. Although the chances for such an attack to work are extremely low (the attacker has to be able to return to the JUMP instruction, which will in all likelihood be prevented by CPM in the first place), CPM specifically adds protection to counter this threat.

The solutions to this problem depends from architecture to architecture. For example, CPM can reserve a register that is used exclusively to perform the masking of code pointers. This will make sure that the attacker can never influence the contents of this register. The impact of this particular solution will differ from processor to processor, because it increases the register pressure. However, as the performance evaluation in Section 5.1 shows, on the ARM architecture this *is* a good solution. And because both the Intel 64 and AMD64 architectures sport additional general purpose registers, a similar approach can be implemented here as well.

3.5   Masking the Global Offset Table

A final class of code pointers that deserves special attention are entries in the *global offset table (GOT)*. The GOT is a table that is used to store offsets to objects that do not have a static location in memory. This includes addresses of dynamically loaded functions that are located in libraries.

At program startup, these addresses are initialized to point to a helper method that loads the required library. After loading the library, the helper method modifies the addresses in the GOT to point to the library method directly. Hence, the second time the application tries to call a library function, it will jump immediately to the library without having to go through the helper method.

Overwriting entries in the GOT by means of indirect pointer overwriting is a common attack technique. By overwriting addresses in the GOT, an attacker can redirect the execution flow to his shellcode. When the application unsuspectedly calls the library function whose address is overwritten, the attacker's shellcode is executed instead.

Like the other code pointers, the pointers in the GOT are protected by masking them before they are used. Since all libraries are loaded into a specific memory range (e.g. 0x4NNNNNNN on 32 bit Linux), all code pointers in the GOT must either be somewhere in this memory range, or must point to the helper method (which is located in the program code memory). CPM adds instructions that ensure this, before using a value from the GOT.

3.6   Masking Other Code Pointers

CPM protects all code pointers in an application. This section contains the code pointers that have not been discussed yet, and gives a brief explanation of how they are protected.

On some systems, when an application shuts down it can execute a number of so-called destructor methods. The *destructor table* is a table that contains pointers to these methods, making it a potential target for a code injection attack. If an attacker is able to overwrite one of these pointers, he might redirect it to injected code. This code will then be run when the program shuts down. CPM protects these pointers by modifying the routine that reads entries from the destructor table.

Applications might also contain a *constructor table*. This is very similar to the destructor table, but runs methods at program startup instead of program shutdown. This table is not of interest to CPM, because the constructors will have already executed before an attacker can start attacking the application and the table is not further used.

The C standard also offers support for *long jumps*, a feature that is used infrequently. A programmer can save the current program state into memory, and then later jump back to this point. Since this memory structure contains the location of where the processor is executing, it is a potential attack target. CPM protects this code pointer by adding masking operations to the implementation of the longjmp method.

4   Implementation

This section describes the implementation of the CPM prototype for the ARM architecture. It is implemented in gcc-4.4.0 and binutils-2.20 for Linux. For GCC, the machine descriptions are changed to emit the masking operations during the conversion from RTL[5] to assembly. The implementation provides the full CPM protection for return addresses, function pointers, GOT entries, and the other code pointers.

---

[5] RTL or *Register Transfer Language* is one of the intermediate representations that is used by GCC during the compilation process.

4.1   Function Epilogue Modifications

Function returns on ARM generally make use of the LDM instruction. LDM, an acronym for 'Load Multiple', is similar to a POP instruction on x86. But instead of only popping one value from the stack, LDM pops a variable number of values from the stack into multiple registers. In addition, the ARM architecture also supports writing directly to the program counter register. Hence, GCC uses a combination of these two features to produce an optimized epilogue. Listing 1.3 shows what this epilogue looks like.

Listing 1.3. A function prologue and epilogue on ARM

```
stmfd    sp!, {<registers >, fp, lr}
...
ldmfd    sp!, {<registers >, fp, pc}
```

The STMFD instruction stores the given list of registers to the address that is pointed to by the *sp* register. <*registers*> is a function-specific list of registers that are modified during the function call and must be restored afterwards. In addition, the frame pointer and the link register (that contains the return address) are also stored on the stack. The exclamation mark after the *sp* register means that the address in the register will be updated after the instruction to reflect the new top of the stack. The 'FD' suffix of the instruction denotes in which order the registers are placed on the stack.

Similarly, the LDMFD instruction loads the original values of the registers back from the stack, but instead of restoring the *lr* register, the original value of this register is copied to *pc*. This causes the processor to jump to this address, and effectively returns to the parent function.

Listing 1.4. A CPM function prologue and epilogue on ARM

```
stmfd    sp!, {<registers >, fp, lr}
...
ldmfd    sp!, {<registers >, fp}
ldr      r9, [sp], #4
bic      r9, r9, #0xNN000000
bic      r9, r9, #0xNN0000
bic      r9, r9, #0xNN00
bic      pc, r9, #0xNN
```

Listing 1.4 shows how CPM rewrites the function epilogue. The LDMFD instruction is modified to not pop the return address from the stack into PC. Instead, the return address is popped off the stack by the subsequent LDR instruction into the register *r9*. We specifically reserve register *r9* to perform all the masking operations of CPM. This ensures that an attacker will never be able to influence the contents of the register, as explained in Section 3.4.

Because ARM instructions cannot take 32-bit operands, we must perform the masking in multiple steps. Every bit-clear (BIC) operation takes an 8-bit operand, which can be shifted. Hence, four BIC instructions are needed to mask the entire 32-bit address. In the last BIC operation, the result is copied directly into *pc*, causing the processor to jump to this address.

The mask of a function is calculated in the same way as explained in Section 3.3, with the exception that it is negated at the end of the calculation. This is necessary because our ARM implementation does not use the AND operator but the BIC operator.

Alternative function epilogues that do not use the LDM instruction are protected in a similar way. Masking is always done by performing four BIC instructions.

4.2   Procedure Linkage Table Entries

As explained in Section 3.5, applications use a structure called *the global offset table* in order to enable dynamically loading libraries. However, an application does not interact directly with the GOT. It interacts with a jump table instead, called *the Procedure Linkage Table (PLT)*. The PLT consists of PLT entries, one for each library function that is called in the application. A PLT entry is a short piece of code that loads the correct address of the library function from the GOT, and then jumps to it.

Listing 1.5. A PLT entry that does not perform masking

```
add    ip ,  pc ,  #0xNN00000
add    ip ,  ip ,  #0xNN000
ldr    pc ,  [ ip ,  #0xNNN] !
```

Listing 1.5 shows the standard PLT entry that is used by GCC on the ARM architecture. The address of the GOT entry that contains the address of the library function is calculated in the *ip* register. Then, in the last instruction, the address of the library function is loaded from the GOT into the *pc* register, causing the processor to jump to the function.

CPM protects addresses in the GOT by adding masking instructions to the PLT entries. Listing 1.6 shows the modified PLT entry.

Listing 1.6. A PLT entry that performs masking

```
add    ip ,  pc ,  #0xNN00000
add    ip ,  ip ,  #0xNN000
ldr    r9 ,  [ ip ,  #0xNNN] !
cmp    r9 ,  #0x10000
orrge  r9 ,  r9 ,  #0x40000000
bicge  pc ,  r9 ,  #0xB0000000
bic    r9 ,  r9 ,  #0xNN000000
bic    r9 ,  r9 ,  #0xNN0000
bic    r9 ,  r9 ,  #0xNN00
bic    pc ,  r9 ,  #0xNN
```

The first three instructions are very similar to the original code, with the exception that the address stored in the GOT is not loaded into *pc* but in *r9* instead. Then, the value in *r9* is compared to the value 0x10000.

If the library *has not* been loaded yet, the address in the GOT will point to the helper method that initializes libraries. Since this method is always located on a memory address below 0x10000, the CMP instruction will modify the status flags to 'lower than'. This will force the processor to skip the two following ORRGE and BICGE instructions, because the suffix 'GE' indicates that they should only be executed if the status flag is 'greater or equal'. The address in $r9$ is subsequently masked by the four BIC instructions, and finally copied into pc.

If the library *has* been loaded, the address in the GOT will point to a method loaded in the 0x4NNNNNNN address space. Hence, the CMP instruction will set the status flag to 'greater than or equal', allowing the following ORRGE and BICGE instructions to execute. These instructions will make sure that the most-significant four bits of the address are set to 0x4, making sure that the address will always point to the memory range that is allocated for libraries. The BICGE instruction copies the result into pc.

4.3   Protecting Other Code Pointers

The protection of function pointers is similar to the protection of the return address. Before jumping to the address stored in a function pointer, it is first masked with four BIC operations, to ensure the pointer has not been corrupted. Register $r9$ is also used here to do the masking, which guarantees that an attacker cannot interfere with the masking, or jump over the masking operations.

The *long jumps* feature of C is implemented on the ARM architecture as an STM and an LDM instruction. The behavior of the longjmp function is very similar to the epilogue of a function. It loads the contents of a memory structure into a number of registers. CPM modifies the implementation of the longjmp function in a similar way as the function epilogues. The LDM instruction is changed that it does not load data into the program counter directly, and four BIC instructions are added to perform the masking and jump to the masked location.

4.4   Limitations of the Prototype

In some cases, the CPM prototype cannot calculate the masks without additional input. The first case is when a function is allowed to return to library code. This happens when a library method receives a pointer to an application function as a parameter, and then calls this function. This function will return back to the library function that calls it.

The prototype compiler solves this by accepting a list of function names where the masking should not be done. This list is program-specific and should be maintained by the developer of the application. In the SPEC benchmark, only one application has one method where masking should be avoided.

The second scenario is when an application generates code or gets a code pointer from a library, and then tries to jump to it. CPM will prevent the application from jumping to the function pointer, because it is located outside the acceptable memory regions. A similar solution can be used as described in the previous paragraph. None of the applications in the SPEC benchmark displayed this behavior.

5 Evaluation

In this section, we report on the performance of our CPM prototype, and discuss the security guarantees that CPM provides.

5.1 Compatibility, Performance and Memory Overhead

To test the compatibility of our countermeasure and the performance overhead, we ran the SPEC benchmark [15] with our countermeasure and without. All tests were run on a single machine (ARMv7 Processor running at 800MHz, 512Mb RAM, running Ubuntu Linux with kernel 2.6.28).

Table 1. Benchmark results of the CPM countermeasure on the ARM architecture

SPEC CPU2000 Integer benchmarks					
Program	GCC (s)	CPM (s)	Overhead	Avg. Mask size	Jump surface
164.gzip	808	824	+1.98%	10.4 bits	2.02%
175.vpr	2129	2167	+1.78%	12.3 bits	1.98%
176.gcc	561	573	+2.13%	13.8 bits	0.94%
181.mcf	1293	1297	+0.31%	8.3 bits	1.21%
186.crafty	715	731	+2.24%	13.1 bits	3.10%
197.parser	1310	1411	+7.71%	10.7 bits	1.18%
253.perlbmk	809	855	+5.69%	13.2 bits	1.51%
254.gap	626	635	+1.44%	11.5 bits	0.57%
256.bzip2	870	893	+2.64%	10.9 bits	3.37%
300.twolf	2137	2157	+0.94%	12.9 bits	3.17%

All C programs in the SPEC CPU2000 Integer benchmark were used to perform these benchmarks. Table 1 contains the runtime in seconds when compiled with the unmodified GCC on the ARM architecture, the runtime when compiled with the CPM countermeasure, and the percentage of overhead.

Most applications have a performance hit that is less than a few percent, supporting our claim that CPM is a highly efficient countermeasure. There are no results for VORTEX, because it does not work on the ARM architecture. Running this application with an unmodified version of GCC results in a memory corruption (and crash).

The memory overhead of CPM is negligible. CPM increases the size of the binary image of the application slightly, because it adds a few instructions to every function in the application. CPM also does not allocate or use memory at runtime, resulting in a memory overhead of practically 0%.

The SPEC benchmark also shows that CPM is highly compatible with existing code. The programs in the benchmark add up to a total of more than 500,000 lines of C code. All programs were fully compatible with CPM, with the exception of only one application where a minor manual intervention was required (see Section 4.4).

5.2 Security Evaluation

As a first step in the evaluation of CPM, some field tests were performed with the prototype. Existing applications and libraries that contain vulnerabilities[6] were compiled with the new countermeasure. CPM did not only stop the existing attacks, but it also raised the bar to further exploit these applications. However, even though this gives an indication of some of the qualities of CPM, it is not a complete security evaluation.

The security evaluation of CPM is split into two parts. In the first part, CPM is compared to the widely deployed countermeasures. Common attack scenarios are discussed, and an explanation is given of how CPM protects the application in each case. The second part of the security evaluation explains which security guarantees CPM provides, and makes the case for CPM by using the statistics we have gathered from the benchmarks.

CPM versus Widely Deployed Countermeasures. Table 2 shows CPM, compared in terms of security protection to widely deployed countermeasures (see Section 2). The rows in the table represent the different vulnerabilities that allow code injection attacks, and the columns represent the different counter-measures.

Each cell in the table contains the different (combinations of) attack techniques (see Section 2) that can be used to break the security of the counter-measure(s). The different techniques that are listed in the table are *return-into-libc/return-oriented programming (RiC)*, *information leakage (IL)*, and *heap spraying (HS)*. CPM is the only countermeasure that offers protection against all different combinations of common attack techniques, albeit not a provably perfect protection.

Applications that are protected with the three widely deployed countermeasures can be successfully attacked by using a combination of two common attack techniques. If the application leaks sensitive information [3], the attacker can use this information to break ASLR and ProPolice, and use a Return-into-libc attack, or the newer but related Return-oriented Programming attacks, to break No-Execute. If the application does not leak sensitive data, the attacker can use a variation of a typical heap spraying attack to fill the heap with a fake stack and then perform a Return-into-libc or Return-oriented Programming attack.

CPM protects against Return-into-libc attacks and Return-oriented Programming attacks [9] by limiting the amount of return sites that the attacker can return to. Both attacks rely on the fact that the attacker can jump to certain interesting points in memory and abuse existing code (either in library code memory or application code memory). However, the CPM masks will most likely not give the attacker the freedom he needs to perform a successful attack. In particular, CPM will not allow returns to library code, and will only allow returns to a limited part of the application code. Table 1 shows for each application the jump surface, which represents the average surface area of the program code memory

---

[6] CVE-2006-3459 and CVE-2009-0629.

Table 2. An overview of how all the widely deployed countermeasures can be broken by combining different common attack techniques: Heap spraying (HS), Information leakage (IL) and Return-into-libc/Return-oriented programming (RiC).

	ProPolice	ASLR[1]	NX[2]	Combination[3]
Stack-based buffer overflow	IL	HS, IL	RiC	IL+RiC
Heap-based buffer overflow	N/A	HS, IL	RiC	IL+RiC, HS+RiC
Indirect pointer overwrite	N/A	HS, IL	RiC	IL+RiC, HS+RiC
Dangling pointer references	N/A	HS, IL	RiC	IL+RiC, HS+RiC
Format string vulnerabilities	N/A	HS, IL	RiC	IL+RiC, HS+RiC

[1] = This assumes the strongest form of ASLR, where the stack, the heap, and the libraries are randomized. On Linux, only the stack is randomized.
[2] = This assumes that all memory, except code and library memory, is marked as non-executable. On Linux, this depends from distribution to distribution, and is often not the case.
[3] = This is the combination of the ProPolice, ASLR and No-Execute countermeasures, as deployed in modern operating systems.

that an attacker can jump to with a masked code pointer (without CPM, these values would all be 100%).

Protection against spraying shellcode on the heap is easy for CPM: the masks will never allow an attacker to jump to the heap (or any other data structure, such as the stack), rendering this attack completely useless. An attacker can still spray a fake stack, but he would then have to perform a successful return-into-libc or return-oriented programming attack, which is highly unlikely as explained in the previous paragraph.

CPM can also not be affected by information that an attacker obtained through memory leaks, because it uses no secret information. The masks that are calculated by the compiler are *not* secret. Even if an attacker knows the values of each individual mask, this will not aid him in circumventing the CPM masking process. It can give him an idea of which memory locations can still be returned to, but due to the narrowness of the masks it is unlikely that these locations will be interesting.

Like many other compiler-based countermeasures, all libraries that an application uses must also be compiled with CPM. Otherwise, vulnerabilities in these libraries may still be exploited. However, CPM is fully compatible with unprotected libraries, thus providing support for linking with code for which the source may not be available.

CPM was designed to provide protection against the class of code injection attacks, but other types of attacks might still be feasible. In particular, data-only attacks [16], where an attacker overwrites application data and no code pointers, are not protected against by CPM.

CPM Security Properties. The design of CPM depends on three facts that determine the security of the countermeasure.

CPM masks all code pointers. Code pointers that are not masked are still potential attack targets. For the ARM prototype, we mask all the different code pointers that are described in related papers. In addition, we looked at all the code that GCC uses to emit jumps, and verified whether it should be a target for CPM masking.

Masking is non-bypassable. All the masking instructions CPM emits are located in read-only program code. This guarantees that an attacker can never modify the instructions themselves. In addition, the attacker will not be able to skip the masking process. On the ARM architecture, we ensure this by reserving register *r9* and using this register to perform all the masking operations and the computed jumps.

The masks are narrow. How narrow the masks can be made differs from application to application and function to function. Functions with few callers will typically generate more narrow masks than functions with a lot of callers. The assumption that most functions have only a few callers is supported by the statistics. In the applications of the SPEC benchmark, 27% of the functions had just one caller, and 55% of the functions had three callers or less. Around 1.20% of the functions had 20 or more callers. These functions are typically library functions such as *memcpy*, *strncpy*, ... To improve the masks, the compiler shuffles functions around and sprinkles a small amount of padding in-between the functions. This is to ensure that return addresses contain as many 0-bits as possible. With this technique, we can reduce the number of bits that are set to 1 in the different function-specific masks. Without CPM, an attacker can jump to any address in memory (2^{32} possibilities on a 32-bit machine). Using the techniques described here, the average number of bits per mask for the applications in the SPEC benchmark can be brought down to less than 13 bits. This means that by using CPM for these applications, the average function is limited to returning to less than 0.0002% of the entire memory range of an application.

CPM has the same high-level characteristics as the CFI countermeasure, but it defends against a somewhat stronger attack model. In particular, non-executable data memory is not required for CPM. If the masks can be made so precise that they only allow the correct return sites, an application protected with CPM will never be able to divert from the intended control flow. In this case, CPM offers the exact same guarantees that CFI offers. However, in practice, the masks will not be perfect. Hence, CPM can be seen as an efficient approximation of CFI.

The strength of protection that CPM offers against diversion of control flow depends on the precision of the masks. An attacker can still jump to any location allowed by the mask, and for some applications this might still allow interesting attacks. As such, CPM offers fewer guarantees than CFI. However, given the fact that the masks are very narrow, it is extremely unlikely that attackers will be able to exploit the small amount of room they have to maneuver. The SPEC benchmark also shows that CPM offers a performance that is much better than CFI[7]. This can be attributed to the fact that CPM does not access the memory in

---

[7] CFI has an overhead of up to 45%, with an average overhead of 16% on the Intel x86 architecture. Results for CPM are measured on the ARM architecture.

the masking operations, whereas CFI has to look up the labels that are stored in the memory. Finally, CPM offers support for dynamically linked code, a feature that is also lacking in CFI.

6   Discussion and Ongoing Work

CPM overlaps in part with other countermeasures, but also protects against attacks that are not covered. Vice versa, there are some attacks that might work on CPM (i.e. attacks that do not involve code injection, such as data-only attacks), which might not work with other countermeasures. Hence, CPM is complementary to existing security measures, and in particular can be combined with popular countermeasures such as non-executable memory, stack canaries and ASLR[8]. Adding CPM to the mix of existing protections significantly raises the bar for attackers wishing to perform a code injection attack. One particular advantage of CPM is that it offers protection against a combination of different attack techniques, unlike the current combination of widely deployed countermeasures.

When an attacker overwrites a code pointer somewhere, CPM does not detect this modification. Instead it will mask the code pointer and jump to the sanitized address. An attacker can still crash the application by writing rubbish in the code pointer. The processor would jump to the masked rubbish address, and will very likely crash at some point. But most importantly, the attacker will not be able to execute his payload. CPM can be modified to detect any changes to the code pointer, and abort the application in that case. This functionality can be implemented in 7 ARM instructions (instead of 4 instructions), but does temporarily require a second register for the calculations.

The mechanism of CPM can be ported to other architectures. A second prototype exists for the x86 architecture, but is not reported on in this paper because of page limit constraints and because it is still incomplete. However, protection of the largest class of code pointers — the return address — works, and its performance is comparable to the performance on the ARM architecture.

A promising direction of future work is processor-specific enhancements. In particular, on the ARM processor, the conditional execution feature may be used to further narrow down the destination addresses that an attacker can use to return to. Conditional execution allows almost every instruction to be executed conditionally, depending on certain status bits. If these status bits are flipped when a return from a function occurs, and flipped again at the different (known) return sites in the application, the attacker is forced to jump to one of these return addresses, or else he will land on an instruction that will not be executed by the processor.

7   Related work

Many countermeasures have been designed to protect against code injection attacks. In this section, we briefly highlight the differences between our approach

---

[8] As implemented in current operating systems, where only the stack and the heap are randomized.

and other approaches that protect programs against attacks on memory error vulnerabilities. For a more complete survey of code injection countermeasures, we refer the reader to [17].

Bounds checkers. Bounds checking [18] is a better solution to buffer overflows, however when implemented for C, it has a severe impact on performance and may cause existing code to become incompatible with bounds checked code. Recent bounds checkers [19,20] have improved performance somewhat, but still do not protect against dangling pointer vulnerabilities, format string vulnerabilities, and others.

Probabilistic countermeasures. Many countermeasures make use of randomness when protecting against attacks. Many different approaches exist when using randomness for protection. Canary-based countermeasures [13] use a secret random number that is stored before an important memory location: if the random number has changed after some operations have been performed, then an attack has been detected. Memory-obfuscation countermeasures [14] encrypt important memory locations using random numbers. Memory layout randomizers [21] randomize the layout of memory by loading the stack and heap at random addresses and by placing random gaps between objects. Instruction set randomizers [22] encrypt the instructions while in memory and will decrypt them before execution.

While these approaches are often efficient, they rely on keeping memory locations secret. Different attacks exist where the attacker is able exploit leaks to read the memory of the application [3]. Such memory leaking vulnerabilities can allow attackers to bypass this type of countermeasure.

Separation and replication of information. Countermeasures that rely on separation or replication of information will try to replicate valuable control-flow information or will separate this information from regular data [23]. These countermeasures are easily bypassed using indirect pointer overwriting where an attacker overwrites a different memory location instead of the return address by using a pointer on the stack. More advanced techniques try to separate all control-flow data (like return addresses and pointers) from regular data [12], making it harder for an attacker to use an overflow to overwrite this type of data.

While these techniques can efficiently protect against buffer overflows that try to overwrite control-flow information, they do not protect against attacks where an attacker controls an integer that is used as an offset from a pointer.

Another widely deployed countermeasure distinguishes between memory that contains code and memory that contains data. Data memory is marked as non-executable [21]. This simple countermeasure is effective against direct code injection attacks (i.e. attacks where the attacker injects code as data), but provides no protection against indirect code injection attacks such as return-to-libc attacks. CPM can provide protection against both direct and indirect code injection.

Software Fault Isolation. Software Fault Isolation (SFI) [24] was not developed as a countermeasure against code injection attacks in C, but it does have some similarities with CPM. In SFI, data addresses are masked to ensure that untrusted code cannot (accidentally) modify parts of memory. CPM on the other hand masks code addresses to ensure that control flow can not jump to parts of memory.

Execution monitors. Some existing countermeasures monitor the execution of a program and prevent transferring control-flow which can be unsafe.

Program shepherding [25] is a technique that monitors the execution of a program and will disallow control-flow transfers that are not considered safe. Existing implementations have a significant performance impact for some programs, but acceptable for others.

Control-flow integrity, as discussed in Section 5.2, is also a countermeasure that is classified as an execution monitor.

8   Conclusion

The statistics and recent high-profile security incidents show that code injection attacks are still a very important security threat. There are different ways in which a code injection attack can be performed, but they all share the same characteristic in that they all overwrite a code pointer at some point.

CPM provides an efficient mechanism to strongly mitigate the risk of code injection attacks in C programs. By masking code pointers before they are used, CPM imposes restrictions on these pointers that render them useless to attackers.

CPM offers an excellent performance/security trade-off. It severely limits the risk of code injection attacks, at only a very small performance cost. It seems to be well-suited for handheld devices with slow processors and little memory, and can be combined with other countermeasures in a complementary way.

Acknowledgements. This research is partially funded by the Interuniversity Attraction Poles Programme Belgian State, Belgian Science Policy, and by the Research Fund K.U.Leuven.

References

1. National Institute of Standards and Technology, National vulnerability database statistics, http://nvd.nist.gov/statistics.cfm
2. Etoh, H., Yoda, K.: Protecting from stack-smashing attacks. tech. rep., IBM Research Divison (June 2000)
3. Strackx, R., Younan, Y., Philippaerts, P., Piessens, F., Lachmund, S., Walter, T.: Breaking the memory secrecy assumption. In: Proceedings of the European Workshop on System Security (Eurosec), Nuremberg, Germany (March 2009)
4. Lhee, K.S., Chapin, S.J.: Buffer overflow and format string overflow vulnerabilities. Software: Practice and Experience 33, 423–460 (2003)
5. Bhatkar, S., Duvarney, D.C., Sekar, R.: Address obfuscation: An efficient approach to combat a broad range of memory error exploits. In: Proceedings of the 12th USENIX Security Symposium, USENIX Association (August 2003)

6. Shacham, H., Page, M., Pfaff, B., Goh, E.J., Modadugu, N., Boneh, D.: On the Effectiveness of Address-Space Randomization. In: Proceedings of the 11th ACM Conference on Computer and Communications Security (October 2004)

7. Gadaleta, F., Younan, Y., Joosen, W.: BuBBle: A javascript engine level countermeasure against heap-spraying attacks. In: Massacci, F., Wallach, D., Zannone, N. (eds.) ESSoS 2010. LNCS, vol. 5965, pp. 1–17. Springer, Heidelberg (2010)

8. Wojtczuk, R.: Defeating solar designer non-executable stack patch. Posted on the Bugtraq mailinglist (February 1998)

9. Shacham, H.: The geometry of innocent flesh on the bone: Return-into-libc without function calls (on the x86). In: Proceedings of the 14th ACM Conference on Computer and Communications Security, pp. 552–561. ACM Press, Washington, D.C., U.S.A (2007)

10. Skape, Skywing.: Bypassing windows hardware-enforced data execution prevention (Uninformed) vol. 2 (September 2005)

11. Abadi, M., Budiu, M., Erlingsson, U., Ligatti, J.: Control-flow integrity. In: Proceedings of the 12th ACM Conference on Computer and Communications Security, pp. 340–353. ACM, Alexandria (2005)

12. Younan, Y., Pozza, D., Piessens, F., Joosen, W.: Extended protection against stack smashing attacks without performance loss. In: Proceedings of the Twenty-Second Annual Computer Security Applications Conference (ACSAC 2006), pp. 429–438. IEEE Press, Los Alamitos (2006)

13. Cowan, C., Pu, C., Maier, D., Hinton, H., Walpole, J., Bakke, P., Beattie, S., Grier, A., Wagle, P., Zhang, Q.: StackGuard: Automatic adaptive detection and prevention of buffer-overflow attacks. In: Proceedings of the 7th USENIX Security Symposium, USENIX Association, San Antonio (1998)

14. Cowan, C., Beattie, S., Johansen, J., Wagle, P.: PointGuard: protecting pointers from buffer overflow vulnerabilities. In: Proceedings of the 12th USENIX Security Symposium, pp. 91–104. USENIX Association (August 2003)

15. Henning, J.L.: Spec cpu2000: Measuring cpu performance in the new millennium. Computer 33, 28–35 (2000)

16. Erlingsson, U.: Low-level software security: Attacks and defenses. Tech. Rep. MSR-TR-2007-153, Microsoft Research (2007)

17. Younan, Y., Joosen, W., Piessens, F.: Runtime countermeasures for code injection attacks against c and c++ programs. ACM Computing Surveys (2010)

18. Oiwa, Y., Sekiguchi, T., Sumii, E., Yonezawa, A.: Fail-safe ANSI-C compiler: An approach to making C programs secure: Progress report. In: Proceedings of International Symposium on Software Security (November 2002)

19. Akritidis, P., Costa, M., Castro, M., Hand, S.: Baggy bounds checking: An efficient and backwards-compatible defense against out-of-bounds errors. In: Proceedings of the 18th USENIX Security Symposium, Montreal, QC (August 2009)

20. Younan, Y., Philippaerts, P., Cavallaro, L., Sekar, R., Piessens, F., Joosen, W.: Paricheck: An efficient pointer arithmetic checker for c programs. In: Proceedings of the ACM Symposium on Information, Computer and Communications Security (ASIACCS), ACM, Bejing (2010)

21. The PaX Team, Documentation for the PaX project.

22. Barrantes, E.G., Ackley, D.H., Forrest, S., Palmer, T.S., Stefanović, D., Zovi, D.D.: Randomized instruction set emulation to disrupt binary code injection attacks. In: Proceedings of the 10th ACM Conference on Computer and Communications Security (CCS 2003), pp. 281–289. ACM, New York (2003)

23. Chiueh, T., Hsu, F.H.: RAD: A compile-time solution to buffer overflow attacks. In: Proceedings of the 21st International Conference on Distributed Computing Systems, pp. 409–420. IEEE Computer Society, Phoenix (2001)

24. Mccamant, S., Morrisett, G.: Evaluating SFI for a CISC architecture. In: Proceedings of the 15th USENIX Security Symposium, USENIX Association, Vancouver (2006)

25. Kiriansky, V., Bruening, D., Amarasinghe, S.: Secure execution via program shepherding. In: Proceedings of the 11th USENIX Security Symposium, USENIX Association, San Francisco (August 2002)

Operating System Interface Obfuscation and the Revealing of Hidden Operations

Abhinav Srivastava[1], Andrea Lanzi[2],
Jonathon Giffin[1], and Davide Balzarotti[2]

[1] School of Computer Science, Georgia Institute of Technology
[2] Institute Eurecom
{abhinav,giffin}@cc.gatech.edu, {andrew,davide}@iseclab.org

Abstract. Many software security solutions—including malware analyzers, information flow tracking systems, auditing utilities, and host-based intrusion detectors—rely on knowledge of standard system call interfaces to reason about process execution behavior. In this work, we show how a rootkit can obfuscate a commodity kernel's system call interfaces to degrade the effectiveness of these tools. Our attack, called *Illusion*, allows user-level malware to invoke privileged kernel operations without requiring the malware to call the actual system calls corresponding to the operations. The Illusion interface hides system operations from user-, kernel-, and hypervisor-level monitors mediating the conventional system-call interface. Illusion alters neither static kernel code nor read-only dispatch tables, remaining elusive from tools protecting kernel memory. We then consider the problem of Illusion attacks and augment system call data with kernel-level execution information to expose the hidden kernel operations. We present a Xen-based monitoring system, *Sherlock*, that adds kernel execution *watchpoints* to the stream of system calls. Sherlock automatically adapts its sensitivity based on security requirements to remain performant on desktop systems: in normal execution, it adds 1% to 10% overhead to a variety of workloads.

1 Introduction

Honeypots and other utilities designed to audit, understand, classify, and detect malware and software attacks often monitor process' behavior at the system-call interface as part of their approach. Past research has developed a widespread collection of system-call based security tools operating at user or kernel level [7, 10, 14, 22, 30, 33] and at hypervisor level [6, 11, 23]. Employing reference monitors at the system-call interface makes intuitive sense: absent flaws in the operating system (OS) kernel, it is a non-bypassable interface, so malicious code intending to unsafely alter the system will reveal its behavior through the series of system calls that it invokes.

Current malware often makes use of kernel modules, also known as rootkits, to conceal the side-effects of a malicious user-level process. Rootkits are attractive for attackers because they combine a high-privilege kernel component with an

T. Holz and H. Bos. (Eds.): DMIVA 2011, LNCS 6739, pp. 214–233, 2011.

easy-to-use, and easy-to-update application. This trend is supported by a recent report from the Microsoft Malware Protection Center[37], that estimates that Rootkits are responsible for around 7% of all infections reported from client machines. Many rootkits, for example *adore* [24] and *knark* [25], provide functionalities to hide processes, network connections, and malicious files by illegitimately redirecting interrupt or system call handling into their kernel modules. However, this class of attacks can be prevented by making the interrupt descriptor table (IDT), system service descriptor table (SSDT), system-call handler routines, and kernel dynamic hooks write protected, as proposed by Jiang et al. [11, 44]. Systems like above assume that protections against illegitimate alteration of these objects will force malicious software to follow the standard system-call interface when requesting service from the kernel.

Unfortunately, this assumption does not hold true. In the first of two principal contributions of this paper, we show how a rootkit can obfuscate a commodity kernel's system-call interface using only *legitimate functionality* commonly used by benign kernel modules and drivers. In particular, we present an attack, *Illusion*, that allows malicious processes to invoke privileged kernel operations without requiring the malware to call the actual system calls corresponding to those system operations. In contrast to prior attacks of the sort considered by Jiang et al. [11, 44], Illusion alters neither static kernel code nor kernel dispatch tables such as the IDT or SSDT. As a consequence, during the execution of malware augmented with the Illusion attack, an existing system-call monitor would record a series of system operations different from the ones actually executed by the malware.

Using rootkits augmented with the Illusion's obfuscation capability, attackers can execute malicious behaviors in a way that is invisible to most of the current security tools and malware analyzers that monitor the processes behavior at the system call level [6, 18, 21]. And since Illusion does not make any changes to kernel code and data structures, it cannot even be detected by Kernel integrity checkers [28].

The Illusion attack is possible because current analyzers depend on the standard system-call interface to represent the underlying changes that a process is making to the system. Importantly, they do not take into account the actual execution of the requested system call inside the kernel. In our second principal contribution, we present a defensive technique to detect Illusion attacks and recover the original system calls that the malware would have invoked had the Illusion attack been absent. To demonstrate the feasibility of our defense, we have developed a prototype system called *Sherlock* using the Xen hypervisor and a fully-virtualized Linux guest operating system. Sherlock tracks the kernel's execution behavior with the help of *watchpoints* inserted along kernel code paths that are executed during the service of a system call. Mismatches between the system call invoked and the service routine's execution indicate that an Illusion attack has altered the internal semantics of the system-call interface.

Sherlock is an adaptive defensive system that tunes its own behavior to optimize performance. It is important to note that Sherlock itself does not provide detection capability for attacks other than the Illusion attack; rather, it augments existing system call analyzers with information about hidden kernel operations. When watchpoints match the expected execution of the requested system call, then traditional system call monitoring indeed observes the correct events. When Sherlock detects the Illusion attack, however, a system call monitor records a faulty series of system calls. Sherlock will then assist the monitor by switching into a deep inspection mode that uses the execution behavior of the kernel to reconstruct the actual system call operations executed by the malware. As soon as the malicious invocation of the system call completes, Sherlock switches back into its high performance mode.

During benign execution with watchpoints enabled, Sherlock imposes overheads of 10% on disk-bound applications, 1%–3% on network-bound software, and less than 1% on CPU-bound applications.

In summary, this paper makes the following contributions:

- It presents the Illusion attack, a demonstration that malicious software can obfuscate a commodity kernel's system-call interface using only the legitimate functionality used by benign modules and drivers. The malicious software controls the obfuscation, so every instance of malware using the Illusion attack can create a different system call interface.
- It discusses the design and implementation of Sherlock, a hypervisor-based kernel execution monitor. Sherlock uses watchpoints and models of system call handler execution behavior to reconstruct privileged operations hidden by an Illusion attack.
- It shows how our adaptive kernel execution monitoring technique balances security and performance by deeply inspecting the kernel state only when the kernel executes hidden operations.

2   Related Work

If defenders know *a priori* about offensive technologies used by attackers, then they can develop appropriate remedies. To this end, researchers have performed various attack studies to better understand how attackers can evade host-based security tools. Mimicry attacks [41, 43] against application-level intrusion detection systems [10] escape detection by making malicious activity appear normal. Baliga et al. [2] proposed a new class of kernel-level stealth attacks that cannot be detected by current monitoring approaches. David et al. [5] created a rootkit for the ARM platform. The rootkit was non-persistent and only relied on hardware state modifications for concealment and operation. We apply this style of attack reasoning to system-call monitors. Like previous literature, we also assume the perspective of an attacker who is trying to undetectably execute malicious software. By taking this view, we hope to help defenders understand and defend against the threat of system call API obfuscation. Our obfuscation does not require any modification to existing operating systems' code and data, in contrast to earlier attacks that modified the system-call or interrupt tables [4, 17].

We use a hypervisor to observe the behavior of a kernel executing within a virtual machine. Jones et al. [12] developed a mechanism for virtualized environments that tracks kernel operations related to specific process actions. With their system, process creation, context-switch, and destruction can be observed from a hypervisor. Srivastava et al. [39] created a system that monitors the execution behaviors of drivers. In contrast, Sherlock allows for arbitrary kernel behavior tracking based upon watchpoints inserted into relevant kernel code execution paths.

Insertion of additional state exposure events into existing code has been a recurring idea in past research [20, 40]. Payne et al. [26] developed a framework that inserted arbitrary hooks into an untrusted machine and then protected those hooks using a hypervisor. In a similar way, Windows filter drivers allow hooking and interception of low-level kernel execution events. Giffin et al. [9] used null system calls to improve the efficiency of a user-level system-call monitor. Xu et al. [45] inserted waypoints into applications; execution of a waypoint adds or subtracts privilege from an application so that it better adheres to access restrictions based on least privilege. Sherlock uses its watchpoints to gain a view of the system call handler execution behavior, and it expects that these watchpoints will be protected via standard non-writable permissions on memory pages containing kernel code.

Sophisticated attackers may attempt to bypass the portions of kernel code containing watchpoints by altering execution flow in a manner similar to that used to execute application-level mimicry attacks [15]. These attacks abuse indirect control flows and could be prevented using techniques such as control flow integrity [1, 29, 35] and kernel hooks protection [44] that guard indirect calls and jumps. Sherlock does not provide such protections itself.

3   System Call Obfuscation via Illusion Attacks

3.1   Motivation

In the first part of the paper we adopt an offensive role and target system-call based monitoring software such as those used to analyze malware, track information flows among processes, audit suspicious execution, and detect attacks against software. The goal of this work is to investigate attackers capabilities to hide the behavior of their malicious code executing on the users' systems.

In this section we present the Illusion attack, a powerful way to extend the functionality provided by rootkits to enable them to blind system-call based detectors. An alternative way of defeating these detectors would be to design malware completely running in kernel-space. In this case, a malicious driver would perform all activities using the kernel code, hence bypassing the existing system-call interface. Though this approach may seem attractive, as shown by Kasslin [13], attackers still prefer a rootkit-based design because it is easier to develop, use, and maintain [32].

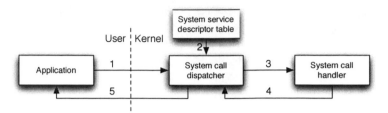

Fig. 1. Normal System-call Execution Path

3.2 Abilities of the Attacker

We use a threat model that reflects current, widespread attacks and state-of-the-art monitoring systems. To launch the Illusion attack, the attacker must install a malicious kernel module or driver; this may occur by acquiring a signature for the module, loading the module on a system that does not check signatures, loading the code via an exploit that circumvents module legitimacy checks [3], or enticement of a naïve user. A legitimate signature is the most capable technique, as it evades cutting-edge defenses against kernel-level malicious code [31]. This fact is demonstrated by the recent Stuxnet worm that stole the digital signature of two companies to install its malicious driver [16, 27]. The loaded module can access and alter mutable data in the kernel, but we assume that it cannot modify static kernel code and data because those changes can be detected by current monitoring systems [34]. This threat model is sufficient to allow the design of our Illusion attack, though we will revisit this model with additional expectations when presenting the Sherlock defensive system.

3.3 Attack Overview

Illusion attacks obfuscate the sequence of system calls generated by a malicious process requesting service from the kernel. The malicious process must still receive the desired service, else the malware would fail to have an effect beyond CPU resource consumption. The Illusion attack must enable the malicious process to execute the same system call requests that it would make in the absence of the Illusion attack, but the particular calls should not be revealed to a system-call monitor.

Figure 1 depicts normal in-kernel system call dispatch with the following steps. (1) When an application invokes a system call, it issues a software interrupt or system call request. The CPU switches from user to kernel mode and begins executing the system call dispatch function. (2) The dispatch function reads the system call number, which indicates the type of system service requested, and uses it as an index into a table of function pointers called the system service descriptor table (SSDT). Each entry in the SSDT points at the system call handler function for a particular system call. (3) After reading the pointer value from the SSDT, the dispatch function transfers execution to that target system call handler in the kernel. (4) When the handler completes, it returns its results to the dispatch function, which then (5) copies them back into the application's address space and returns control to the application. We call this flow the *normal system-call execution path*. An attack that alters system call dispatch—steps 2 and 3—will not succeed, as our threat model does not allow an attacker to alter the entries in the SSDT without detection.

However, a number of system calls allow *legitimate* dispatch into code contained in a kernel module or driver. Consider `ioctl`: this system call takes an arbitrary, uninterpreted memory buffer as an argument and passes that argument to a function in a kernel module that has registered itself as the handler for a special file. Benign kernel modules regularly register handler functions for such files; a malicious module performing the same registration exhibits no behaviors different from the benign code. However, a call to `ioctl` will be directed into the malicious module's code together with the buffer passed to `ioctl` as an argument.

In our construction, this argument contains the original system call request in a serialized form. The malware will marshal the original system call into a memory buffer that it subsequently passes to the `ioctl` system call. The handling function within a malicious kernel module will unmarshal the buffer to identify the actual operation requested by the malware and will then directly call the system call handler for that operation. With this interface illusion in place, the kernel still executes the same operations that the malware instance would have executed without the obfuscation. However, system call monitoring utilities would observe a sequence of `ioctl` requests and would not realize that malicious operations had occurred.

This attack has properties appealing to an attacker:

- The attacker can select from a collection of mechanisms offering legitimate dispatch to module code, such as shared memory, netlink sockets, the proc filesystem, virtual filesystem (vfs) dispatch, or a character device. A particular instance of an Illusion attack may use any or all of these operations in combination as replacements for existing system calls.
- The attacker controls marshaling and unmarshaling operations. Although a system call monitor knowledgeable of a system call marshaling format could recover the original system call sequence by unmarshaling arguments, the attacker can continually change the marshaling format to prevent the monitor from gaining this knowledge. This continual change is similar to the effect of polymorphic engines or packers upon malicious code.
- The attacker does not need to obscure all system calls; she only needs to obscure the set of system calls performing operations that would reveal the malicious intent of her malware to security tools that reason about the malicious behavior. Other system calls executed by the malware, including dummy calls that could be inserted for confusion or mimicry, need not be obfuscated. This reduces the rate of calls to the Illusion attack's dispatching operation and increases the apparent normalcy of the system call sequence, making the attack stealthier.

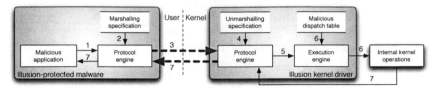

Fig. 2. Alternative System-call Execution Path

- The attacker can automatically convert a malware instance invoking traditional system calls into a malware instance using an Illusion attack. A straightforward source-to-source transformation can simply replace a malware's system calls with a marshaling operation and a call to an Illusion dispatching system call. Similar automated transformation could occur at the binary level at any system call site whose arguments can be recovered via static binary analysis.
- The attacker could define new system calls executable through the Illusion attack but having no counterpart in the traditional system-call interface.

Although a system-call monitor is able to know that system-calls are occurring, it cannot evaluate the semantic meaning of the operations.

3.4   The Illusion Kernel Module

The Illusion attack creates an *alternative system call execution path* that executes system operations requested by malicious applications. By using an alternative execution path, malware is able to perform any system operation without raising the actual system call event that normally invokes that operation. Our design uses a kernel module, a cooperating malware instance, and a communications channel between the two. The kernel module is composed of two engines: the protocol engine and the execution engine. The protocol engine unmarshals an argument buffer into a system operation request and interprets the semantics of that request. The execution engine actually executes the requested system call operation. The execution engine can execute the system operations in several different ways, including: (1) a direct call to the corresponding system-call handler, (2) a direct call to any exported kernel function with similar behavior, or (3) execution of code within the kernel module followed by a jump into low-level portions of the kernel's handler, such as device driver code that accesses hardware of the computer.

Figure 2 shows how the alternative system-call execution path alters a kernel's processing of system call operations. (1) Malware sends an operation request to the protocol engine. (2) The protocol engine obfuscates the request by using the marshaling specification. (3) The malware sends the obfuscated request to the kernel module via the particular communication channel used by this instance of the Illusion attack. (4) The protocol engine in the kernel receives the request, unmarshals the argument using the specification, and (5) sends the requested operation to the execution engine. (6) The execution engine invokes the appropriate kernel operation, using one of the three execution methods described above. (7) When the function returns, it passes the results to the protocol engine which then returns them to the malware. If needed by the malware, the protocol engine can obfuscate the response, which would then be deobfuscated by the corresponding engine in the user-level malware.

3.5 Implementations

We have built two different prototypes of the Illusion attack: one for Windows and one for Linux. In order to validate the effectiveness of the attack to obfuscate system call sequences, we also developed *Blinders*, a Qemu-based system-call tracer for Windows designed using the same principles of Jiang and Wang [11]. In the rest of the section we describe the details of the Windows implementation. However, the Linux code follows a nearly identical design.

Our Windows Illusion attack uses the `DeviceIoControl` system call as its entry point into the kernel. This function exchanges data between a kernel driver and an application through a device. It receives parameters that include a device handle for the device and a memory buffer to pass information to the driver. We used this buffer to pass serialized system operation requests according to the marshaling protocol.

The execution engine within our Windows kernel driver implements all three execution methods described in Section 3.4. For method 1, the kernel driver prepares the stack layout according to the requirements of the system-call handler function. After extracting the handler's function pointer from the system-call dispatch table, it directly calls the handler. For the second method, the driver directly calls exported kernel functions; for example, a call to the function `ZwCreateFile` performs a file creation operation. The last method is more subtle in that the driver executes some part of the code inside itself and only then jumps into the kernel code midway along the control-flow path of the requested operations. We copied a piece of the original function's assembly code from the kernel into the driver as inlined assembly. We equipped our kernel driver to execute two operations: creation of a file and creation of a registry key.

For our experimental marshaling protocol, the user-space malware constructed a sequence of comma-separated fields. We defined two static fields: the first contained the unique number for a system operation, and the second contained a value that identified the number of parameters for the operation. All subsequent values represented the values of parameters.

We executed a prototype malware instance using our Illusion attack together with Blinders inside Windows XP. We issued a request from the user-space malware component for file and registry key creation. The system calls issued by the user-space component were identified by Blinders as the incorrect call, as expected. The system-call tracer was only able to see the system call used to communicate with the driver, which was `DeviceIoControl` in this experiment.

We implemented a similar attack prototype for the Linux 2.6 kernel. In this version, the kernel module directly called exported kernel functions to perform requested operations, and it provided unmarshaling for open, read, write, socket,

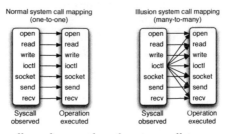

Fig. 3. System calls and examples of system call-to-operation mappings

connect, send, and receive requests. The attack used `ioctl` as the hidden system call entry point to the Illusion dispatch functionality. We ran the Linux prototype, executed all operations, and used the standard system call logging tool *strace* to observe the issued system calls. When an experimental malware instance executed any of the hidden calls, *strace* only showed the `ioctl` system call in its log.

3.6   Foundation

The Illusion attack can be understood by reasoning about system call mapping operations. In a correct trace, there is a one-to-one mapping between a system operation invoked by a process and the operation observed by the monitor. The Illusion attack breaks trace correctness by creating a new many-to-many relation, unknown to a monitor, between the system call invoked and the real system operations executed.

Figure 3 shows two different mappings between a system operation observed by interposing on the normal system call mechanism and the real system operation executed within the kernel. The first mapping is a normal one-to-one relation, where for each system-call invocation there is only one corresponding system operation executed by the kernel. The second mapping, many-to-many, is an example mapping created by the Illusion attack and not known to the monitor. In fact, even if the monitor were aware that system calls were obfuscated through such a relation, it would be unable to reverse the many-to-many relation without additional information to disambiguate among the collection of actual system calls that all map to the same observed call.

3.7   Discussion

Our attack diminishes the ability of system call monitors to understand actual malicious process behavior.

Hypervisor-based system-call analyzers: Due to the prevalence of kernel malware, hypervisor-based system-call monitoring tools have been proposed [11, 23]. Although these tools provide tamper-resistance, they still depend on the normal system-call execution path to record system operations. Illusion is able to obfuscate the system call mechanism and will hide the system operations from these tools.

Malware unpackers and analyzers: A similar effect can be seen on system-call based malware unpacking and analysis [6, 18]. Martignoni et al. [18] proposed an unpacker that monitored the execution of suspected malware and assumed that the code was unpacked when the application issued a dangerous system call. In another work, Martignoni et al. [19] presented a behavioral monitoring system that relied on system calls. The system intercepted system calls as a low-level event and tried building high-level behavioral model. Since the Illusion attack hides the malicious calls, the system would never be able to build high-level model.

Anti-virus tools and intrusion detectors: Some anti-virus software and IDS tools [21] use the system-call interception mechanism to detect a malware infection. Such tools modify the system-call dispatch table in order to intercept the system calls. Even in this case, the Illusion attack is able to hide the system call information without triggering the sensors set by the security application.

Many common security tools such as kernel memory scanners or system-call based anomaly detectors do not detect Illusion attacks. The Illusion attack does not modify a kernel's static data structures or dispatch tables, which allows it to remain stealthy to security tools that monitor these data. Illusion augments malicious software that would not be protected by application-specific anomaly detection systems. Importantly, an attacker can always bolster an unusual system call sequence of Illusion requests with unobfuscated nop system calls to create an undetectable mimicry attack sequence.

4   Sherlock

We developed a hypervisor-based prototype system called *Sherlock* that detects the presence of an Illusion attack and determines the actual system operations executed via the hidden interface. It is designed to achieve the following goals:

- **Secure system:** Sherlock provides security by exposing hidden operations happening inside the operating system. It uses watchpoints, or state exposure operations within kernel code, to track kernel execution. The watchpoints reveal the hidden behaviors of an Illusion attack's kernel module executing within the kernel.
- **Tamper resistant:** Attackers controlling the operating system should not be able to alter Sherlock's execution. It uses a hypervisor-based design to remain isolated from an infected system. It may protect its watchpoints inside the guest OS by making the kernel's static code write-protected to prevent tampering [34].
- **High performance:** Sherlock should not unreasonably slow the execution of benign software. Its design permits adaptive execution, where performance-costly operations will be invoked only when an Illusion attack may be underway.

Our system-call API obfuscation detection operates in two phases. In the first phase (offline preparation), we analyze the kernel source code and insert watchpoints along kernel code paths that execute during the service of a system call.

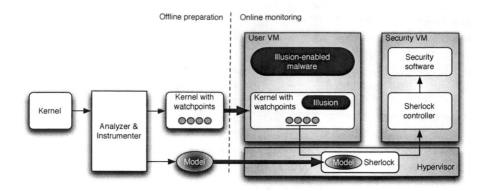

Fig. 4. Sherlock's Architecture

We create models of system-call handler execution behavior to detect Illusion attacks. The second phase (online monitoring) divides the system into three components: an untrusted user virtual machine (VM), a trusted security VM, and a modified Xen hypervisor (Figure 4). The user VM runs a guest operating system (OS) instrumented with watchpoints; our prototype implementation uses Linux. Each watchpoint notifies the hypervisor-level Sherlock monitor of kernel execution behavior via a VMCALL instruction, and Sherlock determines if the watchpoint is expected or suspicious. Suspicious watchpoints are passed to the security VM for deep analysis.

4.1   Threat Model

We expand on the threat model previously described in Section 3.2. As Sherlock uses virtualization, we assume that an attacker is unable to directly attack the hypervisor or the security VM, an expectation that underlies much research in virtual machine based security. Sherlock relies on kernel code instrumentation, and so we expect that an Illusion attack's kernel module will be required to call into the existing instrumented code of the kernel at some point in its handling of hidden operations. Our belief is that while a module may carry some fragments of duplicated kernel code containing no watchpoint instrumentation, it cannot predict all possible configurations of hardware and file systems and must eventually make use of the existing code of a victim's instrumented kernel. Although malicious modules could read and duplicate the kernel's existing code, W⊕X protections would prevent them from executing the copied code. While these protections do not address the problem of object hiding via direct kernel object manipulation (DKOM), such attacks are not Illusion attacks and would be best detected with kernel integrity checkers [46].

4.2   Exposing Kernel Execution Behavior

Sherlock monitors the kernel's execution behavior with the help of watchpoints inserted along the kernel code paths. These watchpoints expose kernel-level

Table 1. Watchpoint Placement (Linux 2.6)

Operation	Functions
Open	sys_open, sys_open, open_namei
Road	sys_read, sys_read, do_sync_read generic_file_aio_read
Write	sys_write, sys_write, do_sync_write, generic_file_aio_write
Socket	sys_socket, sys_socket, _sock_create, inet_create, tcp_v4_init_sock
Connect	sys_connect, sys_connect, net_stream_connect, tcp_connect_init
Send	sys_send, sys_send, _sock_sendmsg, tcp_sendmsg
Receive	sys_recv, sys_recv, _sock_recvmsg, tcp_recvmsg

activities and are implemented using the `VMCALL` instruction. In order to distinguish among watchpoints, each watchpoint passes a unique identifier to Sherlock's hypervisor component that helps Sherlock identify the operation being performed. For example, in the case of a *read* operation in Linux, a watchpoint on the execution path of the read system-call handler sends a unique watchpoint `do_sync_read` whenever it executes. When the hypervisor component receives the `do_sync_read` watchpoint, it infers that a read operation is being performed.

We chose where to place watchpoints by performing a reachability analysis of kernel code. Our analysis finds all functions reachable from the start of the system-call handler down to the low-level device drivers. This analysis yields a set of functions that may legitimately execute subsequent to the entry of the system call handler. We anticipate that inserting watchpoints in all these functions would adversely impact the performance of the operating system. We instead find a set of functions that dominate all other functions in the reachability graph, with separate dominator functions chosen from separate OS components. A function v in the call graph for a system-call handler dominates another function w if every path from the beginning of the call graph to function w contains v. We define a component as a (possibly) separately-linked code region, namely the core kernel and each distinct module. For example, the components involved in the execution of a *read* operation are the core system-call handler, the filesystem driver, and the disk driver. We insert a watchpoint in the middle of each selected dominator. Continuing the *read* example, we insert watchpoints in `sys_read`, `do_sync_read` and `generic_file_aio_read`. Table 1 shows the list of operations and corresponding functions where watchpoints were placed.

We perform this analysis by inspecting the source code of the kernel. During this process, we insert watchpoints inside the kernel functions corresponding to different system calls and ran user-space applications to stimulate our watchpoints. This process has given us confidence that the watchpoints are at the correct locations. To reduce errors that may be introduced by the manual analysis, an automated approach is desirable. Previous research has already performed automatic analysis of the kernel source code to find locations of hooks and security specifications [8, 42], and these systems can also be suitable for selection of Sherlock watchpoint instrumentation locations. For these reasons, we do not consider such analysis as our contribution, but we built a detection system on the top of the output of such analysis.

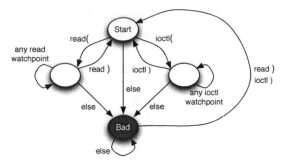

Fig. 5. A portion of Sherlock's Büchi automaton used to distinguish between benign and suspicious operations. All states are accepting. The figure shows the portions of the automaton corresponding to the system calls **read** and **ioctl**; the patterns for other system calls are similar. Whenever the automaton enters the *Bad* state, the internal kernel operations are not matched with a requesting system call, an indicator that an Illusion attack is underway.

Sherlock depends upon watchpoints to know about the state of the executing kernel. To defeat attacks in which an attacker may try to confuse Sherlock by executing fake **VMCALL** instructions, Sherlock identifies the code position (instruction pointer) from where a **VMCALL** instruction is invoked. With this knowledge, Sherlock discards **VMCALL** instruction that does not correspond to the set of our watchpoints.

4.3   Modeling System Call Handler Execution

Sherlock's goal is to reveal hidden system operations. It must distinguish between a normal system call and a suspicious system call. A call is suspicious if it was altered by a many-to-many mapping, as described in Section 3.6. We detect altered system call operations by comparing the sequence of watchpoints executed by the running kernel against an automaton model describing the expected behavior of each system call handler function in the kernel.

To know when system calls are legitimately invoked by an application, we insert two watchpoints in each system-call handler function to know the start and end of the system operation. When a benign application invokes a system operation, execution reaches the system-call handler along the normal execution path and the first watchpoint in that handler executes. Sherlock's hypervisor component receives the watchpoint and traverses an opening bracket "(" transition indicating which system call was invoked. It then receives subsequent watchpoints that had been inserted along the control-flow path of the system operation. Every time it receives a watchpoint, it verifies that the watchpoint was expected given the invoked system call. It performs this step repeatedly until it sees the watchpoint ")" corresponding to the end of the system call request. However, if any received watchpoint should not have occurred given the system call request, then an Illusion attack may have obfuscated the system call interface.

The language of allowed watchpoint sequences is omega-regular, so a finite-state automaton can easily characterize the expected and suspicious sequences. Figure 5 shows a portion of the automaton used by Sherlock to distinguish between benign and suspicious operations, with all individual system calls aggregated into a single model. Whenever a watchpoint executes and is not part of the system operation, Sherlock will take the *else* transition and reach the *bad* state. At the bad state, any operation can be executed until the system call completes, taking Sherlock back to the *start* state. A kernel runs forever, so Sherlock's model is a Büchi automaton with all states final.

4.4   Adaptive Design

Sherlock tunes its performance to match the current security condition of the monitored kernel. Its hypervisor-level component receives watchpoints from the guest operating system and operates the Büchi automaton to identify the suspicious activities. If the automaton is not in a suspicious state, then the kernel is executing in an expected way. Sherlock's hypervisor component immediately discards all received watchpoints, as they would provide no additional information to a traditional system call monitor at the standard interface given the absence of an Illusion attack. Otherwise, Sherlock concludes that this is a suspicious activity and starts logging subsequent watchpoints until the conclusion of the system call. During this process, it pauses the user VM and extracts parameters involved in the operation at each watchpoint. This data gathering helps Sherlock rebuild information about the actual system operation underway. Sherlock unpauses the user VM when an analyzer in the security VM completes the inspection of the state of the VM.

The security VM has a user-level controller process that controls Sherlock's operation and runs infrequent, performance-costly operations. The controller starts and stops the user VM as needed to perform system call identification during an active Illusion attack. The controller passes attack information to existing security software, pauses the user VM, performs detailed analysis of the unexpected watchpoint, and then restarts the guest.

Consider again our example of the *read* system call and corresponding in-kernel execution behavior. Suppose malware uses the Illusion attack to invoke the *read* via arguments marshalled through the *ioctl* system call. The Illusion kernel module may invoke the read operation by directly calling the filesystem driver's read function do_sync_-read. As Table 1 indicates, we inserted a watchpoint in this function. Sherlock receives the beginning marker event "ioctl(" followed by the watchpoint do_sync_read. Since these events correspond to two different operations, they do not match and the automaton enters the *Bad* state. Sherlock's hypervisor component reports this mismatch to the controller along with an indication that *read* is believed to be the actual system call operation underway. This report activates the controller's deep analysis mode – pause the user VM, extract the information from the user VM, and pass the computed system call to higher-level monitoring utilities and security software in the security VM.

5   Evaluation

We paired Sherlock with the Illusion attack to measure its impact on a typical system. We first provide an empirical false positive analysis of Sherlock in Section 5.1. We expect Sherlock to slightly diminish system performance and carry out experiments measuring its effect in Section 5.2. Finally, we discuss future work to address the current limitations of Sherlock in Section 5.3.

5.1   False Positive Analysis

We empirically analyze the ways in which Sherlock may erroneously believe interface obfuscation is underway or fail to recognize the presence of an Illusion attack. A false positive may arise if our model of kernel system call handlers is incorrect and omits allowed behavior. For example, Linux uses the `write` system call for both writing to a file and writing to a socket. If a `write` is executed to write to the socket, it invokes watchpoints both corresponding to the write operation and socket operation. In this case, Sherlock would observe watchpoints corresponding to two different system operations. Even though a naïve automaton model would cause Sherlock to conclude that this is suspicious activity, simple refinements to the model can remove these false positives and improve Sherlock for all future use of the system.

5.2   Performance

As a software mechanism that intercepts events that may occur at high rates, we expect Sherlock's monitoring to impact the execution performance of guest applications. To measure its performance, we carried out several experiments involving CPU-bound, disk-bound, and network-bound workloads. For all experiments, we used Fedora in both the security VM and user VM running above Xen 3.0.4 operating in fully virtualized (HVM) mode. Our test hardware contained an Intel Core 2 Duo processor at 2.2 GHz, with VT-x, and with 2 GB of memory. We assigned 512 MB of memory to the untrusted user VM. All reported results show the median time taken from five measurements. We measured microbenchmarks with the x86 `rdtsc` instruction and longer executions with the Linux `time` command-line utility.

We measured the time to process a single watchpoint both with and without an Illusion attack underway. Whenever a watchpoint executes, the control reaches the hypervisor and Sherlock's hypervisor component checks whether or not the watchpoint is due to a hidden operation. If so, it then pauses the guest VM and sends information to the Sherlock controller. Otherwise, it discards the watchpoint and sends control back to the VM. With no Illusion attack underway, each watchpoint cost $3.201\mu s$ of computation. With the attack, Sherlock's per-watchpoint cost increased to $39.586\mu s$. The adaptive behavior of Sherlock is well visible: its watchpoint processing is fast for the benign case and an order of magnitude more costly when deep inspection is performed due to the detection of a hidden operation. We note that hidden operation processing shows a best-case cost, as our experiment performed a no-operation inspection into the

Table 2. Single operation processing costs

Operation	Normal VM Time (μs)	Sherlock Time (μs)	Sherlock + Illusion Time (μs)	# of Watchpoints Inserted	Executed
Open	17.946	26.439	61.752	3	1
Read	19.419	30.537	60.970	4	1
Write	27.025	37.807	90.656	4	2
Socket	24.515	45.558	115.106	5	3
Connect	1879.894	1905.336	1984.419	4	2
Send	717.391	746.416	838.440	4	2
Receive	8.377	20.958	79.488	4	2

guest OS. An analyzer performing a more detailed analysis may take more time before resuming the guest VM's execution.

Sherlock expects multiple watchpoints for each system call. We next measured the time to execute a single system call in the presence of watchpoints. We measured the time to execute open, read, write, socket, connect, send, and recv, as these correspond to the handlers that we instrumented. We wrote a sample test program to invoke each of these calls and measured execution times in three ways: without Sherlock, with Sherlock during benign execution, and with Sherlock during an Illusion attack. Table 2 presents the result of this experiment, and it also shows the number of watchpoints inserted for each operation and the number of watchpoints executed during an Illusion attack. It can be seen from the table that for open and read operations, Sherlock is able to detect the presence of the Illusion attack even with the execution of a single watchpoint.

Finally, we tested Sherlock with real workloads to measure its overhead upon the guest operating system's applications (Table 3). We carried out experiments with disk-, network-, and CPU-bound workloads. In our disk I/O experiment, we copied the 278 MB kernel source code tree from one directory to another using Linux's cp command. To test Sherlock against network workloads, we performed two different experiments. In the first experiment, we transferred a file of size 200 MB over HTTP between virtual machines using Xen's virtual network. We used a small HTTP server, thttpd, to serve the file. We repeated the file transfer operation on the same file using the physical network to a nearby machine. We measured the time taken by these file transfers with and without Sherlock and show results in Table 3.

Finally, we performed a CPU bound operation. Since we mainly instrumented I/O-related system calls (both disk and network), we did not expect significant overhead with CPU workloads. To measure CPU-bound cost, we used the bzip2 utility to compress a tar archive of the Linux source tree. The result of this operation is again shown in Table 3. These results show that Sherlock is indeed an adaptive system that creates small overhead during the execution of benign applications.

As expected during the execution of these benign applications, Sherlock did not report any hidden operations.

Table 3. Performance measurements. "Normal VM" indicates Xen without Sherlock monitoring; "Sherlock" includes monitoring time.

Operations	Normal VM (sec)	Sherlock (sec)	% Overhead
Disk I/O	45.731	49.902	9.12
Network I/O (Virtual Network)	29.005	29.608	2.07
Network I/O (Physical Network)	212.054	213.352	0.61
CPU Bound	102.004	103.383	0.01

5.3 Discussion

Sherlock relies on watchpoints to monitor the execution behavior of the kernel. In its current implementation, it requires the kernel's source code to calculate the watchpoints placement. This requirement makes it difficult to be used with closed source operating systems such as Windows. To address this problem, we plan to adopt an alternative design that uses driver isolation. In this new design, Sherlock would isolate the untrusted drivers in a different address space separate from the core kernel and prevent drivers entering into the kernel at arbitrary points; kernel code invocation would only be allowed through the exported kernel functions. This design is implemented by Srivastava et al.[38] to log the behavior of untrusted kernel drivers. With this design, we could correlate system calls with the kernel code execution behavior without requiring the source code or watchpoints.

In an extreme scenario, an attacker may bring the entire malicious functionality inside the malicious driver, copy the existing kernel code and remove watchpoints, or bring program slices of code for specific system calls to avoid hitting watchpoints inserted in the existing code. Though this kind of attacks are possible, it is difficult to launch as it requires the prediction of all possible configurations of hardware and file systems present on the victim systems. These kind of attacks can be defeated by monitoring the untrusted driver's interaction with the hardware by using techniques similar to BitVisor [36] to know what operations are performed by the driver.

6   Conclusions

In this paper, we first presented an attack called *Illusion* that obfuscates the system-call executed by a malicious program. As a consequence, existing system-call based analyzers are not able to see the real operations performed by malicious code protected by the Illusion attack. Second, we presented a novel detection system named *Sherlock*. Sherlock detects the presence of the Illusion attack and exposes the hidden operations using a set of watchpoints inserted inside the kernel code of the guest OS. Thanks to its adaptive design, Sherlock is able to achieve its goal maintaining an acceptable performance overhead.

Acknowledgment of Support and Disclaimer. We would like to thank our anonymous reviewers for their extremely helpful comments to improve the final version of the paper. We also thank Neha Sood for her comments on the early drafts of the paper. This material is based upon work supported by National Science Foundation contract number CNS-0845309. Any opinions, findings, and conclusions or recommendations expressed in this material are those of the authors and do not reflect the views of the NSF or the U.S. Government.

References

1. Abadi, M., Budiu, M., Erlingsson, U., Ligatti, J.: Control-flow integrity: Principles, implementations, and applications. In: 12th ACM Conference on Computer and Communications Security, CCS (2005)
2. Baliga, A., Kamat, P., Iftode, L.: Lurking in the shadows: Identifying systemic threats to kernel data. In: IEEE Symposium on Security and Privacy (May 2007)
3. Blorge. Faulty drivers bypass Vistas kernel protection, http://vista.blorge.com/2007/08/02/faulty-drivers-bypass-vistas-kernel-protection/ (last accessed 15 Jan 2011)
4. Chew, M., Song, D.: Mitigating buffer overflows by operating system randomization. In: Technical Report CMU-CS-02-197, Carnegie Mellon University, Pittsburg (December 2002)
5. David, F., Chan, E., Carlyle, J., Campbell, R.: Cloaker: hardware supported rootkit concealment. In: IEEE Symposium on Security and Privacy, Oakland, CA (May 2008)
6. Dinaburg, A., Royal, P., Sharif, M., Lee, W.: Ether: Malware analysis via hardware virtualization extensions. In: 15th ACM Conference on Computer and Communications Security, CCS (October 2008)
7. Forrest, S., Hofmeyr, S.A., Somayaji, A., Longstaff, T.A.: A sense of self for UNIX processes. In: IEEE Symposium on Security and Privacy (May 1996)
8. Ganapathy, V., Jaeger, T., Jha, S.: Automatic placement of authorization hooks in the Linux security modules framework. In: 12th ACM Conference on Computer and Communications Security (CCS), Alexandria, Virginia (November 2005)
9. Giffin, J.T., Jha, S., Miller, B.P.: Efficient context-sensitive intrusion detection. In: Network and Distributed System Security Symposium (NDSS), San Diego, CA (February 2004)
10. Hofmeyr, S.A., Forrest, S., Somayaji, A.: Intrusion detection using sequences of system calls. Journal of Computer Security 6(3), 151–180 (1998)
11. Jiang, X., Wang, X.: "Out-of-the-box" monitoring of VM-based high-interaction honeypots. In: Kruegel, C., Lippmann, R., Clark, A. (eds.) RAID 2007. LNCS, vol. 4637, pp. 198–218. Springer, Heidelberg (2007)
12. Jones, S.T., Arpaci-Dusseau, A.C., Arpaci-Dusseau, R.H.: Antfarm: Tracking processes in a virtual machine environment. In: USENIX Annual Technical Conference (June 2006)
13. Kasslin, K.: Kernel malware: The attack from within. http://www.f-secure.com/weblog/archives/kasslin_AVAR2006_KernelMalware_paper.pdf (last accessed January 15, 2011)
14. Krohn, M., Yip, A., Brodsky, M., Cliffer, N., Kaashoek, M.F., Kohler, E., Morris, R.: Information flow control for standard OS abstractions. In: Symposium on Operating System Principles, SOSP (October 2007)
15. Kruegel, C., Kirda, E., Mutz, D., Robertson, W., Vigna, G.: Automating mimicry attacks using static binary analysis. In: USENIX Security Symposium, Baltimore, MD (August 2005)

16. Last, J. V.: Stuxnet versus the iranian nuclear program. `http://www.sfexaminer.com/opinion/op-eds/2010/12/stuxnet-versusiranian-nuclear-program` (last accessed January 15, 2011)

17. Linn, C.M., Rajagopalan, M., Baker, S., Collberg, C., Debray, S.K., Hartman, J.H.: Protecting against unexpected system calls. In: 14th USENIX Security Symposium (August 2005)

18. Martignoni, L., Christodorescu, M., Jha, S.: OmniUnpack: Fast, generic, and safe unpacking of malware. In: Annual Computer Security Applications Conference, ACSAC, Miami, FL (December 2007)

19. Martignoni, L., Stinson, E., Fredrikson, M., Jha, S., Mitchell, J.C.: A layered architecture for detecting malicious behaviors. In: Lippmann, R., Kirda, E., Trachtenberg, A. (eds.) RAID 2008. LNCS, vol. 5230, pp. 78–97. Springer, Heidelberg (2008)

20. Mavinakayanahalli, A., Panchamukhi, P., Keniston, J., Keshavamurthy, A., Hiramatsu, M.: Probing the guts of kprobes. In: Linux Symposium (July 2006)

21. McAfee Security. System call interception, `http://www.crswann.com/3-NetworkSupport/SystemCall-IinterceptionMcAfee.pdf` (last accessed January 15, 2011)

22. Mutz, D., Robertson, W., Vigna, G., Kemmerer, R.A.: Exploiting execution context for the detection of anomalous system calls. In: Kruegel, C., Lippmann, R., Clark, A. (eds.) RAID 2007. LNCS, vol. 4637, pp. 1–20. Springer, Heidelberg (2007)

23. Onoue, K., Oyama, Y., Yonezawa, A.: Control of system calls from outside of virtual machines. In: ACM Symposium on Applied Computing (March 2008)

24. packetstormsecurity. Adore rootkit, `http://packetstormsecurity.org/files/view/29692/adore-0.42.tgz` (last accessed January 15, 2011)

25. packetstormsecurity. Knark rootkit, `http://packetstormsecurity.org/files/view/24853/knark-2.4.3.tgz` (last accessed January 15, 2011)

26. Payne, B.D., Carbone, M., Sharif, M., Lee, W.: Lares: An architecture for secure active monitoring using virtualization. In: IEEE Symposium on Security and Privacy (May 2008)

27. PCNews. Verisign working to mitigate stuxnet digital signature theft, `http://pcnews.uni.cc/verisign-working-to-mitigate-stuxnet-digital-signature-theft.html` (last accessed January 15, 2011)

28. Petroni Jr., N.L., Fraser, T., Walters, A., Arbaugh, W.A.: An architecture for specification-based detection of semantic integrity violations in kernel dynamic data. In: 15th USENIX Security Symposium (August 2006)

29. Petroni Jr., N.L., Hicks, M.: Automated detection of persistent kernel control-flow attacks. In: ACM Conference on Computer and Communications Security, CCS (November 2007)

30. Provos, N.: Improving host security with system call policies. In: 12th USENIX Security Symposium (August 2003)

31. Riley, R., Jiang, X., Xu, D.: Guest-transparent prevention of kernel rootkits with VMM-based memory shadowing. In: Lippmann, R., Kirda, E., Trachtenberg, A. (eds.) RAID 2008. LNCS, vol. 5230, pp. 1–20. Springer, Heidelberg (2008)

32. Rootkit.com. Rootkit.com, `http://www.rootkit.com/` (last accessed January 15, 2011)

33. Sekar, R., Bendre, M., Dhurjati, D., Bollineni, P.: A fast automaton-based method for detecting anomalous program behaviors. In: IEEE Symposium on Security and Privacy (May 2001)

34. Seshadri, A., Luk, M., Qu, N., Perrig, A.: SecVisor: A tiny hypervisor to provide lifetime kernel code integrity for commodity OSes. In: ACM Symposium on Operating Systems Principles, SOSP (October 2007)

35. Sharif, M., Singh, K., Giffin, J.T., Lee, W.: Understanding precision in host based intrusion detection. In: Kruegel, C., Lippmann, R., Clark, A. (eds.) RAID 2007. LNCS, vol. 4637, pp. 21–41. Springer, Heidelberg (2007)

36. Shinagawa, T., Eiraku, H., Tanimoto, K., Omote, K., Hasegawa, S., Horie, T., Hirano, M., Kourai, K., Oyama, Y., Kawai, E., Kono, K., Chiba, S., Shinjo, Y., Kato, K.: BitVisor: A thin hypervisor for enforcing I/O device security. In: ACM VEE, Washington, DC (March 2009)

37. Some Observations on Rootkits. Microsoft Malware Protection Center, http://blogs.technet.com/b/mmpc/archive/2010/01/07/some-observations-on-rootkits.aspx (last accessed January 15, 2011)

38. Srivastava, A., Giffin, J.: Automatic discovery of parasitic malware. In: Jha, S., Sommer, R., Kreibich, C. (eds.) RAID 2010. LNCS, vol. 6307, pp. 97–117. Springer, Heidelberg (2010)

39. Srivastava, A., Giffin, J.: Efficient monitoring of untrusted kernel-mode execution. In: NDSS, San Diego, California (February 2011)

40. Sun Microsystem. Dtrace, http://wikis.sun.com/display/DTrace/DTrace (last accessed January 15, 2011)

41. Tan, K.M.C., Killourhy, K.S., Maxion, R.A.: Undermining an anomaly-based intrusion detection system using common exploits. In: Wespi, A., Vigna, G., Deri, L. (eds.) RAID 2002. LNCS, vol. 2516, p. 54. Springer, Heidelberg (2002)

42. Tan, L., Zhang, X., Ma, X., Xiong, W., Zhou, Y.: AutoISES: Automatically inferring security specifications and detecting violations. In: USENIX Security Symposium (August 2008)

43. Wagner, D., Soto, P.: Mimicry attacks on host-based intrusion detection systems. In: ACM CCS (November 2002)

44. Wang, Z., Jiang, X., Cui, W., Ning, P.: Countering kernel rootkits with lightweight hook protection. In: ACM CCS, Chicago, IL (November 2009)

45. Xu, H., Du, W., Chapin, S.J.: Context sensitive anomaly monitoring of process control flow to detect mimicry attacks and impossible paths. In: Jonsson, E., Valdes, A., Almgren, M. (eds.) RAID 2004. LNCS, vol. 3224, pp. 21–38. Springer, Heidelberg (2004)

46. Xu, M., Jiang, X., Sandhu, R., Zhang, X.: Towards a VMM-based usage control framework for OS kernel integrity protection. In: ACM SACMAT (June 2007)

Author Index